Isabelle Eberhardt

departures

Selected Writings

Translated from the French and edited by

Karim Hamdy and Laura Rice

City Lights Books

San Francisco

Cover design by Rex Ray
Book design by Robert Sharrard
Typography by Harvest Graphics

Acknowledgments:

Over the years, many people and institutions have supported my work on
Eberhardt and post-colonial relations. The Bunting Institute at Radcliffe
gave me an opportunity, early on, to shift my focus to North Africa, the
English department at Oregon State University gave me time to do
research, the Center for the Humanities there gave me space, and the
National Council on U.S.–Arab Relations and the Fulbright Commission
have provided me with on-going opportunities to visit and learn about
the Arab world. Finally, I would like to thank my children, Rob and John,
for their good-natured support of my work, and to thank the Tunisians
whose hospitality is justifiably celebrated.

Library of Congress Cataloging-in-Publication Data

Eberhardt, Isabelle, 1877–1904.
    Departures: selected writings / by Isabelle Eberhardt ;
translated from the French & edited by Karim Hamdy and Laura Rice.
        p.   cm.
    ISBN 0-87286-288-7 : $12.95
    1. Eberhardt, Isabelle, 1877–1904 — Translations into English.
    2. Africa, Northern — Literary collections.   3. Arab countries —
Literary collections.   I. Hamdy, Karim.   II. Rice, Laura.
III. Title.
PQ2237.E13A24   1994
848' .809 — dc220   94-2797
                                                                              CIP

City Lights Books are available to bookstores through our primary
distributor: Subterranean Company, P.O. Box 160, 265 S. 5th St., Monroe,
OR 97456. 503-847-5274. Toll-free orders 800-274-7826. FAX 503-847-6018.
Our books are also available through library jobbers and regional distribu-
tors. For personal orders and catalogs, please write to City Lights Books,
261 Columbus Avenue, San Francisco, CA 94133.

CITY LIGHTS BOOKS are edited by Lawrence Ferlinghetti and
Nancy J. Peters and published at the City Lights Bookstore,
261 Columbus Avenue, San Francisco, CA 94133.

To the memory of my sister Roberta Rice Kaagan, who also died young, and to the future of her children David and Kyle. — *L.P.R.*

To my late father, Haj Sellami who, like Eberhardt, roamed through Algeria and Tunisia to eke out a living.

To my mother, Hajja Emna, illiterate, yet so capable of nearness to God. — *A.K.H.*

CONTENTS

Au Pays Des Sables
Yasmina, an Algerian Story   1
The Anarchist   29
The Major   38

Pages d'Islam
The Marabout   61
Forced Labor in the South   67
The Seduced   70
Native Exploits   73

Sud Oranais: Part I
Reflections of War   79
Hadjerath-M'guil   85
Ghost Town   93
Little Fathma   95
Meriema   97
Douar of the *Makhzen*   101
At the Home of Bou-Amama's Cousin   117
Figuig   123
The *Djich*   127
Oudjda   131

Sud Oranais: Part II
Ain-Sefra   139
A Halt in the Desert   142
Mirage   145
Bechar   148
Legionnaires and *Mokhaznis*   150
Kenadsa   152
Arriving at the *Zaouiya*   154

The Marabout's Indignation   157
Friday Prayer   160
Saharan Theocracy   163
Twilight   166
Departure   169

Reports from the Sud Oranais
Beni-Ounif, 30 November 1903   172
Beni-Ounif, February 1904   180

Essays on Eberhardt's Work
Mission Civilisatrice. Laura Rice   187
Eberhardt and Gender. Laura Rice   208
Eberhardt and Mysticism. Karim Hamdy   225

Glossary   243

Au Pays des Sables
_____

YASMINA, AN ALGERIAN STORY

She had been raised in a funereal landscape where, at the heart of the surrounding desolation, the mysterious soul of forgotten millennia floated.

She spent her childhood there, in the gray ruins, amid the debris and the dust of a past she knew nothing about.

From the somber majesty of this landscape she seemed to have absorbed an overdose of fatalism and revery. Strange and melancholy among all the girls of her race: such was Yasmina, the Bedouin.

The *gourbis* (huts) of her village rose near the Roman ruins of Timgad, in the midst of a dusty plain, sown with age-old, anonymous stones, debris scattered in the fields of prickly, malevolent-looking thistles, the only vegetation that could withstand the torrid heat of the blazing summers. There were thistles of all sizes, all colors: enormous ones with large blue flowers, silky amid the long, sharp thorns; smaller ones, starred with gold . . . all of them sending

1

out creepers with pale rose-colored flowers. Here and there, a jujube bush or a mastic-tree, scorched by the sun.

A triumphal arch, still standing, spread its sturdy curve on the bright horizon. Enormous columns, some still bearing their capitals, others broken, a legion of columns raised toward the sky as if in angry and hopeless revolt against inexorable Death.

An amphitheater, its tiers recently swept, a silent forum, deserted thoroughfares, the entire skeleton of a defunct city, all the glory of the Caesars vanquished by time and absorbed once more into the jealous entrails of this African land that devours, slowly but surely, all civilization foreign or hostile to her soul.

From dawn when, in the distance, Djebel Aures became iridescent with diaphanous glimmers, Yasmina left her humble *gourbi* and went slowly across the plain, driving before her a meager herd of black goats and grayish sheep.

Usually, she took the herd to the rugged and wild gorge of an *oued* (river), rather far from the *douar* (village).

All the small pastures of the tribe were there. However, Yasmina kept to herself, not mixing at all in the play of the other children.

She spent all her days, in the menacing silence of the plain, without cares, without thoughts, lost in vague, undefinable daydreams, untranslatable into any human tongue.

Sometimes, to amuse herself, she gathered bizarre little flowers, spared from the sun in the dry riverbed, and sang Arab chants.

Yasmina's father, Elhadj Salem, was already old and worn-out. Her mother, Habiba, at age thirty-five was nothing more than a dried-up old mummy, devoted to the harsh work of the *gourbi* and a small field of barley.

Yasmina had two older brothers, both enlisted as spahis. They had both been sent far out into the desert. Her older sister, Fathma, was married and lived in the main *douar* of Ouled-Meriem. Only young children remained at home; Yasmina was the oldest at about age fourteen.

Thus from the radiant dawn to the melancholy dusk, little

Yasmina had seen another spring pass by, just like the others, which mingled together in her memory.

Then, one evening, at the beginning of summer, Yasmina was coming back with her animals, climbing toward Timgad, which was illuminated by the last rays of the setting sun. The plain shimmered, as did she, with a rosy dust of infinitely delicate tone, and Yasmina returned singing a Saharan chant, learned from her brother Slimene who had been back to visit the previous year, and whom she liked a great deal.

> Young woman from Constantine, why have you come here, you are not from my land, you are not made to live in the blinding dunes.
> Young woman of Constantine, you came and you took my heart. . . . You swore you would return, by God most high. . . . But when you return to the land of palms, when you return to El Oued, you will find me no longer in the House of Tears. . . . Ask for me in the House of Eternity . . .

Sweetly, the plaintive song flew into boundless space. And slowly, the overwhelming sun set on the plain.

The solitary and naive soul of Yasmina was so tranquil. Calm and gentle like one of those small, clear pools that the spring rains sometimes create for an instant on the ephemeral African prairies, in which nothing is reflected but the azure blue of an infinite, cloudless sky.

When Yasmina returned, her mother told her she was to be married to Mohammed El Aour, a coffeehouse owner in Batna.

At first, Yasmina cried, because Mohammed was one-eyed and very ugly and because this idea of marriage was so abrupt, so unexpected.

Then, she calmed down and smiled, because it was destined. The days went by. Yasmina no longer went to the pasture. She sewed her humble nomad's wedding trousseau with her own small, clumsy hands.

None of the village women even thought about asking her if she was pleased with this marriage. She had been given to El Aour, as was the custom among the Muslims. That was the way things were done, and thus there was no reason to be especially happy or particularly sad either.

Yasmina knew that her fate would be better than that of some women in the tribe, because she would live in the town where she, like the Moorish women, would be responsible only for her house and the care of her children.

Yet the children sometimes teased her, crying out: "Marte-el-aour!" (The wife of the one-eyed man.) She also avoided going, at nightfall, to get water from the *oued*, with the other women. There was a well in the courtyard of the *bordj* at the archaeological dig, but the Roumi guard did not permit anyone to get the fresh, pure water from it. They were thus reduced to using the brackish river water through which the herds shuffled, morning and evening. From this stemmed the sickly aspect of the people of the tribe who continually contracted malignant fevers.

One day El Aour came to tell Yasmina's father that he could not afford to pay the wedding costs and the bride price until autumn.

Yasmina had finished her trousseau, so when her little brother Ahmed, who had taken her place at the pasture, fell ill, she took up once again the job of shepherdess with its long walks across the plain.

There she pursued the vague daydreams of a simple maiden, which the approaching marriage had not altered.

She hoped for nothing, desired nothing. In her ignorance, she was happy.

There was at that time at Batna a young lieutenant, detailed to the Bureau Arabe, who had just arrived from France. He had requested to be sent to Algeria, because the life of the barracks that he had led for two months, since graduating from Saint-Cyr, had thoroughly disgusted him. He had the soul of an adventurer, a dreamer.

At Batna, he soon took up hunting, drawn by the long rides through the harsh Algerian countryside that, from the beginning, held a singular charm for him.

Every Sunday, alone, he took off at dawn, following by chance the rugged roads of the plain and sometimes the steep paths of the mountains.

One day, overcome by the midday heat, he guided his horse into the wild ravine where Yasmina tended her flock.

Sitting on a rock in the shade of a large reddish boulder where sweet-smelling junipers were growing, Yasmina played distractedly with green twigs and sang a Bedouin plaint in which, as in life, love and death existed side by side.

The officer was tired and this savage poetry pleased him.

When he had found a place in the shade for his horse, he came toward Yasmina and, not knowing a word of Arabic, asked her in French:

"Is there any water here?"

Without responding, Yasmina got up to go, uneasy, almost hostile.

"Why are you afraid of me? I won't do you any harm," he said, already amused by the encounter.

But she fled from the enemy of her conquered race, and she left.

For a long time, the officer followed her with his eyes.

Yasmina had seemed to him slender and slim beneath her blue tatters, with her tanned, oval face in which large black eyes, typical of the Berbers, glistened mysteriously, with a somber and sad expression, in strange contradiction to the sensual yet childish contour of her wide, rosy lips. Passed through the lobes of her delicate ears, two heavy metal earrings framed her charming face. On her forehead, right in the middle, a Berber cross was tattooed in blue, an enigmatic symbol, unexplained even among these native peoples who were never Christian and whom Islam had incorporated, with all their wildness and fetishism, in its great flowering of faith and hope.

On her head, with its heavy, black woolly hair, Yasmina wore a simple red scarf, wound like a wide, flat turban.

Everything about her was marked by an almost mystical charm, whose nature the lieutenant, Jacques, could not define.

He stayed for a long time there, sitting on the rock Yasmina had left. He dreamed about the Bedouin girl and about her whole race.

This Africa, to which he had come voluntarily, still seemed almost chimerical to him, profoundly mysterious, and the Arab people, by all the outward manifestations of their character, plunged him into the utmost astonishment. Because he hardly frequented his comrades from the "mess," he had not yet learned at all to repeat the clichés circulating in Algeria, so clearly hostile, a priori, to all that was Arab or Muslim.

He was still struck by enchantment, by the intoxication of arrival, and he abandoned himself to it eagerly.

Jacques, descendent of a noble family from the Ardennes, raised in the austerity of a provincial religious boarding school, had kept, throughout his years at Saint Cyr, a mountaineer's soul, still somewhat impervious to the "modern spirit," critical and sceptical of prejudice that leads to all the moral failings.

He still knew, then, how to look at things *for himself* and how to give himself over sincerely to his own impressions.

About Algeria he knew only the admirable epic of its conquest and defense, of the heroism ceaselessly deployed by both sides over the course of thirty years.

Being intelligent and not very outgoing, he had already been disposed to analyze his sensations, to classify his thoughts in some fashion.

So, the following Sunday, when he found himself taking the road toward Timgad, he had the clear sensation that he was only going there in order to see the young Bedouin again.

Still very pure and noble, he did not try at all to trick his conscience. He recognized perfectly well that he hadn't been able to resist buying some candy in the hope of making friends with the girl whose strange grace had captivated him so completely, and of whom he couldn't stop thinking all week.

And now, having left at dawn by the pretty road to Lambese, he hurried his horse, gripped by an impatience that astonished even him. It was only the empty space in his heart that had barely left the enchanted limbo of adolescence, his solitary life far from his native countryside, his almost virginal thoughts unsoiled by the debauches of Paris, it was only this profound emptiness that pushed him toward the disturbing unknown he was beginning to glimpse beyond the bare outlines of this Bedouin adventure.

Finally he burst into the narrow, deep gorge of the dry *oued*.

Here and there, in the fawn gray of the underbrush, a herd of goats made a black splash next to the white one made by a herd of sheep.

Jacques looked around almost anxiously for Yasmina.

What is her name? How old is she? Will she talk to me this time, or will she flee as she did the other day?

Jacques asked himself all these questions with growing anxiety. Also, how would he talk to her, when, certainly, she would not understand a word of French and he didn't even know the Sabir language.

At last, in the most deserted part of the *oued*, he found Yasmina lying flat on her stomach amid the lambs, her head resting on her arms.

The moment she saw him, she jumped up, becoming hostile again.

Used to the brutality and the disdain of the employees and the workers at the ruins, she hated all those who were Christians.

But Jacques smiled, and he didn't look as if he intended harm. Also, she saw that he was young and handsome in his simple white cloth uniform.

She had near her a small water flask suspended from three stakes forming a tripod.

Jacques made signs that he wanted a drink. Without answering, she pointed to the skin.

He drank. Then he held out a handful of rose-colored candies. Timidly, without daring to put out her hand, she said in Arabic, with a half-smile and lifting her eyes for the first time to those of the Roumi:

"Ouch-noua? What is it?"

"It is good," he said, laughing at her ignorance, but happy that the ice was broken at last.

She bit into a candy, then, suddenly, with a coarse accent, she said:

"Thank you!"

"No, take them all."

"Thank you, thank you, sir. Thank you."

"What is your name?"

For a long while she did not understand. Finally, when he began to recite the Arabic names of women that he knew, she smiled and said: "Smina" (Yasmina).

Then, he sat next to her to continue the conversation. But, taken by a sudden fright, she fled.

Every week, as Sunday approached, Jacques told himself that he was doing wrong, that he ought to leave that innocent creature in peace, who was so different in every way from him and whom he could only make suffer. But he was no longer free to go to Timgad or stay at Batna, so he left.

Soon, Yasmina was no longer afraid of Jacques. Often she came herself to sit near him, and she tried to explain things to him that he did not understand for the most part, despite her efforts. Then, seeing that he was not going to understand, she burst into laughter. This deep-throated laughter, her head thrown back, revealed the milk-white of her teeth, which filled Jacques with desire and gave him a glimpse of intoxicating sensuality.

In town, Jacques slaved away at the study of Algerian Arabic. His passion made his comrades smile, and they said, not without irony: "There must be a *bicotte* behind all this."

However, what Jacques loved in Yasmina, in his absolute ignorance of her Bedouin soul, was a purely imaginary being, the product of his own imagination, thus someone very unlike the reality.

Smiling, but with a shadow of melancholy in her eyes, Yasmina listened as Jacques poured out to her, clumsily, all the passion that he no longer tried to repress.

"It is impossible, she said with a sadness bordering on grief in her voice. You, you are a Roumi, a kafir, and me, I'm a Muslim. You know, it is *haraam* among us, for a Muslim woman to take a Christian or a Jew; and still, you are handsome, you are good. I like you. . ."

One day, very naively, she took him in her arms and said, with a long, tender look: "Become Muslim. It is easy! Lift your right hand, like this, and say with me: "La illaha illa Allah, Mohammed rassul Allah": (There is no God but God, and Mohammed is his prophet.)

Lightly, as a game, and to please her, he repeated her solemn and singing words that, said *sincerely*, are enough to convert a person irrevocably to Islam. But Yasmina did not understand that these words could be pronounced without belief, and she thought that the profession alone of faith in Islam by her Roumi made him a believer. And Jacques, unaware of these untutored and primitive ideas that the simple people bring to the practice of Islam, did not understand at all the meaning of what he had just done.

＊

That day, as they parted, spontaneously, and with a happy smile, Yasmina gave him a kiss, the first. Jacques felt an indescribable, infinite intoxication.

From then on, whenever he was free and had a few hours, he'd leave at a gallop for Timgad.

For Yasmina, Jacques was no longer a Roumi, a kafir. He had borne witness to the oneness of God and the mission of his Prophet. Then one day, simply, with all the fiery passion of her race, she gave herself to him.

They shared a moment of ineffable annihilation, after which they awoke, their souls illuminated with a new light, as if they had just emerged from the shadows.

Now, Jacques could tell Yasmina almost all the sweet and poignant things that filled his soul, his progress in Arabic had been so rapid. Sometimes, he asked her to sing. Then, stretched out by Yasmina, he rested his head on her knees and, with eyes closed, abandoned himself to a vague and very tender dreaming.

After a while, a singular idea began to haunt him, and although he knew it was childish, and unrealistic, he abandoned himself to it, finding in it a strange pleasure. To leave everything, forever, to renounce his family, France, to stay forever in Africa with Yasmina. Even to resign his commission and take off, always with her, wearing a burnous and a turban, to lead a carefree and easy existence, in some *ksar* (village) of the South. . . When Jacques was far from Yasmina, he recovered all his lucidity, and he smiled at these melancholy, infantile dreams. But as soon as he found himself near her, he let himself go in a sort of intellectual docility that was inexpressibly sweet. He took her in his arms, and plunging her gaze in the shadow of his own, he repeated over and over to her the tender, sweet Arabic word:

"Aziza! Aziza! Aziza!"

Yasmina never asked herself what would be the outcome of her love affair with Jacques. She knew that many girls of her race had lovers, that they hid these affairs carefully from their families, but that generally they ended in marriage.

She lived. She was happy in a simple way, without reflection or any other desire than to see her happiness last eternally.

As for Jacques, he saw clearly that their love affair could not go on that way, indefinitely, because he understood the impossibility of a marriage between himself, with a family over there in his country, and this little Bedouin whom he would never dream of transporting to a new milieu, to a distant and foreign soil.

She had told him that she was to be married to a *cahouadji* in the town, toward the end of autumn.

But that was so far away, the end of autumn. So he also abandoned himself to the happiness of the moment.

"When they wish to give me to the one-eyed man, you'll come get me, you'll hide me somewhere on the mountain, far from the town, so that they will never find me. I'd love to live on the mountain, where there are tall trees older than the oldest of men, and where there is always fresh, clear water running in the shade. And then, there are birds with red, green, and yellow feathers that sing.

"I want to hear them, and to sleep in the shadows, and to drink fresh water. You will hide me on the mountain and you'll come see me every day. I'll learn to sing like a bird and I'll sing for you. Then I'll teach them your name so that they can sing it to me in your absence."

Yasmina spoke to him in this way sometimes, looking at him, her strange gaze ardent and serious.

But, she said, the birds of Djebel Touggour are Muslim birds. They won't know how to sing the name of a Roumi. They'll only know how to sing a Muslim name, and I will be the one to give you a Muslim name. You will be called Mabrouk, that will bring you happiness.

For Jacques, the Arabic language had become a sweet music, because it was her language, and everything about her intoxicated him. Jacques no longer thought, he lived.

And he was happy.

✳

One day, Jacques learned that he was to be sent to a post in the Sud Oranais.

He read and reread the implacable order that had no meaning for him other than that of going away, leaving Yasmina, leaving her to marry the one-eyed café owner and never seeing her again.

For days and days, full of despair, he looked for a way not to go, to switch places with a comrade, but in vain.

Until the final moment, so well had he kept a feeble ray of hope alive, he had hidden from Yasmina the misfortune about to strike them.

Through nights of fever and insomnia, he had arrived at extreme solutions: at times he decided to risk the noisy scandal of elopement and marriage, at times he dreamed of resigning his commission, abandoning everything for Yasmina, of becoming in reality the

Mabrouk she had dreamed of making him. But one thought always intervened to stop him: he had, back in Ardennes, an old white-haired mother and father who would certainly die of grief if their son, "the handsome lieutenant Jacques," as he was known there, carried out all the things that passed through his fevered brain during the slow hours of those wretched nights.

Yasmina had noticed the growing sadness and disquiet of her Mabrouk, and, not daring to tell her the truth yet, he told her that his old mother was ill, far away, *fil Fransa*.

And Yasmina tried to console him, to teach him her tranquil fatalism.

"Mektoub," she would say. "We are in the hands of God and we all die to return to Him. Do not cry, ya Mabrouk, it is written."

"Yes," he would think bitterly, "we are all, one day or another, going to be separated from everything that is dear to us. Why not let fate, this *mektoub* she tells me about, separate us prematurely, while we are still both living?"

Finally, just before the day irrevocably fixed for his departure, Jacques left for Timgad. He went, filled with fear and anguish, to tell the truth to Yasmina. However, he did not want to tell her that their separation would probably, even certainly, be forever.

He spoke to her only of a mission that would take two or three months.

Jacques awaited the explosion of torturing despair.

But, standing before him, she didn't flinch. She continued to look at him, as if she wished to read his most hidden secrets . . . and this heavy look, without comprehensible meaning for him, troubled him greatly. My God! Was she going to think he was abandoning her willingly?

How could he tell her the truth, how could he make her understand that he was not master of his fate? To her, a French officer was almost all-powerful, absolutely free to do as he pleased.

And Yasmina continued to look Jacques full in the face, eye to eye. She remained silent.

He could no longer bear her gaze that seemed to condemn him. He took her in his arms:

"O Aziza! Aziza!" he said." You are angry with me! Can't you see that my heart is breaking, that I would never go, if I had the choice to stay!"

She knit her black brows.

"You lie!" she said." You lie! You no longer love Yasmina, your mistress, your woman, your servant, the one whose virginity you took. You're the one who has decided to leave! No, you will never come back, never, never!"

And this word, repeated stubbornly in a solemn tone, seemed to Jacques to be the death knell of his youth.

Abadan! Abadan! There was, even in the sound of the word, something irrevocable, inexorable and fatal.

"Yes, you're going. You'll marry a Roumia back there in France."

And a somber light flamed in her large, round, nomad eyes. She tore herself almost brusquely from his embrace, and she spit on the ground, with disdain, in a savage gesture of indignation.

"Dogs and sons of dogs, all you Roumis!"

"Oh! Yasmina, how unjust you are to me! I swear to you that I begged all my comrades, one after the other, to take my place, and they did not want to."

"Ah! You know very well that when an officer doesn't want to go, he doesn't go!"

"But they are my comrades, and I was asking them to take my place. They are not answerable to me, while I am answerable to the general, the Ministry of War."

But unbelieving, Yasmina remained hostile and withdrawn.

Jacques wished that the agony of despair he had so feared on the way there had happened after all.

They remained that way for a long time, silent, separated by an abyss, by everything European that dominated his life, and that she, Yasmina, would never understand.

Finally, his heart overflowing with bitterness, Jacques cried, his head on Yasmina's knees.

When she saw him sob so despairingly, she understood that he was sincere. She hugged his dear head to her breast, crying, at last, herself.

"Mabrouk! Apple of my eye! My light! O heart of my heart! Don't cry, my master. You will not go, ya sidi. If you leave, I will lie across your path and die. Then, you will need to pass over Yasmina's dead body. Or, if you must leave, absolutely, take me with you. I will be your slave. I'll take care of your house and your horse. If you fall ill, I will cure you with the blood of my veins, or I will die for you. *Ya* Mabrouk! Ya sidi! Take me with you. . ."

And as he said nothing, shattered by the impossibility of what she was asking, she said again:

"Look, then, put on Arab clothes. We'll save ourselves in the mountains, or better yet, even in the desert, in the country of the Chaamba and the Touareg. You will become Muslim, and you will forget France."

"I cannot. Don't ask for the impossible. I have aging parents, far away, in France, and they would die of sorrow. Oh! God only knows how much I long to keep you by my side, forever."

He felt Yasmina's warm lips caress his hands, in the flow of their mingled tears. This touch awoke in him other thoughts, and they shared a momentary joy more profound, more absolute than they had ever before experienced during the tranquil days of their happiness.

"Oh! How can we leave each other!" sobbed Yasmina whose tears still flowed.

Twice more Jacques returned, and they found once more the inexpressible ecstasy that seemed to bind them to each other, irrevocably and forever.

But at last, the hour of the final parting came, those goodbyes that one knew, and the other sensed, were forever.

In their last kiss they put all their souls.

For a long time, Yasmina heard the echo of the hoofbeats of Jacques's galloping horse. When she no longer heard them, and the plain had returned to its accustomed silence, the small Bedouin threw herself face down on the earth and sobbed.

*

A month had passed since Jacques's departure, and Yasmina was living in a sort of dull stupor.

All day long, alone then in the savage *oued*, she lay on the ground, immobile.

In her, there was no rebellion against *mektoub* to which, from her infancy, she had been accustomed to attributing everything that happened to her, whether good or evil. There was only an infinite grief, a continual suffering, without respite or peace, just the cruel and unjust suffering of unconscious beings, children or animals, who haven't even the bitter consolation of understanding why and how they suffer.

Like all nomads, of mixed race where Asiatic blood is mingled and lost among that of indigenous tribes, Chaouiya, Berber, and so on, Yasmina had only a vague idea of Islam. She knew — without ever really knowing what it meant — that there was one God, alone, unique, eternal, who created all things and who is Rab-el-Alemine (Ruler of Worlds), that Mohammed is his Prophet, and that the Koran is the written expression of the religion. She knew also how to recite two or three short Suras from the Koran that every Muslim knew.

The only French people that Yasmina knew were those who guarded the ruins and worked at the excavations, and she knew as well all that her tribe had suffered. From that, she concluded that all Roumis were irreconcilable enemies of the Arabs. Jacques had done his best to explain to her that there were French people who did not hate Muslims. But inside, he knew it took only a couple of ignorant and brutal bureaucrats to make France despicable in the eyes of the poor, illiterate, humble villagers.

Yasmina had heard Arabs from the surrounding area complain about having to pay crushing taxes, of being terrorized by the military administration, of being robbed of their goods. And she concluded from that that perhaps the good, humane French people of whom Jacques spoke did not come to her country, but stayed somewhere far away.

All this, in her poor, untutored mind, whose living forces were in deep sleep, was very vague and did not absorb her at all then.

She had just begun to think, very vaguely, of the time when she was in love.

Before, when Jacques left her to go back to Batna, she would daydream. What was he doing? Where did he live? Did he see other women, Roumias who went out without a veil and wore dresses of silk and hats like she'd seen the visitors to the ruins wear? And a dim jealousy would flame up in her heart.

But, since Jacques had left for the faraway province of Oran, Yasmina had suffered a great deal and her intelligence began to assert itself.

Sometimes, in her desolate solitude, she would begin to sing the plaintive songs he'd loved, and then she would cry, her heart-rending sobs interrupting the melancholy couplets, calling her dear Mabrouk by all the sweet names she used to give him, begging him to return, as if he could hear her.

She was illiterate, and Jacques could not write to her, because she would not dare show the letter from the officer to anyone to have them read.

So she remained without any news of him.

One Sunday, while she dreamed sadly, she saw a native soldier, mounted on a spirited, gray horse, approach from the direction of Batna. The cavalry man, who wore the uniform of the indigenous officers of the spahis, guided his horse into the *oued*. He seemed to be looking for someone. Seeing the young girl, he called to her:

"Are you Smina ben Hadj Salem?"

"Who are you and how do you know my name?"

"Then, it's you! Me, I'm Cherif ben Ali Chaambi, sub-lieutenant of the spahis, and a friend of Jacques. So you're the one who was his mistress?"

Horrified to see that a Muslim knew her secret, Yasmina wanted to flee. But the officer grabbed her by the wrist and forced her to stay.

"Where are you going, daughter of sin? I came all this way to look you in the face and you try to run?"

In vain she tried to get free.

"Let me go! Let me go! I don't know anyone, I wasn't the mistress of anyone!"

Cherif began to laugh.

"Yes, you were his mistress, daughter of sin! And I ought to cut off your head for that, even though Jacques was like a brother to me. Come over here to the far end of the riverbed. No one should see us. I have a letter from Jacques for you and I'm going to read it to you."

Joyfully, she clapped her hands.

Jacques told her she could trust Cherif completely and, if any trouble should come to her, she should let him know. He said he thought only of her, that he'd remained faithful to her. He ended by promising her to love her always, to never forget her and to come back one day to get her.

Beautiful, young vows; *irrevocable* resolutions that time would erase and destroy quickly enough, like all the rest!

Yasmina asked Cherif to write back to Jacques that she would love him always, that she would be faithful as long as she lived, that she would stay his obedient and loving slave, and that she longed *to be the earth beneath his feet.*

Cherif smiled.

"If you'd fallen in love with a Muslim, he said, he would have married you according to the law, and you would not be here crying."

"Mektoub!"

And the officer remounted his gray stallion and left at a gallop, stirring up a cloud of dust.

Jacques was afraid of arousing the suspicions of the village people and he waited a long time before sending his second letter to Yasmina, so long that when he wanted to write to her, he learned that Cherif had left for a post in the Sahara.

Little by little, after the great despair he'd suffered at first, peace entered Jacques's heart.

In the *ksar* where he lived in the province of Oran, he'd made important French friends, very cultivated, one of whom possessed quite a large library. Jacques began to read, to study questions that, until that time, had been completely foreign to him. New horizons opened in his mind.

Later, he changed posts. At Geryville, he met a young Spanish girl, quite pretty, with whom he fell in love.

And so, the charming image of Yasmina faded into the vague distance of memory, where everything mists over and ends by foundering in darkness of final oblivion.

＊

Mohammed El Aour came finally to say that he could provide for the wedding expenses.

The date fixed for the ceremony was quite soon.

Passive, Yasmina gave herself over to her fate.

Her instinct as a passionate lover told her that Jacques had forgotten her, and that it was all the same to him.

However, anguish gripped her heart at the thought of this marriage, because she understood all too well the ways of her people not to foresee the anger her husband would feel when he found that she was no longer virgin.

She was certain she would become the wife of the one-eyed coffeehouse owner when, suddenly, a dispute over conflicting interests broke out between Hadj Salem and El Aour.

A few days later, Yasmina learned that she was to be given to a man whom she had only glimpsed once, a spahi, Abd-el-Kader ben Smail, young and handsome, who was considered audacious, recalcitrant, a troublemaker by the military, but honored among the native leaders for his courage and intelligence.

He chose Yasmina out of love, having found her very beautiful, in the bloom of her fifteen years. He had offered Hadj Salem a bride price higher than the one promised by El Aour. Besides, it flattered the ego of the old man to give his daughter to this boy who was from a good family in Guelma, even though he had quarreled with his parents following the engagement.

The wedding celebrations lasted three days, first in the *douar*, then in the town.

At the *douar*, gunshots were fired, fireworks were set off, and skinny horses were raced with loud cries that intoxicated both man and beast.

In the town, the women had danced to the sound of *bendir* and to the Bedouin horn, the *r'aita*.

Yasmina, dressed in layers of white muslin blouses with long, wide sleeves, a kaftan of blue velvet laced with gold, a *gandoura* of rose-colored silk, and topped with a small, pointed cap, a *chechia* of cherry red and green, and adorned with silver and gold jewelry, was enthroned on the only chair in the room, in the midst of the women, while the men made merry in the street and on the benches of the Moorish café across the street.

From the women, Yasmina learned of the departure of Cherif Chaambi, and the last flicker of hope that she still retained went out: she would never know anything more of her Jacques.

That evening, when she was alone with Abd-el-Kader, Yasmina didn't dare raise her eyes to her husband. Trembling, she thought of his imminent anger and the scandal that would follow, if he did not kill her immediately.

She still loved her Roumi, and the substitution of the spahi for El Aour did not make her happy. On the contrary, she knew that El Aour was considered well behaved, while Abd-el-Kader had the reputation of being a violent and terrible man.

When he learned what Yasmina could not hide from him, he flew into a rage that was all the more terrible because he was so in love with her. He began by beating her cruelly, then he demanded that she tell him the name of her lover.

"He was an officer, a Muslim. It was a long time ago, he is gone now."

Terrified by the threats of her husband, she gave him the name of the lieutenant Chaambi: since he was no longer there, what did it matter? She hadn't wanted to reveal the truth, say that she was the mistress of a Roumi, which would have aggravated her fault in the eyes of Abd-el-Kader.

But the spahi's passion was stronger than his anger. After all, the lieutenant certainly hadn't talked, he was gone, and no one would ever know the secret.

Abd-el-Kader kept Yasmina, but he became the terror of *douar* Hadj Salem, where he went often to demand money from his parents-in-law who were afraid of him and who regretted not having given their daughter to the tranquil Mohammed El Aour.

Yasmina, always sad and silent, spent her days sewing large shirts of cotton that Doudja, the spahi's old aunt, took to a market in M'zabi.

In the house, there was still Abd-el-Kader's sister, who was to marry one of his comrades.

When the spahi wasn't drunk, he brought gifts to his wife, material for her dress, even jewelry, fruit, cakes. All his pay was spent this way. But at other times, Abd-el-Kader returned home drunk, and then he beat his wife for no reason.

Yasmina remained indifferent to both his caresses and his blows, and kept quiet. Only she was strangling inside the four white walls of the Moorish courtyard in which she was enclosed, and she missed bitterly the immense freedom of her native plain, and the large, menacing ruins, and her *oued* in the wilderness.

Abd-el-Kader saw quite clearly that his wife did not care for him at all, and that exasperated him.

At those times, he would beat her ferociously.

But seeing her cry, he would take her in his arms and cover her with kisses to console her.

Yet Yasmina obstinately continued to love her Roumi, her Mabrouk . . . and her thoughts turned ceaselessly toward the Sud Oranais which she hardly knew and where she thought he still was.

She asked herself in anguish whether her Mabrouk was ever going to return, and when no one was watching, she would cry, for long periods of time, silently.

✳

Jacques had forgotten long ago the romance he had had, at the dawn of his life, in the desolate plain of Timgad, which had only lasted one brief summer.

✳

Barely a year after their marriage, Abd-el-Kader was condemned to ten years of hard labor for assaulting a superior after work. His sister had followed her husband into the South, and the old aunt was dead.

Yasmina was alone and without any means of support.

She had no desire to return to her tribe.

She remained as strangely silent and somber as she had been since Jacques's departure. She did not want to be married again, now that she was a widow. She wanted to be free to await her Mabrouk.

For her, too, time had softened the suffering of her heart, but she had found nothing to take the place of this love, and she continued to love the absent Jacques whom, for a long time now, she had not dared to hope to see again.

When the last pennies that Abd-el-Kader had left her were spent, Yasmina packed up her worn belongings and returned the key of the house to the landlord.

At nightfall, she headed toward the Village-Noir, only about five hundred meters from Batna — a wasteland near the mosque.

This village was a chaotic collection of hovels built of wood or masonry, dirty and crumbling, inhabited by prostitutes, Negresses, Bedouin women, Moorish women, Jewesses, and Maltese women, living there, crowded together haphazardly with all sorts of more or less suspect types, pimps and old offenders for the most part.

There were Moorish cafés there, where the women danced and sang until ten in the evening, and where kif was smoked all night behind closed doors. This was the place of entertainment for the soldiers of the garrison.

While she was living alone, Yasmina had become acquainted with a Moorish woman who lived in the Village-Noir, with a Negress from Oued Rir'.

Zohra and Samra worked in a music hall run by one Ali Franc who claimed to be a Muslim from Tunisia, but whose name seemed to indicate other origins. Besides, he was a previous offender always under surveillance by the police.

The two singers had often advised Yasmina to share their room, making their supposedly advantageous circumstances shine in her eyes.

So when she felt herself completely alone and abandoned, Yasmina joined her two friends who welcomed her gladly.

That evening, Yasmina was supposed to appear at the café to sing.

It was a long, smoke-filled room with a low ceiling, a floor of beaten earth, and white walls that had been covered with inscriptions and designs, most of them brutishly obscene, the work of clients. All along the parallel walls on two sides were tables and benches, leaving a large empty space in the middle of the room. At the far end, a wooden table served as the cashier's desk. Behind it was a sort of platform of beaten earth, covered with old, worn-out mats.

The singers were crouched there. There were seven of them: Yasmina, her two friends, a young Bedouin named Hafsia, a woman from Bone named Aicha, and two Jewesses, Stitra and Rahil. The last one, from Kef, wore a Tunisian dancer's costume, styled in the Egyptian fashion: full, white pants, a short jacket of colored silk, and loose hair tied back only by a large red ribbon. On her feet were small, white, open-toed, satin shoes with high heels.

They all wore gold jewelry and heavy rings in their ears.

However, the Bedouin and the Negress wore a Saharan costume, a large, dark blue veil fastened at the shoulders, forming a sort of tunic. They wore complicated hair styles involving large tresses of red wool braided with their own hair, wound about their temples, covered by scarves secured by jewels attached with small chains. While one got up to dance in the room, between the rows of spectators, the others sang on the platform, clapping their hands and beating tambourines, while a young man played an Arab flute and a Jew scraped away on a sort of mandolin.

The songs and dances were shamelessly ardent and little by little inflamed the numerous spectators that evening.

Pleasantries and crude compliments rained down, in Arabic, in French, more or less mixed with Sabir.

"You're not a bad looker, girl!" said a reveler, a son of Belleville who'd been exiled to Africa, and who seemed struck with admiration in front of Yasmina when, in her turn, she came down into the room.

Serious and sad, as always, enveloped in her resignation and her dream, she danced for these men whose prey she would become when the den closed.

A native brigadier from the spahis who had known Abd-el-Kader ben Smail and who had seen Yasmina, recognized her.

"I'll be!" he said. "There's Abd-el-Kadir's wife. The man at hard labor, the wife in the bar. . . Life goes on, just the same."

And he was the one who joined Yasmina that night in the black hole that served as her bedroom.

✳

The full moon was rising in the distance, to the East, behind the somber peaks of the Aures mountains. . .

A blue light was gliding over the walls and the trees, casting deep shadows into all the recesses and crannies that looked like chasms.

In the middle of the dry wasteland that stretched between the gray walls of the town and the Lambèse Gate on one side, to the slopes of the mountains on the other, rose the mosque alone. Without style or grace during the day, in the magic light of the moon, it appeared diaphanous, almost translucid, bathed by the indistinct rays.

In the Village-Noir, muffled sounds of the *bendir* and the *gasba* echoed. In front of the café of Ali Franc, a woman was seated on a wooden bench, her elbows on her knees, her head in her hands. She accosted the passersby, but with an air of profound indifference, almost disgust.

Extremely thin, her cheeks a dark red, her eyes sunken and strangely glittering, her lips thin and sadly pinched, she seemed to have aged ten years, this charming and fresh little Bedouin girl from the ruins of Timgad.

Nonetheless, beneath this mask of grief, almost of agony, even, the existence she had led for three years had only left a deeper shade of sadness. And, despite everything, she was still beautiful, her ailing beauty all the more touching.

Often, her chest was gripped horribly by a long, terrible cough that tinted her handkerchief red.

Sadness, alcohol, and a thousand other deleterious agents in the midst of which she lived had gotten the better of the robust constitution of this little nomad accustomed to the pure air of the desert.

✳

Five years after he had left for the south of Oran province, the fluctuations of military life had brought Jacques back to Batna.

He returned there with his young wife, a delicate and pretty Parisian woman: they met and fell in love on the Côte d'Azur one spring when Jacques, ill, had gone to Nice to take a rest cure.

Jacques remembered clearly what he now called his "Bedouin idyll" and had even spoken of it to his wife. But now it was all so long ago, and the man he had become hardly resembled the young officer he had once been.

"I was, at that time, an adolescent full of dreams and enthusiasm.

ʻIf you only knew, my dear, what ridiculous ideas I had then! To say that I'd give up everything for a little savage. If I'd given myself over to that folly, what would have become of me? God only knows!"

Ah! How ridiculous he seemed now, that little lieutenant so sincere and ardent at the beginning!

And he no longer understood that that early incarnation of his conscious self had been better and more handsome than the second, the one he owed to the modern spirit of vanity, egoism, and cynicism that he'd entered into bit by bit.

But, one evening when he'd gone out walking with his wife, who found the four or five square blocks empty of any charm, Jacques said to her:

"Come, I'm going to show you the paradise of the troops. But above all, you must be indulgent, because the scene will sometimes appear of a crude nature."

On the way there, they ran into one of Jacques's friends, also accompanied by his wife. The idea of going to the Village-Noir pleased them, and they found themselves on the way. Careful, with good reason, to light the way, Jacques had gone a bit ahead, leaving his wife on his friend's arm.

But as he passed in front of the café of Ali Franc, Yasmina jumped up and cried out:

"Mabrouk! Mabrouk! It is you!"

Jacques had recognized also, just by the name, that it was Yasmina. An icy cold invaded his heart. He had nothing to say to her, to the one who was so overjoyed by his return.

He cursed himself mentally for having had the bad idea of bringing his wife here. What sort of a scandal would she make, this creature lost in debauchery, when she learned she had nothing more to hope for from him!

"Mabrouk! Mabrouk! Don't you recognize me anymore? It's Smina! Look at me, embrace me! Oh! I know that I've changed, but that will go away, I will get well, now that you are here!"

He would have liked to end it all right then, to cut short this disagreeable encounter. Now, he was in full command of the Arabic language of which she once, had taught him his first words, and he said to her:

"Listen, don't count on me. Everything is over between us. I am married and I love my wife. Leave me alone and don't try to see me again. Forget me. It would be better for both of us."

She stared at him, stupefied, with wide open eyes. So, it was true! The last hope that had kept her alive was going out.

He had forgotten her, he was married and he loved a Roumia, his *wife!* As for her, the woman who had adored him, there was nothing left to do but to lie down in a corner and die like an abandoned dog.

From the obscure depths of her soul, a revolt burst forth against the cruel injustice that was overwhelming her.

She pulled herself up, strong, menacing.

"Well then, why did you come to search me out in the far reaches of the *oued*, in my *douar*, where I lived calmly with my goats and sheep? Why did you pursue me? Why did you try every ruse, every trick to seduce me, to lead me on, to take my virginity? Why did you repeat after me, like a traitor, the words that make those who pronounce them Muslim? Why did you lie to me and promise to return one day to take me back forever? Oh! I still have among my amulets the letter that Lieutenant Chaambi brought to me. (And she pulled from her breast an old envelope all yellowed and frayed, which she brandished like a weapon, like an irrefutable witness.) Yes, why, Roumi, dog, son of a dog, do you come back at this time, with your thrice-cursed wife, to flout me even in this den where you threw me away, abandoning me so that I might die here?

Sobs and a rough, cavernous cough interrupted her, and she threw her bloody handkerchief in Jacques's face.

"Take this, jackal, drink my blood! Drink it and be content, assassin!"

Jacques was suffering. Shame and sorrow seized him in the face of so much misery. But what could he do now? Between this nomad woman and himself, a pit had been dug, deeper than ever now.

To fill it up, and at the same time, to rid himself forever of this sad creature, he thought a bit of money would be enough. He held out his wallet to Yasmina:

"Here, he said. You are poor and sick, you must take care of yourself. Take this little bit of money . . . and goodbye."

He was stammering, ashamed suddenly of what he had just done.

Yasmina, immobile and silent, looked at him for a minute, as she had done once before, long ago, in the dry *oued* of Timgad, at the wrenching moment of their final parting. Then, suddenly, she seized his wrist, twisted it and spilled all the gold pieces in the dust.

"Dog! Coward! Kifir!"

And Jacques, his head bowed low, returned to the group that awaited him not far away, hidden by the hovels.

Yasmina fell back on the bench, overcome by convulsive sobs. Samra, the Negress, had come running at the noise, and carefully gathered up the officer's pieces of gold. Samra wound her black arms around the neck of her friend.

"Smina, my sister, my soul, don't cry. They are all like that, the Roumis, dogs and sons of dogs. But with this gold he has given you, we'll buy dresses, jewelry, medicines for your chest. But, you must not tell Ali, who will take the money from us.

But nothing could console Yasmina any more.

She had stopped crying and, somber and mute, she had taken up her waiting again . . . waiting for what, for whom?

Yasmina waited only for death, resigned to her fate.

It had been written, and there was no purpose in lamenting about it. One must wait for the end, that is all. Everything fell to pieces around her and within her, and nothing had the power any more to touch her heart, to make her happy or sad.

However, her grief was infinite. She suffered most for knowing that Jacques was living and so close to her, so close, but at the same time so far away!

Oh! How she would have preferred knowing he was dead, and buried far away in the cemetery of the Roumis, behind the Constantine Gate.

She could have — unconsciously — relived there the charmed hours of long ago, the intoxicating hours of love lived out in the dry riverbed.

She could have still tasted there a sweet and melancholy joy, instead of undergoing the horrible torments of the present.

And above all, he would not have loved another woman, a *Roumia!*

She knew that she would die there from grievous suffering: Until then, only the obstinate hope of seeing Jacques again one day, only the ferocious will to live to see him again had given her the artificial strength to fight against the rapid, devouring consumption.

Now Yasmina was no more than a lump of flesh abandoned to sickness and death, without resistance. Suddenly, the will to live was broken in her.

No rebellious spirit remained in her almost deadened soul.

It was written, and there is no remedy for what is written.

✳

About eleven o'clock, a spahi on leave passed by. He was astonished to see her still there, her back against the wall, her arms dangling, her head bowed.

"Hey, Smina! What are you doing? Want to go up?"

As she did not answer, the handsome soldier in red retraced his steps.

"Ah well," he said, surprised. "What are you thinking about, girl, or are you drunk?"

He took Yasmina's hand and leaned over her.

The Muslim straightened up, a bit pale.

"Only God in His power is eternal!" he said. Yasmina the Bedouin was no longer.

THE ANARCHIST

The father, Tereneti Antonoff, persecuted in Russia and on the point of being exiled, fled to Algeria, looking for a new land, a chosen country where, under a merciful sky, men would be less encrusted by routine.

Still almost wealthy, he had established a farm in a cheerful corner of the Tell, and there, among his fields and his books, he had pursued his dream of a better humanity. However, he had encountered there the same hostile reception from the European settlers and, little by little, he had had to withdraw, to retreat into himself.

The spirit of his only son, Andrei, already grown, had, because of this sudden transplanting, undergone a profound disturbance. All the vagueness, all the mystery of enchanting, intoxicating, fiery horizons had entered his soul, a soul predestined to be a Nordic man's.

Living apart, it was not at all men, but the land of Africa itself that had profoundly troubled him.

You are a poet of nature, his father used to tell him with an indulgent smile, just as I was a poet of humanity. We complement each other.

But Andrei had a difficult time adapting to the cloistered life that suited the lethargic existence of the old man. The specter of the unknown, nostalgia for a place as yet unknown where he could feel himself to be living harmoniously, without ungratified aspirations, gripped him.

At times, for entire months, he no longer opened a book, spending his days wandering among the Bedouins, sitting with the naive and the infirm who reminded him of the *muzhiks* of his country, whom his father had taught him to love and understand.

The old philosopher did not condemn the error of his ways, the nomadic life whose charm and salutary influence he understood, having once felt them himself.

You are right, go refresh your spirit. Go eat black bread and partake of their misery and obscurity like a brother. It will do you good.

So, little by little, Andrei let himself be captivated forever by the rugged land and the Bedouin life. His spirit languished while remaining keen and inquisitive. His lust for life eased and he looked with disdain at the vanity of all violent efforts, of all devouring activities.

When, having chosen French citizenship, he entered the French Foreign Legion as an infantryman and was assigned to an outpost in the South, his boredom and disgust with being a soldier gave way to the joy of travel and the sudden, blazing revelation of the South.

The more gentle splendors of the Tell seemed to him pale, there in that land of silence and blinding sun.

A *bordj* crowned by a tall, square tower, on a barren hill, in the middle of a frighteningly arid desert.

Not a plant, not a tree marked the burned, tormented ocher-colored land. And every day, inexorably, the same devouring sun, tearing from the earth its remaining humidity, jealous, forbidding it to live outside its capricious patterns, in the opalescent hours of the morning and the gilded purple of the evening.

There, Andrei understood the reverence ancient people had for the great celestial bodies, the all-powerful fire, both generative and destructive.

Andrei loved this *bordj* on whose door ironic revelers had inscribed the name "Eden Purée."

Surrounded by comrades eager to return and for whom absinthe was the only consolation, Andrei withdrew into himself in order to better enjoy the happy transformation that he felt welling up from the depths of his being.

The disquiet, the indefinable suffering he'd been tormented by during his youth gave way, little by little, to a calm, peaceful melancholy, to an uninterrupted dream.

He no longer read, being content to live. He was not, however, abandoning his resolution to become one day the poet of the beloved land, to reflect through his more sensitive Northern soul the sadness, harshness, and splendor of Africa.

But he still felt incomplete, and he wanted his work to be perfect. He looked about him with a lover's eyes, slowly, letting impressions accumulate naturally, by small, thin layers.

And this unappeased instinct to love veiled with a charming melancholy this existence made up of silence and dreaming.

Andrei had finished his year of service and he returned, full of nostalgia for the South, to his father, just in time to see him fall sick and die.

"Always be true to yourself. Do not bend before the hypocrisy of conventions, continue to live among the poor and to love them."

Such was the moral legacy that, in an hour of lucidity granted him by his fever, his father had bequeathed him.

The immense pain of his loss darkened the sunny horizon of Andrei's life for a long time. The smiling and gentle old man, the modest, unacknowledged sage who had taught him to love beauty, to be compassionate and feel empathy for all suffering, the teacher who had jealously made sure that no stain would spread upon the soul of the child or the youth, who had never permitted social hypocrisy to impress its discouraging seal on his heart. . . Terenti was no more. And Andrei felt completely alone and bruised, in the midst of men he felt were hostile or indifferent.

But the obligation he had to put his father's affairs in order was a salutary diversion.

Then, there was this troubling problem: what would become of him? At that moment, Andrei recalled his life in the South and lamented its loss. And he mused: "Why not return there, be free, forever?"

He sold the farm, took his father's books to an old friend, a Polish refugee who practiced the humble profession of midwife in Oran, and, all his debts paid, he had tens of thousands of francs to carry out his project.

He returned to kneel piously at the unmarked grave of the old philosopher, in the small cemetery atop a hill overlooking the bay of Mostaganem.

And then he left.

Andrei thought it was enough to have the precious gift of sorrow to be happy.

He arrived to put down roots there, in the warm shadow of the date palms of Tamerna Djedida, in the salty bed of the underground river Oued Rir'.

He had bought some palm trees, a spring permeated with salt-peter whose clear rivulets brought life to the garden, and a small square house made of red *toub*.

The Bureau Arabe in charge of the oasis had tried, given its hatred of civilians, especially independent ones, to discourage Andrei from his project. They had used all their methods against him, subtle persuasion, intimidation. He clashed with the arrogance, the conceit of these self-styled administrators in braided coats, but his calm resolve conquered their resistance.

He knew, however, that the climate of the region was brutal, that fever reigned there and killed even the local people. But hadn't he spent long months at the end of the valley of the Oued Rir', near its mouth at Chott Mel'riri? He hadn't been sick and he would endure.

He loved this mysterious, visionary country where all the hidden chemistry of matter was spread on the surface of the ground, where the iodized saltwater made whimsical white arabesques on the fragile grasses of the murmuring *seguia*, or tinted rusty red the bottoms of the small *toub* walls that made the gardens into true labyrinths of shadow.

The water ran everywhere, hollowing out holes, profound pools with still, alluring surfaces that reflected the slender fronds of palms, the fleshy leaves of fig trees and the round red fruits of pomegranates.

Then, suddenly, without transition, the desert opened out, flat, immense, blindingly white. The marshy ground was covered by a thin layer of salt with large splotches of brown humidity.

All this was blazing, sparkling to infinity while far on the horizon were tiny black marks — other oases.

And at noon in the summer, mirages played there over the dead plain from which even God's benediction had been withdrawn.

In winter, the *chotts* (salt flats) and the *sebkas* (salt lakes) would fill with clear, milky, or blue water, and the uneven ground made multicolored archipelagos in these dangerous seas.

Dressed like the local people, Andrei lived their life, accepted by them and soon loved, because he was sociable and kind and almost always healed them when, sick, they came to him to ask for advice.

He will become Muslim, they used to say, having heard him say often that Mohammad was a prophet like Jesus and Moses, come to show the true path to all men.

The inhabitants of Tamerna were the 'Rouara, blacks from the Sahara, a taciturn people of somber appearance, and ardent piety mixed with fetishist beliefs in amulets and the dead.

This foreboding magic and the silence of the desert, contrasting with the mystery and live rippling of the flooded gardens, had put their seal on the spirit of the people and darkened among them the simplicity of monotheistic Islam.

Tall and thin in their hooded, floating garments, wearing around their necks long prayer beads of yellow wood, the 'Rouara glided like phantoms through the tangle of their gardens.

To protect their dates from sorcery, they tied fetishes of bone to the ripening clusters. They adorned with grimacing faces the cornices and grooved cupolas of their *koubbas* and their molded *toub* mosques. At the corners of their hivelike houses, they attached the black horns of goats and gazelles. On the night between Thursday and Friday, a night thought to be fatidic, they lit small oil lamps near the tombs scattered throughout the countryside.

They suffered this obsession with the beyond, with questions of night and death.

Andrei opened his heart fully to all beliefs, choosing none, and these naive superstitions did not disgust him at all because, in the end, he saw in them this same need to commune with the beyond that he himself felt.

The dark-skinned women were beautiful, especially those of mixed race, beneath the complicated Saharan costume that gave them the aspect of ancient goddesses. Draped in veils of red or blue, laden with gold and silver, with hairstyles of braids looped high then laid along their cheeks, covering their ears with heavy earrings, they wrapped themselves, to go out, with dark blue cloth that concealed the brilliance of their jewelry.

Their strange charm and the mystery of their gaze attracted Andrei.

Voluptuous, but seeking intoxicating raptures illuminated by the divine glow of the illusion of love, without the brutality of appetite, Andrei had never savored gratifications that lacked even the aura of dreams. What kept him away from these gratifications were the inevitable banality and rancor of an unavoidable and sudden awakening.

And in the fire of the evening, he loved to watch the young girls go by carrying amphoras, walking in procession with rhythmic steps toward the wells with the sweeter water, at the edges of the desert where the dying sun cast their lengthening shadows on the scorched earth.

Andrei's life flowed on in happy tranquillity, monotony without boredom.

He would get up in the early dawn to taste the invigorating freshness of the gentle breeze that rustled the leaves of palms and aromatic garden plants.

On his horse, whom he loved with the pitying tenderness one feels for resigned yet proud animals, he wandered in the desert, pushing sometimes toward neighboring oases, numerous in the valley, adorned in the early light with gold and crimson.

The great open space intoxicated him, the pristine air filled his chest and an immense spontaneous joy revitalized him, dissipating the languor of the hot night that followed the burning heat of the day.

Then he would return and wander in the gardens, watching the bronzed peasants stirring the red mud of the garden plots, removing the salty sediment that obstructed the *seguias*.

It was summer, and the palm groves appeared to him in all their splendor. Under the mighty dome of the palms, clusters of dates were hanging, swollen with sap, richly colored according to their kind. Some, still green, downy with silvery dust, others straw yellow, golden yellow, orange, bright red, or purple, a warm spectrum of matte or shiny tones.

For a long while Andrei leaned over the springs flowing out from the mysterious depths of the invisible river.

Then he would return to the coolness of his simple room and would stretch out on his bed of reeds to abandon himself to the fatal and bewitching languor of the siesta.

When the shadow of the date palms stretched out over the weary earth, Hadj Hafaid, Andrei's servant, would wake him gently, bidding him to go refresh himself with a bath.

At times, gripped with a nostalgia for work, Andrei would write and, from time to time, at long intervals, he would summon his memory of the subtle literary research concerning stories of the fantastic into which he had put a bit of his soul, his life.

On the road to Touggourt, not far from the large, enclosed cemeteries, lived two women, the old one, Mahennia, and her daughter,

Saadia, whose husband had repudiated her because people said that she and her mother were sorcerers.

They lived poorly on the earnings of the old woman, a midwife, herbalist, and skilled bone-setter.

They were respected in the country and feared because of the rumors that had circulated about their sorcery and about the inexplicable death of Saadia's husband soon after their divorce.

Of mixed race, almost Arab, the two women remembered their Semitic heritage and exalted it.

Saadia was beautiful and her warm, olive-tinted, oval face was characterized by the grave melancholy of her eyes.

She lived modestly with her mother, and despite her beauty, the superstitious 'Rouara fled from her.

Andrei, in the course of his solitary walks, saw her many times and the old woman, anxious about the success the Roumi had as a healer, tried not to attract his hostility. She offered him the drink of hospitality, coffee, and she did not hide her daughter from his eyes.

Saadia served him attentively and silently.

Andrei knew the mysterious rumors that circulated about these women and the strangeness of their existence had drawn him to them, and charmed him.

Saadia's beauty and her sadness were for him a delicious discovery and he often returned from then on to the old woman's.

He wanted Saadia and did not fight his desire.

Wouldn't it be an embellishment to his too solitary life to be loved by this mysterious girl; and wouldn't it be a more complete fusion with his chosen land through the medium of this creature of the native soil?

Voluptuously Andrei abandoned himself to the flames of his desire. The impenetrable Saadia did not betray her feelings other than by a heavy-lidded gaze that captivated this blond, gray-eyed man of sweet and dreamy countenance.

All the rebelliousness of her solitary youth, all her need to be loved and not to remain a flower blooming in the silent desert, Saadia transferred to the one man who did not flee her.

Soon becoming less shy, she spoke to him, she told him the names of the dried herbs that hung in bunches from the roof of their house, and explained their virtues and their dangers.

That one is the fragrant *nana* whose juice cures stomach ailments, and that is gray *chih* whose smoke soothes coughs.

Her husky voice, resonant, sometimes staccato, had a strange accent in Arabic, which Andrei now understood.

Other times, Saadia would name for him the jewels she wore. One day, in order to better understand her, Andrei asked her how her husband had died.

"When one's time has come, no one can stop it even for the blink of an eye, and he who would commit injustice incurs God's wrath."

A shadow passed over Saadia's face.

One day, he found her home alone. Their house was isolated and hidden by palms. She smiled and invited him in just the same.

"Will your mother come home soon?"

"No, she won't come. But do you come here to see her only? She is old and her days have run out."

And Andrei, in the painful desire to love, looked at her.

Smiling, her expression becoming softer, she stood before him, welcoming. For the first time, Andrei knew the complete ecstasy of the senses for which he had wisely prepared himself, embellishing it with all his dreams.

When the evening moon filled the room, Saadia sent him away, softly and prudently.

"Go a roundabout way. I don't know if the old one will pardon us. It is better that I sound her out first."

So, Andrei left.

The desert, all red, flamed and a blue shadow stretched out like a veil beneath the palms whose tops were illuminated by plumes of fire.

Andrei stopped, made breathless by the sudden revelation of the beauty of the earth and the fullness of life.

THE MAJOR

Everything, in this Algeria, had been a revelation for him, a source of distress even — of anguish. A sky too serene, a sun too dazzling, an atmosphere in which there languished, like a slow sigh that invited indolence and idle voluptuousness, the solemnity of a people draped in white, whose soul he could not penetrate, the deep green vegetation, contrasting with the rocky gray or red soil, parched and apparently desiccated, and then something indefinable, but bewildering and intoxicating, which emanated from an unknown source, all this had agitated him, had caused to burst forth in him wellsprings of emotion of which he had never suspected the existence.

In coming here, out of duty, just as he had studied medicine in order to support his blind mother, his two sisters, and his frail little brother, just as he had lived and thought until now, he had bowed to necessity, simply, without enthusiasm, without attraction to this land of which he was ignorant.

Nevertheless, once he had been appointed, he had not wished to read anything, before getting to know this land where he had transplanted his silent and sober life, and his sad and limited dreams, before attempting to make any judgment.

He would see, independently, alone, without submitting to any influence.

Since his arrival he had had to listen to the warnings of his new comrades who welcomed him and whom he found ironic, protective, disdainful of callow youth, above all anxious about the impressions they made, anxious to astound him. He listened indifferently to their criticisms and their complaints: no social life, nothing to do, utter boredom. A land without charm, brutal settlers singularly preoccupied with gain, repugnant natives, some aping the settlers, primitive, beneath censure, ridiculous.

He was indifferent to all that, and he made only one acquaintance among these comrades with whom he had to live.

Then, one day, taken by surprise, this child of the green and forested Alps, of clear, defined horizons, entered into the great, desert plain, vague and infinitely monotonous, without foreground, almost without anything that caught the eye.

This was for him at first a discomfort, an annoyance. He felt all the infiniteness, all the imprecision of this horizon invade him, penetrate him, enfeeble his spirit, as if clouding his soul with the vague and inexpressible. Then, suddenly he felt how much his dream was expanding, spreading out, soothing itself into an immense calm, like the surrounding silence. And he saw the splendor of this land where the light alone triumphed, illuminating the plain, the mottled soil, constantly destroying sameness. The light, soul of this harsh ground, was bewitching. He was close to worshiping it, because in its wonderful variety it seemed alive to him.

He knew the happiness, the quiet joy in the diaphanous golds and purples of the morning. The anxiety, the captivating, heavy spell, the anguish even, of the blinding noons, when the intoxicated land seemed to moan beneath the burning caress of the flaming light. The indefinable sorrow, the peaceful resignation of the red-gold evenings, setting the scene for the impending mystery of the nights, obscure and indecipherable, or clear like an uncertain dawn, drowning all things in a blue mist.

And he loved the desert plain.

Pale dunes, heaped up, crowded, surging, changing hues each hour, submitting to the variations of light, but immobile, as if dreaming an eternal dream, surrounded the colorless *ksar*, whose innumerable domes seemed to rise and fall continuously.

Narrow twisting streets, lined with tumbledown adobe houses, some in ruins, now and then the dappled shadow of a date palm playing over things, obeying the light as well, small open spaces leading into quiet passages which gave suddenly, deceptively, onto the incandescent immensity of the desert. A white *bordj*, isolated in the sands, from the terrace of which one could see the infinite swells of the dunes, in the deep hollows between them, the dark velvet of date palms. Here and there, the armature of a primitive well, a beam reaching toward the sky, inclined, ending in a rope like a giant fishing pole. Dominating everything, at the top of the hill, a great square tower, its whiteness shimmering amid the transparent airs at midday, dazzling, and later, in the evening catching the last red rays of the setting sun: the minaret of the *zaouiya* of Sidi Salem.

All around, hidden in the dunes, were solitary villages, sad and dilapidated, whose names had a strange music for Jacques: El-Bayada, Foum-Sahheuine, Oued-Allenda, Bir-Arair.

Jacques's first sensation, sharp to the point of anguish, was that he was imprisoned in all this sand, after all the deserted places through which he had traveled in the last eight days, and which he believed he had understood, and had begun to love. But now all this space, which separated him from Biskra, where he had seen the last barely recognizable landmarks and familiar landscapes, seemed to him overbearing and hostile, almost to the point of despair.

A captain, two lieutenants of indigenous affairs, an officer of the tirailleurs, and an Arab sub-lieutenant of the spahis, an old fossil worn thin by the heavy yoke of duty, these were his new companions. From the time of his arrival among them, he felt a chill gripping his heart. They were courteous, bored, distant from him, so distant. And he found himself alone, sadly, with the anguish of this land that now frightened him. Silent in his dealings with men, always obeying those instinctive impressions that he thought to be fairest, he withdrew into himself. They found him sullen and uninteresting, this pale blue-eyed blond whose gaze was always turned inward. What ended up separating them finally was that he immediately felt superior to them because of his profoundly developed intellect and his advanced education.

He studied the rough, singsong language of the natives conscientiously; its accent immediately appealed to him and he understood its harmony with the burning horizons and the parched earth.

So he would speak with these men who, with eyes lowered and hearts firmly closed, stood up deferentially as he passed by.

"The natives, whoever they are, are required to salute all officers," said Captain Malet, a man just as stiff and absorbed in his harsh career as Rezki the Turk.

"I urge you to never get too familiar with these people, to keep them in their place. Be severe, always, without fail. That is the only way to tame them."

Hard, cold, blindly following orders from above, the Captain never acted spontaneously out of kindness or cruelty. He remained impersonal. Captain Malet had been living among the natives for fifteen years — ignored by them and ignorant of them: a perfect meshing of cogs in the great machine called domination. Of his aides he required the same impersonal attitude, the same extreme coldness.

Jacques, from the outset, rebelled, wanting to be himself and to act according to his conscience, which inevitably led him into mistakes, disillusionment, and perpetual uncertainty.

The captain shrugged his shoulders.

"Here is a new source of problems," he said to his assistant. "The other one (Jacques's predecessor) was a drunkard and made us look ridiculous. This one is here to make innovations, upset everything, judge, criticize. I'll bet he is imbued with 'humanitarian' ideals, social causes, and other things of the same sort. Thank God he's only a doctor and won't have to meddle with administration. But it's annoying just the same. All said and done, the other was better, less of a burden. Why do they send us kids! If only they'd give us settlers."

And the Captain dedicated himself from then on to demonstrating his complete disapproval to the doctor, frankly and coldly. It saddened Jacques. Although he didn't submit to their judgment, he still suffered from their hate, if not their contempt.

More and more what disgusted him most in his dealings with these men was their vulgarity, their dedication to be, think, and act like everyone else, to look like one another, to impose on one another the same orthodox and narrow point of view.

This appropriation of one another's liberty, this meddling in one another's thoughts and actions appalled him. Not content to be nonentities themselves, these people wanted to annihilate his own personality, regiment his ideas, check the independence of his actions. And little by little, despite the natural mildness of his shy and affectionate character, he felt growing within him mute anger, rancor, and revolt. Why did he tolerate the diversity of humanity, why had he wished to be able to advocate the free and fertile blooming of individuality, to promote its unhindered development; why had he no desire to mold other personalities in his image, to imprison their energies in the paths that it pleased him to follow, and why was there, in others, this intolerance, this tyrannical proselytism in the name of mediocrity?

Very quickly, his intellect and his character were being educated, developing in this limited environment in which he saw a microcosm of all the ugliness that had escaped him elsewhere, pervading the motley and shifting crowds.

Nevertheless, the profound disquiet that had arisen in his soul upon the sudden revelation of this land so different from his own was subsiding gradually but perceptibly. There, where he had at first experienced the pain of extreme disquiet, he began to perceive the riches of beneficent peace and fertile melancholy.

At first, he hadn't wanted to "visit" this land where, for at least eighteen months, he had been isolated. As for being a tourist, he had neither the curiosity nor the taste. He preferred to discover the finer details gradually, little by little, by chance, in day-to-day life and during his daily walks without aim or destination. Then, out of this accumulation of impressions, a larger picture would form in his mind, would surge up on its own, naturally.

Thus, he had ordered his life so that he would suffer less and could meditate more.

The day after his arrival, he had to go in the morning to visit the civilian patients, the natives. A young tirailleur, beautiful as a woman, with shadowy and languorous almond eyes, acted as interpreter. At the infirmary, a jovial orderly with a ruddy and beaming countenance helped him.

In a long and narrow courtyard, about twenty natives were waiting, squatting in quiet and relaxed poses.

When Jacques appeared, the feeble-looking patients stood up, and saluted him clumsily.

The women, five or six of them, raised both hands awkwardly over their bowed heads, as if to ask for grace.

In the eyes of these people, he detected a certain fear bordering on distrust.

The group of men in dirty burnouses, their brown faces full of life, their ardent eyes hidden by soiled, ragged kerchiefs. The women were more somber. The lined, toothless faces of the old ones, burdened with braids of white hair dyed with henna, and adorned with tresses of red cotton, with rings, scarves. The sensual but impenetrable faces of the young girls, with pronounced but clear and harmonious features, olive-skinned, fearful eyes open wide — all draped as of old in dark blue-black *mlahfas*.

Attentively, tempering with his mild gaze and his reassuring, affectionate manner the brusqueness with which the infantryman interpreted his questions, Jacques examined his patients, pitiable in the face of all this misery, all this suffering which he was to relieve.

The visit was a long one. He noticed the ironic surprise of the Corporal. The tirailleur was impassive.

However, despite the new attitude of this doctor toward them, the natives did not open up, did not anticipate his actions. Centuries of distrust and servitude were between them.

Upon leaving, Jacques felt clearly that the task, for which he wanted to be a humble worker, was immense, overwhelming. But he did not despair. If everyone were to throw up their arms helplessly in the face of all this work, if no one set a good example, evil would always triumph, irremediably. And besides, Jacques believed in the vital force of truth, in the good redemptive virtue of hard work.

At the barracks, at the hospital, he encountered the same impassive, hard faces, which like that of his assistant were stiff and inhuman. The naked poverty of their lives struck him: mechanical activities, a minimal number of movements and identical gestures infinitely repeated, first out of fear, then out of habit. Beyond that, in their personal lives, they were left with two choices: the numbing of alcohol and the cheap instant gratification of the whorehouse. There, in that narrow circuit, they had spent the best years of their lives.

Eight pale creatures, faded, seated on stone benches in front of a sort of bar, wearing light clothing, stained, torn and dirty, but reeking of perfume. Their flaccid, scarred bodies were worn out from being kneaded by brutal hands on infested wool mattresses. For a few pennies, they submitted to a weary embrace, out of necessity, without the echo or vibration of sympathetic flesh. Bottles of strong alcohol, procuring a borrowed warmth, a false joy that they could not find in themselves, such was the corner of personal life in which these men sought refuge, men who, in exchange for a sure meal and a pallet, had sold their freedom, the last liberty of man: to go where one pleases, to choose the ditch in which one will suffer the agonies of hunger, the bite of the cold.

Jacques naively believed he empathized with their suffering, assuming they felt the same sensations he did. He believed their constant recriminations against their fate resulted from their conscious awareness of their miserable state. Then, he was astonished and troubled to discover that they did not suffer from living like that. "It's a dog's life," "Damned and double damned," they said. "So many days down, and so many to go." They counted the days of misery left. Then, set free at the end of their "leave," they reenlisted, without flinching. If, by chance, they left, at the end of six months, hard up, having led an aimless existence, they returned and put their docile necks back under the yoke. And Jacques pitied them for being thus, for not suffering from their disgrace and their servitude.

Jacques had dreamed of the civilizing mission of France, he had believed he would find in the *ksar* men conscious of their mission, dedicated to ameliorating those lives they controlled so completely. But, to the contrary, he quickly perceived that the system in operation had but one goal — the preservation of the status quo.

Never provoke the least thought in the natives, never inspire in them the least desire, particularly not the least hope for a better destiny. Not only should one not seek to assimilate them but, on the contrary, keep them at a distance, keep them in the shadows, keep them low . . . remain their masters but don't become their educators.

And wasn't it natural? Because when they were in familiar surroundings at the barracks, these people never tried to elevate themselves to the level of the French or to reach out in human fashion to the masses below, the impersonal crowd, because they had become accustomed to being there to squelch any manifestation of independence, any innovation; so how, invited by fate, which they could only consider beneficent because it served at once their self-interests and their ambitions to govern the natives who were doubly estranged, first as *pekins* and then as natives, how then could they help but be faithful to their concept of military duty: discourage individuality, submit these people to the strictest subordination, check any development that would lead them to be less docile.

And he concluded: No, it is not their job to govern civilians. No, they will never be educators. Each one of them, upon departure, will leave things in the same state he found them upon arrival, without improving them at all. It is the reign of stagnation, and the military territories are separated from the rest of the world, from France herself, alive and vibrant, from the true Algeria, by a sort of Chinese Wall, which they maintained and which they would like to raise even higher, make forever impenetrable, an exclusive fiefdom of the army, closed to everything that is not the army.

And a great sadness invaded him at the thought of this task, which could have been so fruitful and which was botched.

What increased the bitterness of his discontent even more was his personal impotence to make anything better, given this state of affairs in which he saw clearly a social and national danger for France.

Occupying a minor position in this hierarchy that dominated everything and was the basis of everything, next to the omnipotent Bureau Arabe, having no authority himself, he had to remain in the role of inactive spectator.

In the beginning, he had tried to speak up at the mess hall, but he ran up against resolute prejudice, against the sincere and obstinate conviction of these people and also against their irony, which silenced him.

"You are young, doctor, and you know nothing of this land, of the natives. When you get to know them, you will think as we do. Captain Malet had said these words in a tone of ironic condescension that had chilled Jacques to the bone.

From the time that he began to understand Arabic and to know how to express himself a bit, he liked to go stretch himself out on a mat in front of a Moorish café to listen to people, to their songs, free-spirited, like the desert and like himself, unfathomably sad, or to their idle conversation. Little by little, the Souafas were becoming used to this Roumi, to this officer who was not strict, not snobbish, who spoke to them with an open smile, who sat among them, who, by a gesture, stopped them when they wanted to get up at his approach to salute him.

Why was he like that? They did not know, did not understand. But they found him helpful in all their miseries, fighting patiently, step by step, their mistrust, their ignorance. Sick people, reassured by the doctor's reputation for goodness, flowed into the Bureau Arabe, talked to him during his walks, disturbed his dreams on the mats of the cafés. Instead of becoming impatient, he saw that progress was being made, and he rejoiced. The difficulty of his task did not discourage him, nor the ingratitude of many.

His favorite hour of rest, full of sweet and melancholy dreams, was during the evening, at sunset. He used to go to a small Moorish café across from the Bureau Arabe, and there, stretched out, would watch with renewed enchantment every day, the mystery of the violet hour.

Across from him, the milky white buildings of the *bordj* turned first rose, then little by little completely red, glowing like embers, wonderful, blinding. All the lines, straight or curved, profiled against the purple sky, seemed mounted in gold. Beyond the blazing domes of the town, the great dunes were flaming. Then, all paled gradually, returning to rose, iridescent. A pale fog, silvery buff in color, glided onto the ledges of the buildings, onto the summits of the dunes. From all over the landscape, along the narrow corridors between the dunes, the violet shadows of night came creeping, climbing toward the flaming summits, damping the fire. Then everything disappeared into the deep navy-blue twilight.

Then, from the great minaret of Sidi Salem and from the small terraces of other dilapidated mosques, the voices of the muezzins rose, hoarse and quite untamed, lingering. With these enchanting voices, the last human rumblings of this town, without pavement, without cars, died out, and every evening a thin Bedouin flute began to whisper melodies of infinitely deep sadness, there in the tiny ruined streets of Messaaba, to the west of El Oued.

Jacques was in a dream.

He loved this land now. The daily tasks he performed satisfied his impatient need for activity. And all the immense sadness, all the mystery that was the enchantment of this land satisfied his need for dreams.

Because of his moral bent, and also out of shyness, Jacques had remained very chaste. But here, much more than at home in France, as life grew more monotonous, he was troubled in his lonely soul by the stirring insatiable urges. He hadn't expected that. However, at first, this desire which, in him, exacerbated the intensity of all his sensations, was sweet, if unappeased. He held his soul open to all delights, to all ecstasies.

But soon his overwrought nerves wearied of this abnormal, exhausting tension, and Jacques felt a vague irritation, an unconquerable oversensitivity, pervade him, disturbing his peace of mind.

He got angry at himself, fought against this excitement of the senses whose nature he could not dissimulate.

Then, one evening he was wandering slowly and aimlessly in the tiny streets of Acheche, in the north part of El Oued, where all the houses were in ruins and seemed uninhabited. He loved this silent, abandoned corner. The inhabitants had died without leaving heirs or had gone into the desert, to Ghadames, to Bar-es-Souf or farther. Night was falling and Jacques, seated on a rock, was dreaming.

Suddenly, he saw in one of the ruins a small, flickering light. A voice rose, rhythmic, accompanied by the clink of bracelets. . . . the voice of a woman softly singing. It seemed an incantation, so mysterious was the sadness in the rhythm of this song. The eternal wind of the Souf whispered through the ruins, and on this warm breeze wafted the scent of benzoin.

The song broke off and a woman appeared in the doorway of a house a bit less tumbledown than the others. Tall and slender in her black *mlahfa*, she leaned gracefully against the wall. Jacques saw her silhouette barely visible against the glow of the violet-tinted evening. A bit faded, almost weary, she was quite beautiful, like a finely sculpted statue.

She saw him and trembled. But she did not go back in. For a long time they looked at one another, and Jacques felt an inexpressible confusion invade him.

"Arouah!" she said, quite low. "Come!"

And he approached her, without hesitation.

She took him by the hand and guided him into the darkness of the ruins, toward a small light suspended on an iron hook driven into the wall; a small antique lamp was burning, flickering: a sort of small square, iron censer containing oil in which a large wick was swimming. Two still habitable rooms opened onto a small interior court. In a corner, on a fire burnt to embers, a pot of water was boiling. A large black cat, curled into a ball, was dreaming in the red glow of the fire, purring gently.

The woman seated Jacques in the doorway and remained standing silently in front of him. Jacques took her hands. His own hands trembled and he felt his head reeling delightfully. His chest tightened and he felt choked by emotion. Never had he felt rapture so poignant and he wanted to prolong this delicious torture indefinitely. But, without knowing, he blurted.

"But . . . who are you, and how is it you are here?"

Her name was Embarka, the Blessed. Her husband, a poor farmer from the tribe of Acheche, was dead. She, an orphan, had only a brother left, a water carrier in the big towns of the Tell, she no longer knew exactly where. Left alone, she followed the tirailleurs and the spahis: she went out and she drank with them. Then, since no one wanted her for a wife anymore, she had sought refuge there, in her brother's old house, and she had been living in it with a blind aunt. She prostituted herself for food. Now, she feared the Bureau Arabe. It all depended on him, the doctor, and she begged him not to force her into a brothel, and to keep her secret. Jacques reassured her. Embarka said little. Her story had been simple and brief. She seemed worried.

She left Jacques for a moment to block up the entrance with boards and stones: sometimes the soldiers came by at night.

Then, she came back and carried the small lamp into an empty, barren room: a table, covered with a cloth and a few rags, made up all the furniture. Suddenly, there was happiness, almost as he had dreamt of. And life seemed to him very simple and very good.

*

In their intimacy, Embarka remained silent, discreet, in absolute submission, yet without opening up. And this veil of mystery in which she unconsciously wrapped herself, far from disquieting Jacques, charmed him. When she saw him dreaming, she kept quiet, squatting in the small yard or attending to chores in her house. Or, she sang and her slow, slightly nasal, low, soft voice matched the cadence of his own dream.

He went there every evening, leaving behind the dull military canteen, and the home of this native prostitute became his own.

From the first day, she had accepted this new life, without any surprise, without any hesitation. She didn't miss anything. In the evenings, the drunken soldiers no longer came to buy her love and to make her suffer, no longer had the right to beat her for a few pennies. Embarka was happy.

In the barracks and at the Bureau Arabe, Jacques noticed much progress. No more dark suspicious looks, no more fear mixed with fierce hatred. And he sincerely believed he had won over all these men.

There certainly was some negligence on their part toward him. They were less eager to serve him, less docile, often disobeying his orders and acknowledging it without fear, because he didn't choose to exercise his power to punish.

Jacques was too discerning to miss all that. But was it not natural? If these men were submissive to his comrades, to the point of complete abdication of human volition, it was fear that coerced them into it. They were more eager to serve him than to obey him.

But they did that too, reluctantly. In his case, even Rezki, usually so stiff and cold, waited on him obligingly. Even in the constant struggle against the ill will of the natives who didn't want to follow his prescriptions, much less improve their hygiene, Jacques had won some victories. He earned the friendship of the most intelligent among them, the marabouts and students. By his respect for their faith, by his clear desire to get to know them, to penetrate their ways of seeing and thinking, he gained their esteem, which opened many other, usually simpler and more obscure, hearts to him.

Why rule by terror? Why inspire fear, which is merely a form of repugnance, of horror? Why insist absolutely on blind, passive obedience? Jacques asked himself these questions and found in all honesty that this entire system of oppression disgusted him. He didn't want to participate in it.

One day the Captain summoned the doctor to his office.

"Listen, my dear Doctor. You are very young, new to this business. You need to be advised. Well! I regret so much to have to say this to you, but you still don't know very well how to conduct yourself here. You are excessively lenient with the men. You understand, as commander, I have to be vigilant about the preservation of discipline.

"However, this breach is still less serious than your attitude toward the natives. You are much too familiar with them; you don't exercise the care necessary to affirm your superiority, your authority over them. Believe me, they are all alike, they need to be ruled with an iron fist. Your attitude could have, in the future, the most unfortunate consequences. It could even stir up trouble in these untamed and fanatic souls. You believe in their claims of devotion, in the alleged friendship of their religious leaders. But all this is nothing but deceit. Watch out! Watch out! As far as I am concerned, it's only for your own good that I tell you this. In addition, I have to anticipate the consequences of your behavior. You understand, I have all the responsibility here!"

Deeply wounded, and moreover annoyed, Jacques felt a surge of anger. At first bewildered, then gloomy, he explained his thoughts, all that he had distilled from his observations, to the Captain.

Captain Malet knit his brows.

"Doctor, with these ideas, it is impossible for you to carry out your service here. Abandon them, I beg you. All that is armchair philosophy, pure literature. Here, with such ideas, we would soon stir up a rebellion."

Faced with this dismal lack of understanding, Jacques was overwhelmed by rage and despair.

"You may think what you like, Doctor, but please, don't put such ideas into practice here. In any case, I cannot tolerate it. There are so few of us French here, that, instead of sowing dissension among ourselves, we should cooperate."

"Right! For a useful purpose, humane and French," cried Jacques.

The Captain replied coldly:

"We are here to defend and maintain the honor and glory of the French flag. And I believe we fulfill that duty loyally, as soldiers and patriots. One cannot do otherwise without failing in one's duty. We are soldiers, just soldiers. Anyway, I just wanted to warn you."

Jacques, his peace of mind disturbed, annoyed and irritated, took his leave. They parted coldly.

But sure of his convictions, Jacques didn't change anything in his attitude.

Day by day, he felt his comrades becoming more hostile. His dealings with them remained courteous, but were reduced to the bare minimum. He was not wanted, he was an embarrassment.

＊

So Jacques withdrew into himself even more and the little house in ruins became dearer to him. There he rested in the surroundings that he loved; there he was far from all that made his life intolerable at the *bordj*. Embarka didn't question him about the causes of his sadness, but, sitting at his feet, she sang him his favorite plaintive ballads or smiled at him.

Did she love him? Jacques couldn't tell. But this uncertainty didn't make him suffer because what attracted and charmed him most about her was the mystery that hovered around her being. She was for him almost the incarnation of her land and race, with her sadness, her silence, her absolute inaptitude for gaiety or for laughter. Because Embarka never laughed.

In her smile Jacques discovered the riches of sadness and voluptuousness. Indeed, he loved her as she was, without understanding her or her mystery, because of the intoxicating prospect that in her he could love his own dream.

In different circumstances, if he had known the land and the Arab race better, and above all, if their strange love had started more simply, perhaps Jacques would have seen Embarka in a different light. Little by little, Jacques became once again calm and courageous, forgetting the Captain's warning, in which he hadn't seen the least danger.

And, sensuously, he let life take its course.

It had already been six months since his arrival. Now he knew the language of the desert, he knew these men who at first had seemed so mysterious to him, but who were, after all, just men like everyone else, no better and no worse, just *different*. And in fact what made Jacques like them was that they were *different*, they didn't possess the thick-headed vulgarity he had detested so much in Europe.

And the gray, sandy horizon surrounding the dreary town didn't distress Jacques any more: his soul communed with the infinite.

*

At dawn, in clear and exhilarating weather, Jacques left the ruins. An overwhelming joy gladdened his heart. He walked happily, drunk with life and youth, in the awakening streets. This land that he loved seemed completely new to him, as if a veil that had hidden it until now had been abruptly rent. El Oued, immutably framed by dunes, appeared to Jacques with so much unsuspected splendor.

Oh! To stay there, forever, never to go away again! To accomplish the good work, at once painful and captivating, for which he was destined; then, at other times, to abandon himself to the exquisite serenity of contemplation. Finally, in the warm nights, to give himself completely to the exquisite rapture of this unbidden love. Jacques didn't know what to think of this adventure, of this woman, of what would become of this fledgling dream; he didn't want to analyze his feelings. When, perchance, he considered ordering these new impressions, his thoughts flooded in, fully, rapidly to the point of incoherence, and he preferred to abandon himself to her sadness and her tranquil serenity that nothing ever came to disturb.

It seemed to him that, in this land, the days and the months passed away more slowly, more harmoniously than elsewhere. His anxiety subsided and his soul rejoiced in the silence of things, full of peace without suffering. He clearly felt he was becoming bit by bit, almost insensibly, inclined to inactivity, but he gave himself over to it voluptuously.

He had decided to ask to stay there forever, because he no longer felt any desire to see cities again, or Europeans, or even solid, wet, verdant earth. He loved his Souf, burning and melancholy, and would have chosen to live out his days there in the serenity and beauty of this peaceful land.

*

Jacques felt singularly apprehensive when, toward the middle of January, the Captain summoned him again. The commander of the outpost was gruff and cold this time.

"I have already warned you several times, Doctor, that your attitude is not becoming to your rank and your duties. Not only that, in your interactions with the people and with your native patients, you didn't heed my advice at all, and moreover, you've been carrying on an affair with a native woman of doubtful character. You've taken her as your mistress and moved in with her. Now you openly advertise your relationship by walking with her in the evening. You must admit that such conduct is intolerable. I beg you, then, to break off this relationship that is as absurd as it is damaging to your prestige, to ours, to everyone's. I beg you, break it off. It is childish behavior and must stop immediately; otherwise, we will all look profoundly ridiculous. Of course you realize how unpleasant it is for me to have to talk to you like this. Excuse my bluntness, but I cannot tolerate such goings on. Imagine! You go sit at a Moorish café, next to those wretches whom you have discouraged from greeting you with proper respect. You have made compromising friendships with marabouts. And then this liaison, this terrible liaison!"

Jacques protested. Was he not even the master of his private life anymore, of his behavior in his free time! How could other officers keep, in the barracks, Negresses given them by native chiefs. How could others bring there European women, repulsive sluts from the disreputable quarters of Algiers or Constantine, who sat insolently around at the mess hall, at the club, even at the Bureau Arabe, and who demanded that the most respectable of the natives bow down to them and that the soldiers obey them!

"None of that stains the honor of these officers in the least. The Negresses are mere servants, maids, that's all. One mustn't make a big deal out of it. As for the European women, a liaison with one of them is not in the least reprehensible, and it is only natural that the natives, whether civilian or in uniform, should be obliged to show the utmost respect toward French women. You should see the difference yourself between the harmless relationships of these officers and yours, so eccentric and so damaging to your prestige."

"Mine is certainly more ethical and more human, Captain."

"Anyway, I will drop this painful discussion and, because you force me, I have to warn you that, if you don't completely change your way of life and your actions, if you don't conform to the customs dictated by reason and by the necessities of occupation, I will find myself under the obligation, disagreeable to me as it is, to ask your superiors to relieve you of your job."

Jacques knew the Captain's harsh, dry character, but he would never have dreamt of this possibility, now so terrible. He went to his room and stayed there for a long time, stock-still and shaken. To change his way of life, to become like the others, to give up his personality and his convictions, to become an automaton, to give up the good work already started . . . to drive Embarka from his life . . . finally, to be annihilated.

What good would it be then to stay here in this town that would have become a prison.

And the need to leave, cruel as the uprooting of a part of his soul and his flesh and bone, dawned on him.

No, he would not submit. He would remain true to himself.

A mournful weariness invaded his heart. But, bravely, he did not change a thing about his way of life.

✳

A new form of suffering awaited him. He noticed that his friends, the marabouts and the native chiefs, were uneasy in his presence, that they didn't enjoy his visits anymore as in the past, that they didn't ask him to stay longer as they used to, or welcome him. They became cold and respectful again. At the café, in spite of his protests, people would stand, they would salute him, and groups dispersed when he arrived.

The joy of his life was interrupted. Again, he was a stranger. Something mysterious and threatening had awakened all his suspicions and fears. His achievements were collapsing lamentably, still unfinished, shattered, abruptly, cruelly.

The hospital orderlies had become blatantly ironic and, in their attitudes, instead of the cheerful good nature he had encouraged, there was at times insolence, almost contempt.

His friends and companions on long journeys, the spahis of the

Bureau Arabe, had become entrenched in deafening silence again, in the distant submission of the early days.

And then, there was Embarka.

But the certainty that all these dreams that had intoxicated him for half a year were coming to an end, that everything was falling apart, that it was the agonizing end of his happiness, disturbed the peacefulness of his place of refuge in the ruins.

Jacques spent exceedingly bitter hours thinking about those happy days, forever vanished, and about the causes of his downfall.

He understood that it would have been enough for the Captain and his assistants to say in front of the native chiefs how much they condemned the doctor's attitude, and how undesirable their association with him was, for these chiefs to feel obliged, because of their absolute subordination, to abandon him.

An overwhelming sadness gripped Jacques's heart. A chance incident hastened the collapse of all that he had built for himself — for his way of life, his way of thinking.

Embarka used to visit a friend of hers who was married to a man of the Messaaba tribe. In her careless way, as an outcast, she didn't veil her face.

One night, on her way back from this part of town, far from her own, she was insulted by Amor-Ben-Dif-Allah, the keeper of a brothel. Self-assured and never fearful, Embarka responded. The women of the house got mixed up in the quarrel and the police took Embarka to prison.

Convicted of clandestine soliciting, she was imprisoned for fifteen days and listed on the register of prostitutes. Jacques protested strongly, broken-hearted to see his dream dragged through the mud.

"Oh! Good God, she was your mistress? I didn't know that it was her . . . oh! how embarrassing!" exclaimed the Captain. "But you see how right I was to warn you! What a scandal. Now everybody will be talking about the doctor's mistress. What are we to do about this?"

"I couldn't release her to you after such a turn of events; if you took up with her again, it would cause a horrible scandal. Oh, you didn't heed my advice at all!"

Trembling with emotion and anger, Jacques answered:

"So, you are going to leave her in jail. Until when?"

"You know that prostitution is very strictly regulated. This woman can only leave prison in order to enter a brothel."

"She was no longer a prostitute because we lived as man and wife together."

"They found her in the vicinity of the brothel, face uncovered, causing a major row. She was arrested. You see, Doctor, the information we have on her proves that she never quit her vile profession. This woman cannot be returned to you, for your own good. I see you are excessively romantic. So what can I do!"

The Captain was getting agitated but wanted to maintain a courteous and conciliatory tone.

All of a sudden, Jacques, for whom this discussion was terribly painful, made a decision, the only option left for him.

"Then, Captain, I am going to dispatch a telegram, this very day, for my replacement — for health reasons."

A glimmer of joy shone beneath the Captain's inscrutable look:

"Maybe you are right. I understand how much this stay at El Oued is painful for you, with your ideas, which I am sure will change before long. We certainly will miss you very much but, for your own sake, it is better that you leave."

"Yes, finally I am leaving with the firm and unalterable conviction that your system of administration is absolutely wrong and represents a growing danger to the French cause."

The Captain shrugged.

"To each his own, Doctor. After all, you are a free man."

"Yes, I want to be free!"

And Jacques left.

Now he waited impatiently for clearance to leave this land that he loved so much, where he had wanted to stay forever. And, oddly enough, now that he knew he was going to leave, it seemed to Jacques that he had already left the Souf, that this town and this land that stretched out around him could have been any town and any land, but certainly not his resplendent and mournful Souf. He looked at the familiar landscape with the same dreamy indifference one feels when looking at a strange port, where one has never been, would never go, from the deck of a ship, during a short layover.

✳

By bribing the guard, he managed to get into Embarka's cell for an instant. It was for him another disillusionment, a new source of rancor: she met him with a torrent of bitter reproaches, tears and sobs. He didn't love her — officer that he was, capable of doing whatever he wanted, he'd left her to be imprisoned, to be listed on the register. She insulted him, becoming cold and hostile in her turn, forever.

Jacques left her.

✳

Everything was truly ended.

He wanted, at least, to see the little house in ruins where he had been so happy.

How alone he was now, and everything that he had thought so solid, so long-lasting, now resembled these crumbling, gray, and useless ruins.

Jacques suffered. Resigned, he left; he felt truly incapable of starting over here, starting another life, stale and devoid of meaning.

✳

Under an azure sky, still transparent and shining, under the heavy burden of summer, the dunes of the Souf spread out, undulating, blue-tinted on the distant horizon. Jacques wanted to leave his beloved land at his favorite hour, at sunset. And, for the last time, he looked at these vistas that he would never see again. His heart ached.

For the last time, before his nostalgic eyes, the great enchantment of transparent evening was unfolding.

When he passed the huge dune of Si Omar, and when El Oued disappeared behind the rising wall of purple sand, Jacques felt a consoling resignation in his heart. He was calm now and he watched the tiny, wretched hamlets, the small *zerbias* (fenced yards) made of palm branches, the domed houses passing in front of his eyes; and the violet shadows of the two red-clad spahis' horses stretching out infinitely against the red light of the evening.

Then suddenly the idea occurred to him that, undoubtedly, he was made that way, and all his enterprises would be aborted, that all his dreams would end like this, and he would go into exile, more or less driven out of all the corners where he would try to live and love.

Indeed, he would never be like the *others*. He would never submit to the tyrannical yoke of mediocrity.

Pages d'Islam

THE MARABOUT

The steep, red mountain walls embraced the deep valley, and dark brush carpeted the gorges and sharp fissures that the torrents of winter had cut into the rock. Wild olive trees, twisted and churlish, the rigid, mastic trees with stiff, motionless branches and metallic leaves, cast their blue shadows over the rugged, hardened ground. In the depths of the valley, Ansar-ed-Dem (Wellspring of Blood) gushed forth from a dark chasm in the midst of a heap of broken rocks and yellow gold stalactites, where, among the black mosses and the slender ferns, the subterranean waters ran in rusty streams. Sometimes, at dawn, the shepherds found in the matted grass along the humid banks of the river traces of nocturnal battles; panthers and hyenas would come there to drink and terrible, bitter quarrels broke out among these great prowlers of the shadows.

On the eastern slope of the mountains enclosing the valley, a *forka* (a tribal splinter group) lived poorly from several meager fields wrested from the inhospitable mountain.

The inhabitants of the region spoke Arabic, but the valley had the Berber name Taourirt and its *forka* the even stranger name Ouled-Fakroun (Sons of the Turtle).

Even the oldest of the peasants did not know the origin of this bizarre name. It was of little importance to them in any case; they were far too busy tilling their thankless fields, grazing their scanty flocks, making charcoal, and on occasion, poaching a bit.

Dominating the huts of the group, on the summit of a barren and rocky hill, rose the somewhat larger and sturdier *gourbi* of Sidi Bou Chakour (Man with a Hatchet), an ancient marabout who was revered in the region. Near his *gourbi* grew a branching palm tree, its strange parasol fanning out to shade the mat where the pious old man liked to sit and meditate, tell his prayer beads, or receive pilgrims.

However, Sidi Bou Chakour did not scorn the humble, hard work of the peasant. He tilled and sowed his own field and watched over his herd, which children took to graze on the mountain.

The Bedouins called their livestock by a characteristic name: *el mel* (fortune), an old tradition harking back to nomadic, pastoral times of long ago.

Sidi Bou Chakour was a tall, thin, but robust old man. His bronzed, oval face, genuinely Arab in its beauty, was illuminated by the lively flame of his gaze: under his white brows, the black eyes of the marabout shone as in the days of his youth.

When Sidi Bou Chakour felt the approach of old age, he dismissed his two young wives, without any discord or harshness, and kept Aouda who was wise and gentle.

"An old man is like the trunk of a young tree that has reached its maturity: he bends no more.

"The river down which God leads us, we will never go up again, and it does not become an aging creature to try to rejuvenate himself. The time has come," he said, "for me to leave all that is not necessary for existence, and to devote myself exclusively to the worship of God Most High, and to his service in the path of goodness and righteousness."

But the peasants of Ouled Fakroun obliged their marabout not to abandon all worldly matters. They had great faith in him and, in all difficult circumstances, used to consult him.

In truth, the old man wasn't subservient to anyone, not even to the *hokkam* (authorities). When a cause seemed just to him, he spoke out courageously to defend it and, often, he had suffered because of his independent spirit which, if it had been emulated, would have been a sure sign of renaissance for his race.

Sidi Bou Chakour had often had disputes with the various caids who had succeeded each other for thirty years among the Beni-bou-Abdallah, the tribe of which the Ouled-Fakroun was a member. But these men, themselves Bedouins, had a deep respect for the marabout at the same time that they feared his foresight and the freedom of his speech, and they preferred to maintain courteous relations with him.

One day, the authorities sent as caid to the Beni-bou-Abdallah a young man of good stock who owed his nomination to the long-standing subservience of the family. This man, who crawled before authority, was all the more harsh with the defenseless peasants he governed.

Son of a naturalized father, raised in a school in Oran where, incidentally, his performance was deplorable, and named caid at an early age thanks to his high connections, Caid Salah was an ambitious man who was deeply disdainful of his race and completely unscrupulous.

These ragged Bedouins, reluctant when it came to paying up *douros*, loquacious when defending themselves, irresolute but stubborn, were seen by the caid only as stupid cattle to be driven harshly and exploited as much as possible. For them, he did not have any fraternal feeling, and he had the astonishing and ridiculous naïveté to think of them as savages, as members of an *entirely different race*.

While exhibiting a groveling servility before the authorities, Caid Salah was haughty toward the poor whom he governed. Through this harshness toward those he referred to with disdain and complete carelessness as the "Arabs," and by his servility, he hoped to obtain what are wrongly called *honors:* decorations and, who knows, perhaps one day an appointment as some sort of Agha.

Upon beginning his duties, and from his first encounter with Sidi Bou Chakour, the caid sensed that the marabout would be his most obstinate adversary. As was his habit, he scurried to denounce this marabout to his superior and even to Algiers, as having "a very bad attitude toward *our* domination."

But everyone knew what to expect from this caid's police work, and the marabout was left in peace.

Each time the caid tried to meddle in the affairs of the *forka* of the Ouled Fakroun, he ran up against the good sense and resolution of the marabout, who was not about to let him outwit the naive and fearful peasants.

One day, in front of the representative assembly, the marabout even said to the caid, whose cunning words full of hidden menace urged the peasants to give up their lands for colonization: "Strip us bare, but don't say you are our benefactor."

Caid Salah's hatred toward the marabout became more poisonous with all these failures. Despite the apparent false "Parisianism" of the caid, the battle that ensued from the first days between himself and Sidi Bou Chakour was entirely Bedouin, ominous and full of snares.

But the most perfect order reigned in the *forka*, the conduct of the marabout was irreproachable, and the administration, despite all the insinuations and venomous informing of the caid, had no reason to crack down. Moreover, Caid Salah, incredibly mistaken about the effect of his conduct and actions, thought he was admired when in reality he was held in contempt. The people went to him about matters that would have been imprudent to entrust to others, but they would not make unnecessary enemies in order to placate him.

Unfortunately, the sad and grim Margueritte Affair came to throw panic and chaos into everyone's heart. The caid, taking advantage of the situation, denounced Sidi Bou Chakour as a dangerous fanatic. And one day the old man left, shackled, for the far away Taadmit, the very mention of which caused the Arabs of Algeria to tremble.

Proud and resigned, the marabout answered the perfidious charges of the caid with a precise and dispassionate list of indictments against his accuser, whom France had sent as an envoy into their midst to teach them love and respect for her, and who caused them instead to hate her by committing iniquities in her name.

In the clamor provoked by the Margueritte Affair, the voice of the marabout was drowned out, and he accepted his fate with the simple resignation and strength of a true Muslim.

Far away, in the mountains that overlooked the high plateaus, with many other prisoners, Sidi Bou Chakour, whom no tribunal had judged or condemned, worked at hard labor, slept on the frozen ground without any blanket, eating only meager rations of bread as nourishment.

When her husband was sent into this dolorous exile, the aging Aouda, overcome with sorrow, was hunted down by this *modern* caid with his Parisian gift of gab and his peculiar manners. Despoiled of her small holdings on the grounds that Sidi Bou Chakour did not have an official deed of property, Aouda had to take refuge with the weak and defenseless among the peasants. The Ouled-Fakroun and the rest of the tribe muttered their discontent, but fearing the vengeance of the Roumi caid, they shut up and hung their heads.

Months went by. Inconsolable, the pious old woman soon passed away. When, having been set free through the intervention of a just and righteous functionary from Algiers, Sidi Bou Chakour returned to Taourirt, he was a frail and doddering old man with haggard eyes. He found his small plot was now in other hands, his *gourbi* in ruins, his old companion dead, and his palm tree, in whose shade he used to sit, cut down.

Serene and resigned, without rebelling, the old marabout squatted down under the mastic tree of the *djemaa* (council) and waited, praying to God and asking for alms in his name, for his final hour.

Sidi Bou Chakour died shortly after his return from Taadmit, venerated everywhere by the poor and simple peasants of the *forka* of Ouled-Fakroun. He was buried at Ansar-ed-Dem; his sepulcher became a place of pilgrimage for the Bedouins of the region, because this modest, saintly man had loved and counseled them.

FORCED LABOR IN THE SOUTH

Outside the town, at the foot of the gray dunes, a roofless square of masonry looms up, punctuated by clover-shaped openings, casting a narrow, transparent shadow beneath the almost perpendicular rays of the sun, in the midst of the extraordinary blazing of all that white sand that, like a vast furnace, extends into infinity from the small domed houses to the monstrous flanks of the *Erg* (region of dunes).

A slow, sad chant arises from this singular building, accompanying the continuous, obsessive squeaking of a badly greased wheel and chain.

In the thin band of blue shadow, a man dressed in white wearing a high turban with black cords is reclining, a stick in his hand. He smokes and dreams. From time to time, when the squeaking slows down or gets lower, the man cries out: "Pump! Pump!"

Inside, three or four gaunt men, burned by the sun and clad in white wool, feebly turn a rusty windlass, and the chain hauls up water that spills over with a fresh splashing into shallow, mortar *seguias*.

Round and round they go, worn out, streaming with sweat. The spahi on guard is a good guy, despite the rigor of his official uniform. When he acknowledges their common origins, the poor devils are allowed to stop sometimes to mop their brows. If not, it's pump, pump. And thus all the livelong day in their hearts they agonize over whether today their relatives might bring them a bit of bread or couscous, since the State gives them nothing except crushing work under a leaden sky, upon burning sands. Those who come from far away, wait, more grimly, for the derisive pittance — hardly enough for their subsistence — given to them through *dar-ed-diaf* by the "commune."

"Why are you in jail?" asked the newly arrived spahi, a tall gangly boy with the profile of a bird of prey.

"Yesterday, I was dozing in front of Hama Ali's coffeehouse. The lieutenant of the company tirailleurs passed by and I did not salute him. So, he beat me with his stick and complained to the Bureau Arabe. The captain put me in jail for two weeks and fined me fifteen francs."

The spahi, just arrived from the civilian territories, is surprised:

"So, here the Arabs are required to salute officers just like the rest of us soldiers?"

"Yes, all officers . . . otherwise, you're beaten and imprisoned. We even once had a lieutenant who required women to salute him. Oh, military rule is rigid, awful!"

The spahi, indifferent, continues his questioning.

"And you, old man?" The question is addressed to a little old man, timid and quiet.

"Me? I am from the Ouled-Saoud. When Lieutenant Durand's mistress was going to leave, she had a lot of baggage, so he gave orders to the caids. Mine ordered me to send my camel, but as she had sores on her back, I did not want to lend her. I have been in jail for eight days. The lieutenant, when he was questioning me, slapped me across the face when I said my camel was ill, and no one has told me how much time I have to do. As God is my witness, my camel is sick."

Launched upon the list of his grievances, the old man to whom no one listens any longer, goes on bemoaning his misfortune.

"And me," said a third, "I came to the market where I sold a tub of butter. The next day I was supposed to collect the money, but there was an urgent letter from the sheikh of Debila. So they gave it to me, telling me I was to leave immediately. I begged them in vain, I was threatened with prison. So, in order not to lose the money for my butter, I pretended to leave, waiting until morning. They found out, God knows how, and I have been in jail for two weeks with a fifteen-franc fine."

"You would have done better to lose the cost of the butter, then," the spahi remarked wisely.

But all this, "it's just so many stories!" And he returns to his place in the shade, shouting out to the prisoners: "Pump!"

And the monotonous squeal begins again, as do the continuous, plaintive chants of the prisoners who seem to recount endlessly their sorrows, their timid recriminations against the dreaded power that grinds down and crushes all their race: the enlisted natives.

THE SEDUCED

The bright autumn sun shed a gentle warmth over the yellowed plane trees and the fallen leaves scattered over the sand, dotted with tufts of grass, in Place du Rocher, the most beautiful square in the crumbling town of Tenes. In the resonant clarity of the air, the happy rousing sounds of bugles reverberate, alternating with the more melancholy, more African tones of the Arab *nouba*. Displaying all the false pomp of the military, clad in their least worn jackets, wearing their least faded *chechias*, the tirailleurs walked by. They were permitted to talk with the young men of their race who, either curious or drawn by the colorful display, followed the parade.

And the mercenaries, out of duty but also out of mischievous pleasure, vaunted in glowing terms the advantages of military life to the wide-eyed fellahs, recounting the fantastic particulars of their lives.

Among those who were listening attentively to the soldiers' stories, Ziani Djilali ben Kaddour, a woodcutter from the Charir tribe, stood out because of his height, his chiseled aquiline profile and his proud demeanor.

What struck him most in what the tirailleurs said was their assertion that they did not pay taxes. At first he had been incredulous: as far back as he could remember Arabs had paid taxes to the Beylic.

But Mustapha, the coffeehouse keeper, assured him that what the soldiers said was true. And Djalali thought it over.

His father was getting old. His brothers were still young and, soon, all the work of the farm, the support of the family, the taxes, and the payments to the rich usurer Faguet and to the *Zouaoua* would fall on his shoulders.

How would he manage? Their field was small and badly situated, eaten into on all sides by rock slides and brush. And what finally made his life at home unbearable was his young wife's recent death in childbirth.

To live without worry, to be well-clothed, well fed, not to pay taxes, and to bear arms, all this seduced Djalali, and he enlisted with other young men, gullible like him, eager for the unknown, the pomp.

Old Kaddour, broken by age and illness, a father in rags, followed, lamenting the young recruits' departure for the tirailleurs' base at Blida. Then he returned more broken and dejected to his *gourbi* with its thatch roof, to die there, resigned, because such was the will of God.

At the barracks, Djilali was rapidly disillusioned. Everything that he had been told about military life before enlisting was just so much pretense and fakery. He'd let himself be taken like a bird in a net. At times, he felt the urge to revolt, but he learned to suppress it out of fear of suffering and death. Little by little, he accustomed himself to passive obedience, to monotonous and pointless work, to the harsh yet simple life of a soldier in which the concrete responsibility of real life was replaced with another, artificial one.

Drink and debauchery in seedy dens replaced for him those free and dangerous liaisons in the countryside where it took courage and daring to win the love of a Bedouin woman with dark eyes and a tattooed face.

The heart of the fellah hardened and became numb. He ceased to think about his native farm, about his old father and his young brothers: he became a soldier.

Three years went by.

Autumn returned, the incomparable African autumn with its hesitant regeneration, its green grasses and fragrant flowers hidden in the underbrush. In the shadow of the mountains, the hillsides of Charir turned green, dominating the road to Mostaganem and the harmonious crescent of the great blue gulf, quiet and still, but streaked here and there with rose.

On the road drenched by the first refreshing rains, the tirailleurs out on maneuvers passed by, sullen and filthy. On their hard bronzed faces, sweat and mud are mixed and, often, with an exasperated gesture, a sleeve of rough white fabric wipes a sweaty brow. With a curse, an obscenity or blasphemy, tired shoulders shrugged off the biting pain of the straps of the heavy mule saddle.

Since the time when, by chance, the maneuvers of the company brought them to the mountainous and rugged region of Tenes, Ziani Djilali felt a strange malaise, a mixture of shame and remorse.

But when the company passes by the foot of the hills of Charir, Djilali looks at the hillside where his farm was, near the *koubba* and the cemetery where his old father, who he had abandoned, sleeps. His brothers, scattered, have become day laborers for the settlers: dressed in European rags, barely recognizable, they wander from farm to farm. His *gourbi* has been sold and Djilali stares in disbelief at the fellah who is cutting thorny brush in the field that once had been his, formerly the land of the "Ziani." In this look was all the horrible despair of a trapped beast, the instinctive hatred of a peasant whose land has been taken away, and the sadness of exile.

Oh! Let the lying music resound, now, it no longer fools the peasant nor attracts him. With a heavy heart, he recognizes he has gotten a raw deal and that his place is near his own people, on the nurturing land, beneath the rags of a laborer, in the poor life lived by his ancestors!

And, angrily, with the back of his sleeve, he wipes the sweat and dirt from his brow and the tears from his eyes. Then, he bows his head and continues on his way, for no one can fight *mektoub*.

NATIVE EXPLOITS

Big Pelagie, the servant woman of M. Perez at the settlement Alfred de Musset, had agreed to go out walking the next day, Sunday, with Joseph, the valet at the farm. He wanted to make a good impression, but he was short of money. So, the cunning Mariquita threw a sack over a magnificent goose from the farmer's barnyard and wrung its neck. The baker, a friend of Joseph's, would cook it nicely in the oven that evening. It would be delicious, and never would the Perez family suspect the European had helped.

When Mme. Perez noticed that her most beautiful goose had disappeared, she poured out her lamentations everywhere and ran to alert her husband, who was busy overseeing some Moroccans spading up a piece of land near the *oued*.

"José, someone stole the big goose last night; you know, the gray and black one."

"Oh for Christ's sake! It's those *bicots* again, that's for sure.

Big-boned, angular, and robust, Perez was wearing a corduroy suit, and a round-brimmed, white cork hat. His gestures were violent, his voice loud. Quick to anger, suspicious, always finding that things weren't going well, despite his wealth, Perez, who dealt harshly with the poor, especially with the natives, was a municipal councillor and was considered something of an orator because he held forth more loudly than the others at the coffeehouse and because he always had the most violent opinions.

During the absinthe hour, Perez, in the midst of an attentive, picturesque group, told the story of the theft of his goose, the second in six months. If things kept going this way, colonization was done for and they'd all have to get out. Native banditry was growing by the day. It was enough to discourage even the hardiest souls.

"Yes," said Durand, a friend of the councillor's, "but over there in France they could care less about it. There's nothing left for us — only for the *bicots*. They acquitted the assassins at Margueritte, they want to strip us of our disciplinary courts and allow the natives to crush us. . . ."

"Right, and the hell with us. Let them rob us blind, pillage us, not even respect us anymore, that doesn't mean anything. There are bastards around to tell them they have rights."

"True, but the rest of us are not going to let them get away with it," cried Perez, slamming his fist on the table. "We'll be vigilant, we'll defend ourselves, and we'll plug the first guy who budges. We won't have another Margueritte here. Oh, that verdict, we're going to make them pay dearly for it, those *bicots*. They'd better not start getting too pleased with themselves or we'll give them a rude awakening."

"And me," said Perez, "since I'm getting robbed, I'm going to be my own police, with my gun."

But Dupont, the coffeehouse manager, who had drawn near, had another idea:

"Look out for number one. Perez, you should write down the story and send it to the newspapers, in order to show everyone that we are the victims of these natives."

"Yes, of course," Durand agreed. "You must do that, and besides, it would please our representative. I heard he collects documents like that to answer those who insult the settlers. Our goose could be important."

"Okay. But I'm not a very good writer," said Perez, hesitating.

"No problem, we'll fix it later. Dupont, bring something to write with!"

And Durand put on his glasses and began "composing." Several sheets of paper were torn up; eventually, the final version was written and sent in a sealed envelope to the political journals in North Africa, with the note "please publish this in the interest of colonization and in the defense of honest men."

The letter had been signed by those who were present and by others in the village. The caid of the Beni-Mkhaoufine, a former village policeman always trembling for his job, signed without understanding a word.

A few settlers, however, refused to get mixed up in these "schemes." The Savoyard Jacquet responded to the entreaties of Durand:

"Why should I care? There are always thieves, everyone has to watch out for himself; anyway, there are policemen for this. And besides, I'm busy growing my grapes and my wheat; I could care less about your newspapers and your politics. I never read them, your papers, because they're full of lies. Besides, it's a pain in the neck.

Having read and reread their collective letter, the zealots of the Durand group went their separate ways, shaking hands with a knowing air. Dupont, the coffeehouse manager, returned to his post:

"This way, at least, we would count at election time."

Jacquet shrugged his shoulders.

However, the affair was beginning to take on serious overtones.

After supper, Perez staked himself out on a stool in a dark corner of the courtyard, near the chicken coop, his gun across his knees, with watchful eyes and open ears; Perez even avoided smoking, so as not to be seen. Then, overcome by boredom and sleepiness, he thought he might smoke into his hat, that way no one would see him.

In the course of their day out, the two servants had eaten the roast goose and returned that night. When everyone was asleep, Joseph rejoined Pelagie in her garret.

"You know," she said, smiling, "the boss has got his gun and is guarding his birds."

"Let him keep a lookout, the fresh air will do him good."

And the two servants convulsed with laughter at the idea of the boss freezing his ass off outside.

Two days later, the postman, Claudignon, arrived at the coffee-house, very excited.

"Guess what," he cried, "they printed your letter. Look, here it is in two newspapers! You're in luck, Monsieur Durand, and you, Perez, your name is in the papers!"

And the postman triumphantly unfolded the paper to give the full effect of the format. In large print the headline read: NATIVE EXPLOITS: They write to us from Alfred de Musset:

"Our friends, the *bicots*, are doing quite well. Since the monstrous verdict of Montpellier, and the despicable attacks on disciplinary courts, which are so beneficial but still too lenient in our view, native banditry has been increasing rapidly as has the insolence of the natives toward the settlers.

"They seem to forget that they are beholden to them. The poor settlers are worried sick about their property and their lives, but they'd better not be pushed too far, because their anger could make the Metropole very sorry indeed for these odious attacks against Algeria.

"Just judge from our situation, here in our town, based on this incident which has galvanized the entire European population. In the wee hours between Friday night and Saturday, unidentified robbers stole a magnificent goose from M. Perez, a settler in the town of Alfred de Musset. The very audacity of this theft demonstrates that the culprits responsible are sorry examples of their race which is fundamentally evil-spirited.

"It is fair warning to the friends and defenders of Yacoub and his cohorts."

The style of this article had been corrected a bit by the editors of these arabophobe tabloids, but the vanity of the authors was nonetheless flattered and their prestige swelled.

"What could we do? We couldn't let them assassinate us."

And to finish it all off, Durand, who felt all puffed up with prestige, had a final word of wisdom that everybody understood:

"There are no minor issues in politics."

Sud Oranais: Part I

REFLECTIONS OF WAR

Ain-Sefra, not long ago an ordinary garrison, was slumbering in the routine characteristic of military life during times of peace.

Today, with the troubles in the South and the turmoil rumbling once again across a Morocco in ferment, Ain-Sefra seems to be awakening, to be regaining its former spirit, from the heroic era of Bou-Amama. More troops, more noise, arrivals and departures, delays, even anxiety at times, an unusual commotion fills the sandy, narrow streets.

Commingling in the sun are *goumis* (Arab or Berber soldiers) mounted on their small, wiry horses; *mokhaznis* (horse soldiers of the Moroccan government) in their long black burnouses embroidered in red across the chest, belts bristling with cartridges; tirailleurs in blue; spahis in red jackets; and finally the legionnaires; those blond men from the North, bronzed, tanned by the suns of distant colonies.

In the canteens and the Moorish cafés filled with a joyful din, the most unexpected contrasts jostle one another. Here, bawdy couplets from popular songs and practical jokes blend with the cooing sentimentality of German and Italian romances. And to the side, the cries and howls of the old African *r'aita* come out in strange triplets, accompanying slow chanting, interrupted by a refrain of long, desolate wails.

In the same intoxication of movement and noise, the neighboring worlds, the world of the Europeans and that of the Arabs, rub elbows, mix together, without ever becoming one.

To all these striking dissonances, the Foreign Legion arrives to add still more exotic notes. And with all this din and all these men, in the precariousness and the uncertainty of the moment, Ain-Sefra is beautiful.

✳

I climb up to the hospital in the fortress that dominates the town.

Huge buildings of red brick surrounded by galleries with arcades. The wounded of El-Moungar wander in the shadow, with their stark white bandages, in the idle boredom of their convalescence.

Two or three Frenchmen among the foreigners . . . the rest are Germans or Italians: rough, plucky faces, engaging smiles.

Somewhat flattered to be "interviewed" — a word taught to them — they are also intimidated. Thus, in true military fashion, they end up referring me to their commander, Corporal Zolli.

Young, tall and thin, at ease in a gray hospital gown, he speaks correct, and sometimes even elegant, French. Accustomed to being interviewed, Zolli is not disconcerted.

With clarity and energy, he tells me of the imprudent halt, without precautions, in the valley between El-Moungar and Zafrani, of the fatal carelessness of Captain Vauchez who said laughingly that he would go in shirt-sleeves to Tafilalet, and this only days before his death. The corporal nevertheless vouches for the admirable presence of mind of the captain who, mortally wounded, found the strength to pencil several words to send as a warning to Captain de Susbielle at Taghit.

Through the narrative of the Corporal there also passes the silhouette of the Danish officer, Lieutenant Selkauhausen, who had come to serve in the Foreign Legion, at his rank, in order to learn, and who went to his death far away, in this forgotten corner of the Sud Oranais.

It seems that the lieutenant was engaged to be married back home, adds the corporal. All the same, it is sad, that death.

Zolli knows how to bring to life the terrors of that fierce day-long battle, his men outnumbered, far from all reinforcements. He is modest, not exaggerating his own role, acknowledging the wound to his right hand that, from the beginning, prevented him from firing.

A former soldier under General Menotti Garibaldi, in Macedonia, Zolli loves warfare: he always manages to be where the fighting is.

Sometimes even the roughest of men take courage and dare to relate a simple and poignant memory or some anecdote about their own misfortune.

"We were godawful thirsty that day," says one of them, who seems to remember nothing else. "And, as there wasn't no water, we got ourselves a bunch of bottles of strong wine, in the evening, when it was all over. So, that sent us sky high, and made us drunk."

How congenial these poor devils are who have suffered and almost died for causes that are not their own, that leave them profoundly indifferent.

On the ground floor, wounded tirailleurs occupied a small room.

There, stretched out from boredom, lay Mouley Idriss, a tall *mokhazni*, bronzed, muscular, lean, with the regular and lively features of a nomad.

This *mokhazni* was wounded several days before El-Moungar by a *djich* (armed group). Very simple and, at first, very shy, Mouley Idriss finally becomes reassured and smiles. He explains what all the

Arabs from the Southwest think. For them, it is neither a question of war with Morocco, nor above all a holy war. The region has always been *bled-el-baroud* (Land of Gunpowder), and the tribes of this vague frontier have always raided each other. Mouley Idriss designated the enemy by a significant term: *el khian*, the robbers, the bandits. He thinks of the current military operations quite simply as counterraids and reprisals against the *djiouch*.

This explains well why the valuable native auxiliaries, the *mokhaznis*, the *goumis*, the cavalry messengers, *sokhars* (camel drivers), most of whom are recruited from the local nomad population, feel no repugnance at fighting the bandits, and are examples of valor, endurance and devotion beyond all praise.

Mouley Idriss, without dwelling on what he had suffered at the hands of the enemy, condemns the acts of those he calls bushwhackers and jackals.

Deep down, he must not sincerely want this to come to an end: he is a nomad, thus a man of gunpowder, and he loves to fight.

Mouley Idriss belongs to the *makhzen* (administrative center) of Sidi Mouley ould Mohammed, agha of the Amour of Ain-Sefra, one of the most congenial of the local personalities of the Southwest and one of the most devoted to the French cause.

While I chat with Mouley Idriss, his fellow tirailleurs gather round.

Half naked with their ill-fitting hospital gowns and their shaved heads, they are comical. Their pranks and bursts of laughter contrast with their hardy builds and their virile faces.

All this small, suffering world awaits with impatience the day when the authorities will decide to release them, even if partially cured: Arabs consider the hospital a funereal place, a prison.

✳

Eight o'clock in the evening, oppression hovers over Ain-Sefra, in the dark, closed shops, barricaded cafés, and similarly in the great evenings of epic drunkenness when the Legion hits town. No civilians in the street, a heavy silence, almost the impression of a town in danger.

The shopkeepers and the *mercantis*, as they are called by the Arabs, assemble behind closed doors, around the green field of deserted billiard tables. They look grave and serious. There are prolonged grievances, the endless exaggeration of things, fear blown out of proportion. They talk of strategy; they find the garrison ridiculously insufficient; they calculate the risks of waking up the next day with the railroad and the telegraph lines cut. Someone announces a *harka*, a great hoard of bandits approaching from the direction of Sfissifa. Someone even goes so far as to estimate the distance between the village and the fort, a safe haven.

There is almost panic this evening at Ain-Sefra. And all this because a patrol was attacked at Teniet-Merbah, some twenty kilometers from here, and because a *mokhazni* had been killed. In addition, they noted the passage of a *djich* close to the station of Mekalis.

In a *mozabite* shop where I had come looking for a little light and gaiety, a spahi enters, a handsome youth with a sweet, expressive face.

He seems uneasy.

"Farewell," he says, "please excuse me if I wronged any of you."

"But where are you going?"

"Ah! Haven't I taken an oath? Whoever signs up puts his head in a hangman's noose; afterwards, he does as he is ordered, without thinking of his tent or his friends. As for me, it is not death that I fear. One only dies once. It is to walk alone through the night, without another human being to talk to. I am being sent to take a letter to Beni-Yaho."

Everyone there embraces the spahi, remembering the *mokhazni* killed that morning.

And that is the one really sad and poignant note in the whole scene of that frightened village — the departure of the poor soldier who, himself, is really risking his life in the threatening darkness and the silence of the countryside.

Everything goes very well, however, and the slow hours of the night run out without the slightest alert, without any echo of gunfire.

Day breaks, radiant, dispersing all the phantoms evoked during the night.

Someone tells me that the spahi Abdelkader had not been attacked. And everything calms down and the dull village returns to its routine.

HADJERATH-M'GUIL

A railway station, an isolated keep amid jagged rocks.

At fifteen hundred meters, dominating several hovels made of planks, a fortress of *toub* on a rocky slope at the foot of the last spurs of Djebel Beni-Smir.

An *oued* invaded by alfa grass and oleanders, a few scattered palms. Beyond the fortress, on the riverbank, two small French tombs.

One is already three years old; the other very recent, on which several poor wreaths are fading: the tomb of the spahi brigadier Marschall, killed a month ago in the Chaabeth-Hamra pass, among the Beni-Smir, while pursuing a *djich*.

The graves of these two soldiers look forsaken and infinitely sad with their crosses of black wood, abandoned and out of place against the harsh expanse of the desert.

At the station, where I get off the train by chance, without even knowing the direction of the fortress where I am going, I find a dark Bedouin, a handsome Arab typical of the high plateaus, who is unloading a saddle and a harness. Despite his white robe, I easily recognized in him the soldier, the spahi in civilian dress, or the *mokhazni*.

I decide to speak to him because he inspires trust. I tell him a story to explain who I am and why I'm here, and we soon become friends with all the open congeniality of the Muslims.

Taieb ould Slimane of the Rzaina tribe of Saida is leaving the spahis and signing up for the *makhzen* of Taghit. This very day he is going to Oued-Dermel to buy a horse.

"If you want to, come with me, and we'll have coffee with my former comrades at the fortress. You can do your business there, then we'll spend the night at Oued-Dermel, if you are able to go on foot. Tomorrow, we'll be given the horses and then return here to catch the train for the South."

That seems all right, and I agree.

We head off, first along the railroad tracks and then along the slope of a ravine.

At the fortress, a comical scene happens.

The head of the fort, a captain from the Legion, looks at me, stupefied. He does not see the link between my card as a woman journalist and the young Arab handing it to him. We end up coming to an understanding, however.

It is impossible to interview legionnaires without authorization from higher up. Over all, I am not disappointed, and I join Taieb with the spahis.

Beneath a long roof of wood planks and masonry, they sit on straw mats arranged on the ground. The troops in cotton uniforms with red belts joyfully surround their liberated comrade, and as I am with him, they welcome me too.

They quickly spread out blankets and ask us to sit. Then, after extensive Arab greetings, and repeated well-wishing, they offer us four or five cups of coffee, a kind of clear, odorless juice like the infusion of licorice herbs given at hospitals.

However, we dare not refuse this coffee offered with such good-will . . . and besides, we have already had a lot worse!

We do not stay for long, despite the spahis' insistence that we stay the night.

✳

Taieb comes up with an idea: he wants to look for a certain Tidjani, originally from Bou-Semrhoun, a worker at the train station who has a mule.

Behind the fortress, beneath a ragged tent, we find Tidjani's wife, a withered woman tanned by the sun, but who must have been beautiful once.

She still knows how to drape herself gracefully in her tatters of red wool.

Taieb, who believes firmly in the reality of Si Mahmoud the Constantine, winks at me smiling, dropping the air of gravity he had earlier.

Hassouna is from Djebel-Amour, the country of beautiful girls.

Taieb leans back on his elbow on an old woolen cushion in order to see the Bedouin woman better, to whom he says with practiced tenderness:

Do you remember, two years ago, at Duveyrier?

Hassouna denies it energetically, but with an uneasy laugh that belies her.

"What about Duveyrier? You're crazy, and you lie. Between you and me there's merely a good feeling."

"That's right! And is any feeling as good as the one we had? Go on and chatter like a lying bird who lays eggs and flies away disowning them! If I don't know you, then who does?"

"The father that sired me!"

"But not as well as I do having possessed you when you were young and fresh!"

They continue their crude flirtation, yet without any obscene language.

I really think that if I had not been there, Taieb would have pushed things further, in spite of the incipient decrepitude of Hassouna.

She serves us coffee while looking slyly at Taieb, who makes an expressive gesture of embracing her and crushing her in his arms.

Tidjani arrives. He does not seem to be at all surprised to find us in his tent with his wife.

Tidjani is wearing ragged old European cast-offs and a *chechia*.

He is nevertheless one of the unknown heroes of the battle of Chaabeth-Hamra in which Corporal Marschall died.

Tidjani, a simple civilian, voluntarily borrowed a gun from a Jew and left on foot, running after the mounted spahis, in pursuit of a *djich*.

While her husband goes to look for a mule, the wily temptress chats with us in a friendly way, and tells us about herself.

She lives there, where gunpowder is always talking, yet she maintains the most astonishing indifference. She laughs while talking about some *djiouch* camped nearby in the underbrush of Beni-Smir.

She jokes that, among the Ouled Abdallah bandits, there are handsome, proud young men, and says that she would welcome them gladly if she didn't fear her husband's knife.

She says all this with a thousand innuendos aimed at Taieb. On occasion, however, a fleeting shadow of nostalgia passes over her aging face, when she speaks of the hills of her birthplace at Djebel-Amour.

What a strange apparition, that common, worn-out woman, amid a landscape of rocks and blowing sands, in these troubled days!

*

We leave, taking turns riding Tidjani's lame mule.

The good man talks to us endlessly to prove that his beast is good just the same.

Not paying any attention to him, Taieb, carefree, sings of beautiful tattooed Amouriat, of long journeys across arid wastes, of skirmishes, and of all-powerful destiny.

As for me, I watch the contours of the countryside widen out, become more serene and more harmonious, upon leaving the labyrinth of rocks that the railroad passes through almost all the way from Ain-Sefra.

The wall of the Beni-Smir stretches toward the west and the valley opens up. Red sandy earth, sightly undulating, with gray tufts of *drinn*, the grass of the South, tougher and drier than even the alfa grass of the high plains.

On the surface of the sand, a recent wind has traced small grooves, slight waves that lend to this desert site a marine appearance.

At the foot of the rounded peak of Djebel-Tefchtelt, we found the *douar* of the Oued-Dermel *makhzen:* some twenty low nomad tents striped black and gray hug the ground, as if cowering timorously.

The *mokhaznis*, recruited from everywhere among the branches of the Amour, are camped there, with women and children, to watch over the railroad and the surrounding mountains where bandits are dug in.

The small horses hobbled between the tents are grazing despondently on armfuls of *drinn*.

A few black goats are playing with the children and the dogs who, on our approach, come running, hackles up, ferocious, with blood in their eyes.

A great feeling of solitude and sadness reigns over this encampment of Muslim soldiers.

The village sheikh, Abdelkader-Ould-Ramdane, still young, with an intelligent but impassive face, receives us gravely.

The good *mokhaznis* extend us their hospitality under a large tent carpeted with red wool *haiks*. They serve us Moroccan mint tea, flat cakes, and butter. They tell me about the continual alerts, the attacks and pursuits into the mountains, the ruses of the prowlers, as if they were quite ordinary, natural things.

Here again, there was not the least notion of warfare, in the true sense of the word, no struggle of race against race, or religion against religion.

The *mokhaznis* spoke only of looters and of thieves. In the grand, slow-changing ways of all nomads, these people are quite simple and primitive, shepherds and camel-drivers who continue their familiar existence, almost unchanged, beneath the black burnouses of the Ain-Sefra *makhzen.*

Taieb characterizes them with a French word, a bit disdainful and typically spahi, which means, "They aren't shrewd."

✳

It is hot under the tent, where the crowd of men recline, resting their elbows on their knees or amicably on a neighbor's shoulder.

In the other half of the tent, behind hangings of richly colored purple wool, the rustling of women and their whispers intrigue my companion. However, he forces himself to remain impassive and not to notice anything that reveals the nearby presence of women.

We leave the stifling shadow of the tent, and Taieb follows us reluctantly. We stretch out on a mound of sand, above the dry *oued* that, for the *mokhaznis*, represents the *hadada*, the problematic frontier of Morocco.

A light breeze plays over the fine sand, barely rustling the *drinn* and the spiny jujube trees, clumped together, bristling and impenetrable, like aquatic plants.

A great silence weighs upon this forsaken country, on this *douar,* and on our small group. Around me, a dozen *mokhaznis* are reclining, their profiles patient and energetic, their features of striking purity.

The sun sinks toward the golden crests of the mountains and a rose-colored glow dances over the sand, lighting plumes of fire beneath the harsh vegetation. Another hour of rest, like a respite in my life, an hour of escape and melancholy dreaming, troubled by neither regret nor desire.

The day is fading. Then, suddenly, appearing from behind a bush, a ragged Bedouin approaches the chief of the *makhzen,* Abdelkader-Ould-Ramdane, to whom he speaks in a low voice.

The chief gets up, a serious look on his face.

Get up! You, over there, go right away and herd all the animals into the middle of the *douar*. There is a *djich* from Ouled-Abdalleh half an hour from here.

A *djich!* At first, that does not seem very serious to me. Besides, would those bandits dare attack a *douar* where there were twenty rifles?

However, the *mokhaznis* obey. They leave, grumbling a bit, to gather their horses, mules, and goats who are pasturing near by: all the sheep are in safekeeping north of Ain-Sefra.

Eight o'clock. The moon is not up yet. We are resting, leaning back on our elbows on a rug, inside the tent. It is pitch dark: Abdelkader gives us scarcely the time to gulp down some barley couscous and a few cups of tea, then he puts out all the lights. The chief has also stationed sentinels to lay in wait at the four corners of the *douar*. The *mokhaznis* have raised the flaps of the tent on the desert side, and they are lying down, their loaded rifles at hand.

They scan the darkness with their lynx eyes.

All this seems more serious now.

Thus begins the long watch. We speak in low voices; we hide when smoking. The silence is heavy, barely broken next door in the women's area, by the muffled, monotone song of a woman rocking her little one.

Suddenly, the dogs begin growling. The startled *mokhaznis* stop their chatting and banter. The dogs grow more excited. Soon, there is tumult. They leap against the sides of the tent, barking furiously, and run about covering us with dust.

"You see," Taieb says to me, "the dogs are barking in all directions: it's them, they have us surrounded right now. Ah! Si Mahmoud, if only you and I had rifles!"

The sensation I feel is not fear; but the whole scene, the din of the dogs, the people who are after us, who are there in the night, so close but unseen, all of that produced in me the bizarre impressions of a troubled dream. Nevertheless, I feel a childish desire for the attack to happen, for something to happen.

This goes on for more than two hours.

Taieb ends up getting sleepy, and he grumbles:

"Let them come or let them go to the devil!"

One of the *mokhaznis* teases him:

"Go tell them to get out of here, you'd be doing us a favor!"

We all end up joking, laughing at this rather annoying adventure, at these people who don't want to attack and won't go away.

"There must not be many of them, and besides, as there are no lights in the *douar*, and no animals outside, they know that we are ready," says Abdelkader, still quite serious.

Were it not for their fear of the chief, the *mokhaznis* would have started mocking and calling out insults to the invisible *djich*.

Little by little, however, calm returns, the dogs quiet down, and we fall asleep.

In the middle of the night, yet another alert; the dogs rush out above our heads, howling. The *mokhaznis* swear bluntly: we are not going to get any sleep tonight!

We watch; we wait. Nothing. Once more, silence, like the coolness before dawn, falls over the *douar*. This time, we fall into a deep, exhausted sleep.

It is dawn, the most radiant time in the desert. I am wakened by the low murmur of the *mokhaznis* praying outside, bathed in the iridescent glow of the breaking day.

We come out and get on our horses to return to Hadjerath.

Around the *douar*, at about two hundred meters, the *mokhaznis* find the traces of the *djich:* some twenty men on foot.

We leave again, climbing the jagged rocks of Hadjerath M'guil.

GHOST TOWN

Once again the small train moves slowly through the desert. Stations pass after long stops.

Djenien-bou-Rezg, the burning plain, a huge reddish fortress, several scattered huts.

Now it is Duveyrier, the Arab Zoubia, in its amphitheater of hills, of black rocks.

Not long ago, the Saharan train used to stop there, and the new village, completely European, had grown from this traffic. Low houses, painted with grayish clay, multiplied with the songs of the Legion's exiles; canteens and bars opened, hovels made of planks and old gasoline drums; a courageous duenna had even brought several worn ladies of the night, rejects from the den of Saida and Sidi-bel-Abbes.

Strings of camels knelt in the sandy streets before going to supply the remote outposts of the South.

Duveyrier was the source of this river of abundance flowing toward the Sahara. An apparent prosperity reigned there for several months. People were getting rich, coming from just about everywhere, drawn by the lure of an easy if troubled traffic in goods.

During certain transactions, a name was whispered that had

reverberated in the Sud Oranais for twenty-five years — the ancient, almost legendary name that sounded more strangely troubling here where it was real: Bou-Amama.

Then, one day, the stubborn little railroad — two iron rails that took off, gleaming and alone, across the desert — went beyond Duveyrier to stop farther on, across from the enchanting Figuig. Overnight another village sprang up, precocious as the grasses of the Sahara after the first winter rains. And the short-lived existence of Duveyrier ended, displaced by the newcomer: Beni-Ounif-of-Figuig.

Today, in the iridescent light of the morning, Duveyrier seems prematurely abandoned: houses with new walls, but no roofs, the black empty sockets of gaping doors and windows; the merchants have taken away all that they could — girders, boards, crossbeams, tiles — in their hasty exodus. The closed or disemboweled bars are already falling into ruin and filling up with sand. It seems like some calamity — fire or flood — has befallen this new-born market town and returned it to the silence of the desert.

There is a poignant sadness to this corner of the world, an abandoned ruin.

Only the small garrison still suggests life in Duveyrier, where along the street the striking poppy-red burnous of a spahi or the blueberry uniform of a tirailleur spring up.

At the train station, everyone comes by in pursuit of melancholy amusement, watching the train go by . . . and life moving on elsewhere.

At Duveyrier, a surprise, a symptom of the months of unrest: a squad of armed tirailleurs boards the train, in case of attack.

And again, despite that, just as in Ain-Sefra and Oued-Dermel, there is no real feeling of danger amid the great quiet of the smiling, sunlit plain.

LITTLE FATHMA

Children, the only lively note, the only happy note in the deathly silence, in the town's nostalgic sadness.

The littlest ones are especially comical, blacks for the most part, naked under their short little shirts, a long woolly ponytail entwined with small white shells or amulets at the top of their shaved heads.

They have already learned to beg for pennies from passing officers. They jump around them, stamping their feet, persisting with graciousness or wheedling like kittens. Then, they fight ferociously over the copper coins thrown on the ground, diving after them and rolling around in the dust.

The ringleader is little Fathma.

She must be about eleven years old. Her prepubescent body, sleek as a cat's, disappears beneath green woolen rags, held upon her frail chest by a superb clasp of chased silver, ornamented with oddly shaped red coral.

Little Fathma is of mixed race. Her round face, with downy cheeks of a warm copper hue, is both brazen and sweet, with caressing eyes and already voluptuous lips. In a few years, Fathma will be quite beautiful and quite shameless.

Guiding the stampede of the amber and black children, she

gallops through the ruins, overflowing with laughter like a wild nymph. She appears suddenly, hazardously poised on the edge of a decaying terrace, or on the top of a shaky wall. She begs, she poses, she smiles.

One day, I saw her, feigning thanks, take the hand of a Roumi, an officer, between her little hands, and say to him with troubling seriousness: "I like you very much, ya sidi." The man smiled and attributed the caress to the desire to get more coins. The little Fathma, chagrined, shook her head, chiding. "No, no, not that. I just like you, by the grace of god." This meant, in Arabic, that her sudden tenderness was disinterested.

What a strange, little creature whose charming heart is as deceiving and fugitive as the reddish ruins.

MERIEMA

A low sky, opaque, incandescent, a dull sun that burns nonetheless. On the dust that covers everything, on the white or gray facades of the houses, heat reverberates, burdensome, blinding, seeming to emanate from an interior hearth. On the angular crests of the dry hills, dark flames brood, and reddish smoke is gathering behind the mountains of Figuig.

Nothing shines, nothing lives in all this blazing. Only now and then a gust of dry heat comes, as if from a distant furnace, to lift up whirlwinds of dust that flee, rapidly, toward the east, and dissipate in the valley.

At the station, between the black train cars and the gaping fences, people are waiting for the train, exhausted Europeans and Arabs who gesture tiredly.

Miserable horses and mules hang their heads, drooping to the ground, nostrils bleeding.

And over all this reigns a palpable, oppressive silence that suggests neither rest nor sensuality: it is a deathly enervation reaching the point of anguish.

That was one of my first impressions of Beni-Ounif.

No guide, no alien perspective interferes between my senses and the surroundings, no trivial explanations, while I was wandering all by myself through this corner of the country new to me.

At the edge of the village, near the station, a section of high wall, an ardent gray, the color of metal in fusion. Further on, beyond the blue rails ending in a red trench, nothing, a plain sown with black rocks, more dust, a scorching, endless nakedness. At the very bottom of the wall, a narrow band of tawny shadow, transparent and without coolness.

There, I saw Meriema, squatting in front of a small heap of old metal and debris of all sorts.

A naked body, twisted and decayed, sagging empty breasts, black skin, bent by age, soiled by filth and dirt. A woolly head shaved like a boy's, a thin and wrinkled face, a large, thick mouth covering strong yellow teeth and protuberant eyes, the poor eyes of a sick beast: a miserable simian mask full of suffering, fear, and disorientation.

She was nodding her head in an odd manner while combing through her pile of scraps and sweepings with her long bony fingers.

She talked nonstop, addressing an invisible audience, in an incomprehensible tongue full of barbaric consonants that I later learned to be Kouri, a strange, black dialect from the Sahara or the Sudan.

I spoke to her in Arabic. She continued murmuring, rising to a sort of angry lamentation.

I held my hand out to her. She pulled my fingers one after the other, without interrupting her ramblings. Nightmarish grimaces twisted her face.

A man from Figuig who was looking at her said to me: "You know, that woman is not from here. She was a slave of some Muslims, at Mecheria; she was married, she had a son called Mahmoud. You see how destiny works: this Meriema was pious, serene, and sensible. She enjoyed among the women a reputation for being virtuous. Then, one day, God took her son from her. Thus she became demented and fled, alone and naked. She stopped speaking Arabic and returned to the language of her ancestors, from far away, from beyond Touat even. She went on like that along the roads and through the villages, living from charity given by the faithful. Several times, someone took her to the *ksar* at Oudarhir, at Figuig, where pious Muslims took care of her. But she always comes back to Beni-Ounif. She lives under a pile of boards. There, however, the kids persecute her and make fun of her. Sunday nights, when the legionnaires and tirailleurs get drunk, they forget that she is a poor innocent and they violate her, despite her pleading and cries. A drunk man is like a savage beast . . . God preserve us from misery like the fate of this creature!"

A morning of light. The sirocco abated on the plain where, for a number of burdensome days, it had been scattering reddish cinders.

At dawn, a light wind from the north shook the dust from the date palms, making the valley green once more all around the ocher *ksar*.

In the midst of these green transparencies, the sun rises. The tirailleurs pass through going toward the riverbed, where several palms and oleanders are growing from red veins of *toub*.

The musicians, dressed in their white linen, with their brass that catches the sun giving off sparks of gold, with the less flashy instruments for the Arab *nouba*, are going to rehearse, rousing the dead valley until nine o'clock with the echoes of trumpets, the plaintive, nasal notes of the *r'aita*, the dull hammering of the drums.

They cross the village, and the glory of the morning hour puts a white-toothed smile on their bronzed faces, a caress on their naked, muscular necks.

With a dry, mechanical gesture, all the arms lift the brass in unison, and a rousing music, full of careless joy, bursts forth.

Suddenly, emerging from the shadows, like a black puppet, Meriema appears. Someone had dressed her up in a ragged *gandoura* and an old straw hat with faded blue ribbons.

Out in front of the laughing group of tirailleurs, she dances, jumps around, making short cries like an irritated monkey. Little by little, speeding up her movements, with frenetically swinging hips, she tears off her ragged *gandoura* and continues to dance naked, with only her hat held by a string.

All the way to the clay pits, Mariema accompanies the music of the tirailleurs who enjoy themselves in the cloudless morning.

A quiet day in the silent desert, in the village. A faint white mist covers the sky where migratory birds are flying. In the *oued*, among the black flagstones, beneath the angular fronds of the blue date palms, Meriema is sitting.

With multicolored tatters picked up in the streets, she has decorated the bushes, as if to celebrate some bizarre ritual of a fetishist cult.

Keeping time, her long, thin, knotted brown arms raised above her head, she is beating an old can like a tambourine.

She sings an unintelligible chant in a shrill, falsetto monotone.

Acrid smoke rises in gray spirals from a small fire made of camel dung that the madwoman has lit in front of the trees.

From the earth, however, there rises the stale odor of the charnel house, bones lay around, a large pool of iridescent blood putrefies . . . this place serves as a slaughterhouse.

But Meriema does not see the sorry carnage, unclean pigs digging through the bloody debris with their avid snouts, licking up the coagulated blood. She does not smell the terrifying odor of death. She prays, she chants, she cries, cut off forever from communion with other humans, plunged in the lugubrious solitude of her own darkened soul.

I met Meriema for the last time on the eve of my departure. It was very late; the waning moon was rising, livid, almost furtive, over the blue plain. And Meriema was dancing, completely naked, completely black, alone, on a low dune.

DOUAR OF THE *MAKHZEN*

Like Oued-Dermel, like Ain-Sefra, like all the outposts in the region, Beni-Ounif has its *douar* of the *makhzen*, with its striped tents pitched on the gritty barren land.

This *douar*, isolated at the southeast end of the *ksar* at the edge of the gardens, seems calm and somnolent. Nevertheless, it hides intrigues, unfolding plots, even dramas.

Coming from the Amour of Ain-Sefra, the Hamyan of Mecheria, the Trafi of Geryville, many of the *makhzen* (administrators) are married and have trailing behind them their *smalahs* of women and children whom the demands of military service cause them to abandon for months on end.

Volunteers in the cavalry, without official uniforms or any military training, are *mokhaznis*. Of all the Muslim soldiers recruited by France in Algeria, these men, under their blue burnouses, remain the most traditional, preserving their local customs.

They remain attached to their Muslim faith, unlike most of the tirailleurs and many of the spahis.

Five times a day, one sees them withdraw into the desert to pray, grave, indifferent to all that surrounds them; and they have a certain beauty in their noble gestures at this hour as they become one with themselves again.

However, after mixing with the regular troops, whether tirailleurs or spahis, many *mokhaznis* become a bit careless and playful in spirit like the indigenous soldiers. Without any moral gain, they rid themselves of some of their ancestral traditions, of the reserved speech of the nomads. They also end up in the long run resigning themselves to living in these tents.

And then, given their harsh existence, constantly on the alert, continually exhausted, and uncertain about their tomorrows, their love affairs, so relished in their native *douars*, take on more savor and charm.

Inevitably their mores grow lax here and they openly carry on affairs that, back home, would be hidden beneath a shroud of secrecy, in the obscurity of night where love lies side by side with death.

Every evening, beautiful, tattooed women with bronzed skin and dangerous eyes, and clad in gorgeous tatters of purple or deep blue wool, go in groups toward the *feggaguir* of the *oued*.

They gossip and laugh among themselves and are grave and silent only when some Muslim man passes by.

The soldiers in their blue or red burnouses, who take their wiry little horses to the watering trough, pass as close as they can to those voluptuous springs. Not a word passes between them and the Bedouin women. Nonetheless, invitations, confessions, refusals, promises are exchanged by discreet gestures.

The man sternly passes his hand over his beard. That means: May they shave my beard and strip me of all signs of virility if I don't succeed in possessing you.

The woman responds, with smiling eyes, by shaking her head, just to tease him. Then, furtively, wary of even her companions, she makes a small movement with her hand.

That is enough, the promise is made. It will cost him a few shimmery pieces of cloth bought from the Mozabites, or a few white ones — not much.

Then later, passion will seize the two lovers, an Arab kind of passion, tormented, jealous, seemingly mad, lifting men out of their ordinary impassivity.

Thus, at the same time it is an encampment of brave, hardened men, the *douar* of the *makhzen* is also a small city of dangerous and ephemeral passions, because here shots are fired quickly, and it is easy to believe they were fired by some *djich!* . . . The *bled* has no echo.

The unmarried troops sleep under the stars in the courtyard of a makeshift Bureau Arabe.

Even the night-sentinels sleep rolled in their burnouses, with the absolute calm of the people of the South, accustomed over the years to sense danger close by in the shadows of night.

And it is these isolated *mokhaznis* who haunt most openly the farther reaches of the camp, and who poach most often around the tents of their married companions whom they envy and look down upon for being such miserable husbands.

※

A huge convoy of camels and of *goumi* cavalry, who arrived one gray autumn day, camp in the valley near the palm groves.

A few white tents of officers or of the caid are pitched in the middle of this chaos, between the hobbled, neighing horses, and the kneeling camels who grumble their complaints.

Piles of *gh'rairs* (camel sacks), pieces of carpet, blankets, sooty pots, shaggy goatskins suspended from tripods made of sticks, the flash of shiny mess tins among the heaps of Bedouin rags of bright and somber colors dominated by red and brownish black: all this accumulates and mixes in an unruly and magnificent disorder.

Men wander around, talk with each other, pitch camp.

Goumis in white burnouses, their belts bristling with cartridges; the camel drivers — the *sokhars* — true men of the desert, lean and tanned, hardy under their fraying, dusty cotton shirts, bound at the waist by a strap of untanned leather or a rope, with sandals on their feet, all marked with ancient scars, their heads covered with a simple piece of linen, sometimes with small plaits of hair along their cheeks: men who remain unchanged from the time of the patriarchs and prophets at the dawn of the world.

The head drivers, leaders of groups of sixteen *sokhars*, gallop around on their wiry horses and shout orders.

Within several hours, these newly arrived *goumis* with their convoys of camels bring life to the dull valley which seems to serve as a temporary home for an entire people in migration.

Archaic, fascinating, these heaps of old belongings have not changed over the centuries; robed people with antique gestures arrive, stay for several days, then one morning are on their way again, tying up and carrying away their belongings in the simple and colorful *gh'rairs* of the nomad.

A winter's day dawned on the black rock of the *hamada*. On the horizon, above the dunes of Oued Zousfana, a sulphurous light illuminated the heavy, gray clouds. The mountains, the hazy hills, stood out, a vague silhouette against the gray of the opaque sky. The disheveled crowns of the cool date palms fill with pale dust, and the old mud houses, standing in the midst of ruins, emerge, yellowish, as if stained by the troubled shadows of the valley, beyond the large, isolated cemeteries.

The desert has stripped off its ornaments of light and an immense shroud hovers over it.

In the camps, around the horses covered with silk tatters, around the camels, the *goumis* and *sokhars* wake up. A murmur arises from the heaps of damp burnouses bed-rolled on the hard ground.

Awakened, the jostled camels peevishly start grumbling. In silence, reluctantly, the nomads get up and light their fires. In the dank air, a bleak vapor rises from the palm fronds.

The icy wind sweeps brusquely through the camps; it catches up whirlwinds of dust and smoke and snaps the taut canvas of the *goumi* commander's tent, its tricolor battalion flag.

The silhouette of the French lieutenant passes by. Calm, sad-eyed, hands shoved into the pockets of his blue cotton pants, he smokes his pipe, absent-mindedly observing man and beast.

He too feels oppressed by the strain of beginning yet another day, after months and months of this harsh job as caravan leader, always on the go, as he puts it, always alone with, as his only consolation, this sad pipe in which the monotone hours of his life are going up in hazy smoke.

The nomads prepare coffee in their mess tins, then, against a relentless wind, they get up slowly, lazily, shaking off the sand weighing down their burnouses.

They attend to all kinds of tasks around the camp.

The *goumis* and the *sokhars* throw armloads of alfa grass down in front of their animals. They quickly groom the officer's gray horse. Some, sitting around smoky fires, begin mending their harnesses or their burnouses. Others go up to the village, where they carry on interminable haggling with the Jewish merchants or sip Moroccan tea for hours in the rough rooms of the Moorish coffeehouses.

Some camels grumble and bite at their *gh'rairs*. A horse breaks loose and gallops furiously across the camp. Two men argue over an armload of alfa grass. And that is all, day after day, during the long hours and hours of waiting.

Long ago the nomads forgot the solitude of their traditional lives on the High Plateaus, without other concerns than their herds and the eternal quarrels of rival groups that sometimes ended in shots fired aimlessly.

For a long time, they have been walking across the desert, in columns and convoys, always insecure in this land crisscrossed by hungry bands of marauders, holed up like packs of jackals in the inaccessible gorges of the mountain.

Now winter is coming, somber glacial winter; nights without shelter spent near fires without warmth. And, with the great resignation of their race, they have adapted to this life because, like all things here below, it is God's will.

In these chance meetings, the nomads become friends by sharing bread and shelter in the open; this fraternity among soldiers happens quickly but does not last.

These are small groups of men who tie up their horses together or herd their camels into the same corner of the camp, who eat from the same big wooden bowl, who share the same, humble interests in life: buying provisions, caring for the herds — their only fortune — and sometimes also, clandestine forays to the tents of the coveted beauties in the *douar* of the *makhzen*, even to the tents of the Amouriat Figuig, the skinny dissident prostitutes of Zenaga and Oudarhir.

✳

It is evening, the hour of chants, of monotone, plaintive songs, improvisations, naive and poignant, on war and love, on exile and death, reminiscent of ancient rhapsodies.

> The chiefs tell us of a journey to far away
> My heart sees into the future
> It announces my imminent death.
> Who will witness my death? Who will pray for me?
> Who will remember me with an elegy at my tomb?
> Ah! who knows what divine fate has in store for me!
> My white gazelle will forget me
> Someone else will ride my gentle mare.
> Be still my heart! Eyes, do not cry!
> Tears serve no purpose.
> No one obtains what is not written,
> And what is written, no one will escape.
> Be still, my heart, await God's mercy
> And if you cannot be still, there is always death.

The singers modulate their elegies, accompanied by the sweet *djouak*, a small Bedouin flute, whose mysterious sighing is now and then broken by the wild and strident cries of the *r'aita*.

After a somber, blood-red dusk, under the blackening vault of clouds, night has fallen, heavy and opaque.

A fitful breeze blows; the uncertain glimmers of light draw from the shadows vague, alien shapes, moving groups of phantoms.

The black, angular silhouette of a camel becomes deformed, almost frightening. The shadow of a white horse shakes its long mane.

Around a large, bright fire, a group of Bedouins stand, waving the soft folds of their burnouses like great white wings. Others, sitting in a circle, prepare the evening meal. Among these men with the sharp profiles of birds of prey, some have stern features with clear lines in which the Asiatic blood, less mixed, has preserved its ancient Arab beauty.

In attitudes of abandon and repose, vague groupings of bodies lying on the ground. Then, suddenly, without apparent cause, agitation, grand gestures, beneath the harshly illuminated robes.

For a long time, the nomads keep vigil as if in feverish anticipation of some arrival.

But, on high, on the plateau where the fortress stands, the bugles sound the lingering notes that announce it is time to extinguish fires. Little by little, the fires flicker and die out. Night grows thick around the camp, the nomads roll up in their rags and stretch out on the ground, seeking the oblivion of sleep, their gun or stick beneath their heads, their shoes serving as pillows.

Near the last fire, a young man, with two small locks of black hair hanging over his high cheekbones, stirs the ashes with the tip of his stick, still singing, almost whispering.

Variant

Two *mokhaznis* from the mess at Geryville, very young men from the broad horizons of the alfa grass steppes, sit face to face and begin to sing a plaintive ballad whose keening refrain ends in a sort of grieving sob.

At first they seem to be asleep, their eyes closed, their voices like the murmur of running water:

"Yesterday, all day, I lamented and cried: — I longed for my tent; I longed for my gazelle. — Today the sun shone on me — and sadness left my heart."

Unconsciously, the voices rise, grow stronger, quicker.

"Be still, my heart, and do not weep, my dear eyes! — Tears are useless. — No one can have what is not written — And what is written, no one can escape — Our land is the land of gunpowder — and our tombs are marked in the sand — Be still, my heart, be calm until your wounds are healed — and if they do not heal, take solace, there is death."

Then, from the *mokhaznis'* mess, another voice rises, rough and more hoarse, sobbing a desolate plaint for the fate of Muslim soldiers:

"God has abandoned me because I am a sinner. — I left my tribe and my tent; — I put on the blue burnous; — I have a gun for a wife. — The chiefs tell us about a journey to far away. — My heart sees into the future, it announces my imminent death. — Tomorrow, the hour will sound; — the angel of death will draw near. — Will it be a ragged Guilil or a pitiless Filali whose shot will kill me? That is God's secret. — And who will say the prayer of the dead over me? — Who will cry at my grave? I will die, and no one will have pity on me."

The voices, more numerous now, rise into the tranquil night, and the flutes whisper the sorrows of the soul.

> Yesterday, I cried all day:
> I longed for my tent,
> I longed for my gazelle,
> Today the sun rose and I smiled . . .
>
> There are some who have gone to Tafilalet, to Bechar,
> Others are here, who fought
> in the days of Timmimoun and El-Moungar.
> God protected them.
>
> Others never left their tents,
> And they are dead . . .
> Life is in the hands of God
> And there is only one death.

Think of nothing, hide nothing in your heart.
Our land is the land of gunpowder,
Our tombs are marked in the sand,
And your tomb is open, oh son of Mimoun! . . ."

*

These are the last beautiful days when the desert begins to ready itself for the onslaught of sandstorms.

The pale sky is veiled with milky dust. No wind; a light, mild breeze. At Beni-Ounif, there is a feverish coming and going, an uncommon commotion, as the great convoy of Beni-Abbes, which also supplies the faraway oases of the Sahara, moves out tomorrow.

For the *goumis* of Geryville, the order to depart has arrived: they are going to Bechar. The nomadic city will disperse into the *hamada*, the stony desert in the solitude of the sands.

Squatting in circles in small groups, in the village streets, among the piles of rock and debris, the blue-clad *mokhaznis*, the red spahis and the tawny nomads tumultuously divide up their supplies and their money; before leaving they put an end to their shared lives, always provisional, soon ended.

From the direction of the Zousfana, through the limpid night, dawn breaks. In the midst of the black, chaotic mass of the camps, a few red flames burn again in the hearths of last night. Then a confused murmur, low-pitched and monotone, rises from the already troubled sleep of men and beasts: the nomads praying. They invoke aloud the Master of the dawning day.

The light, hesitant, almost furtive at first, rises to its zenith, and the great stars that shone through the night grow pale and disappear.

Only Bordj-en-Behar, the morning star, glows, a lamp of joy and hope lit at the smiling birth of the day.

Low on the horizon in the east, some light clouds are aglow, swimming in the golden-green, oceanic transparencies.

And there is a stream of opalescent light in the street where life, at this first hour, seems easy and good.

Suddenly the camps fill with confused noises and cries.

The camels, having been aroused against their will, groan their discontent as they go up to the village where they will stand for hours between the railway station and the fortress, in the midst of piles of swollen packs, planks, canteens, and crates bearing faraway addresses: Taghit, Igli, Beni-Abbes, In-Salah, Adrar . . .

At the fortress, the bugle blares several notes of reveille, at first hoarse, then loud and imperious.

In front of the small shanties of the Bureau Arabe still wrapped in sleep, several blue or red burnouses pass by among the green or black tatters of the Jews of Kenadsa, come from the South to sell their handcrafted jewelry.

Finally, after many hours of work, the camels, almost two thousand of them, are gathered in the midst of the cargo to be loaded.

They are standing, and the oblique rays of the sun slide into the massive jumble of large immobile feet, upon swaying heads both curious and attentive, and upon the curves of their backs and their bare flanks of gray, dirty white, brown, or brownish red.

Several comical young camels, their gentle, elongated heads bearing naively infantile expressions, with the grace of great birds covered with dusky feathers, press against their mothers, their shaggy lips searching for the pointed nipples.

Now, the *sokhars* make their camels kneel by tapping them with sticks just below the knees.

The loading begins.

The din is indescribable, quarrels break out around each beast, with furious cries, guttural exclamations, insults and wild gestures, as if the entire mess were going to end up in a massacre.

Some invoke God; others ask the Prophet to bear witness to a palm-fiber string badly tied, to a neck of a sack left open. And all this goes on with no concern for time passing; the din increases steadily.

The grating harnesses of a supply train and the passage of galloping soldiers wreak havoc and terror among the camels who spring up, throwing off their half-loaded burdens and flee, chased by the imprecations of the *sokhars*.

The *bach-hammars*, mounted on their horses since early morning, swagger sticks in their hands, harass and goad their men, clamoring sharp, menacing orders.

From a distance, the nomads call to each other; they communicate with loud, drawn-out cries.

Oh, the throats of the Southern people, of what iron are they made that they do not break or rupture from those profound cries, those calls that resound like the sound of trumpets.

Several camels mutiny, shuffling in place or fleeing clumsily on three feet, the fourth tied up under them.

The horses rear, neighing to mares passing by. The wind rises suddenly making the tatters snap like filled sails. Whirlwinds of dust fill the camp, making eyes sting and lungs burn.

The military uniforms, the blue and red burnouses make pleasing colorful splashes in this surging mass of dull and somber earth tones.

Time passes, and the commanders, losing their patience, run around to get things moving and they, too, start shouting. But their French voices are too feeble to be heard among the Bedouin cries, and they are lost in the din that grows feverishly just before departure.

And the harsh, wild cries, the plaintive grumbling of the camels dominate all this mounting tumult, spreading out over the plain until it meets the eternal silence of the far horizons.

However, this great spectacle of pure desert life will come to an end, and one will no longer see its unforgettable splendor with the advent of colonial "security" and the railroads.

A *goumi* leaves first, rounding the corner of the fort at a trot, heading west, with the tricolor battalion flag flying over the soldiers' off-white burnouses and the dusty caparisons of the horses: It is the Trafi of Geryville who will accompany the small convoy out of Bechar.

Another *goumi*, from the Amour of Ain-Sefra, leads the great convoy of the Beni-Ounif, taking the southern route.

The tirailleurs of the escort, wearing *chechias* on their heads and scarlet belts over their white cotton uniforms, mill around and move out with their large, shuffling herds. The sun glints like white lightning off the steel of the rifles.

The camels, once standing, quiet down, as if meditating, and go down into the valley, walking toward Djenan-ed-Dar. For an hour they stretch out in an endless line that winds along the plain. The sun illuminates the dust. The convoy vanishes over the red horizon above which an iridescent mirage is floating.

Variant

Toward the west, in the distance, several mountains vaguely outlined, their strange forms barely distinguishable: truncated cones, jagged crests, terraces. All around, an infinite plain, burned, red, cracked earth dotted with bunches of alfa grass, green at the bottom, spreading upward into gray tufts at the tips of the dried stems: the somber mottling of a panther pelt spread out under the clear warmth of an autumn sky.

Light breezes blow over the plain, caressing it. On lean horses all bone and tendon with gray, coarse hair, the cavalry approach at a walk. Their black burnouses and their heavy *haiks* of earth-colored wool lend them an imposing air. Their faces are thin, with chiseled lines; their eagle eyes have a wild gleam. Martial bearing, grand gestures, dignified demeanor . . . One might almost mistake them for marabouts, were it not for their rifles which they carry slung across their backs or held upright, the butt end on their knees. *Bach-hammars* for the convoys, they are also, at times, courageous warriors by tradition and profoundly indifferent to death.

Far behind them, scattered in the alfa grass, the nomads are approaching, their foreheads banded by thin fawn-colored cords wrapped around light headdresses, sticks across their shoulders, pushing out their thin, tanned chests, lined with strong muscles, in the gaps between their dusty tatters; they are driving ahead of them the heavy, slow camels, unloaded except for the small triangular pack-saddles.

Their long supple necks sway; their thick-lipped muzzles graze on a few thin, gray shrubs tucked away between the black stones and the tufts of alfa grass.

The camels stop. Then, as the camels take too long, the *sokhars* emit a hoarse cry, a guttural *ah!* that comes from their copper throats, and a short whistle. The undulating necks straighten up again, and the heads resembling both the sheep and the serpent, strangely disdainful heads with gentle eyes, begin again their regular swaying. Their long yellow teeth are chewing cud, continually grinding away.

The herd goes by. The men, smaller, disappear first into the infinite waves of the alfa grass. Then, it's the camels' turn to become distorted, rounded, and to merge into the vague undulations of the ground.

Such caravans come from all the *douars* of the high plateaus, heading south, slowly crossing these happy solitudes, that they alone, shepherds and wanderers, know and love, with the unconscious love of gazelles and wild birds.

These are the last nice days before the sandstorms. The pale sky veils itself with milky haze. No wind, now and then a scant warm gust.

At Beni-Ounif, in the valley near the *ksar*, a sudden burst of noisy life.

Nomads arrive every day, with their long procession of camels, to camp next to the *goumis*.

The camps of the *sokhars* are simpler and more chaotic, but more colorful as well.

It is a jumble of things: *gh'rairs*, long straight sacks of rough gray and black wool that one hangs off the pack saddles of camels, the strips of carpet, the unraveled blankets among the smoky pots, the shaggy goatskins hanging from tripods, the flash of a new metal mess-tin in the pile of Bedouin tatters, of somber or warm colors in which red and rusty black are dominant; all this accumulates and mixes near the fires of dried palm fronds or camel dung, among the kneeling camels who ruminate while the others seem to dream, dominating everything with their tall, angular silhouettes.

The friendships, born of sleeping around the same fire and eating from the same plate throughout the long journey, continue; new ones are born; some end in terrible fights. Sometimes blood is spilled.

And thus it has been with these *sokhars* and their camels in migration, just as in the first ages of the world.

At the fort, the bugle sounds the notes of reveille, at first rusty, then piercing and imperious.

In front of the sleepy shacks of the Bureau Arabe, several blue and red burnouses pass by among the green and black rags of the Jewish nomads from Kenadsa, who come from the South to sell their gold and silver jewelry.

Among the *goumis* there is also an unusual bustle: The Amour from Ain-Sefra are heading off west in a column, to Bechar. The Trafi of Geryville go down toward Taghit and Beni-Abbes to protect a convoy. The names of El-Moungar and Zafrani still evoke deathly shudders of fear.

And finally, after several hours of work and shouting, all the camels, almost two thousand of them, are gathered in the midst of the cargo to be loaded.

They are standing, and the oblique rays of the sun glide over the innumerable folds of their great, immobile feet, on their swaying heads, curious and attentive, on their backs and flanks, fawn-colored, gray, dull white, brown, or red.

Several comical baby camels, with elongated heads, gentle and naive, press against their mothers with the grace of great downy birds, searching with already shaggy lips for the pointed nipples.

Now the *sokhars* make their camels kneel with small taps of a

stick below their knees. The loading begins. The tumult is indescribable as quarrels break out around each camel, with furious
cries, guttural exclamations, insults, and wild gestures, as if all this
must end with a massacre. God is invoked, and the Prophet is called
to witness because of an argument over a string of palm fiber badly
tied, the neck of a sack open.

All this goes on with no notice of time passing.

The longer the loading goes on, the more the din increases.

Grating harnesses, galloping calvary pass, sowing chaos and
terror among the camels who spring up, dumping off their half-
loaded burdens and fleeing, chased by the imprecations of the
sokhars.

The *bach-hammars*, mounted since early morning, riding crop
in hand, hurry their men, harassing them, shouting out orders,
threatening and sometimes even striking out.

Over great distances, the Bedouins call to one another, shout
back and forth, and come to understandings.

Oh, the throats of these men of the South, of what metal are they
wrought that they neither break nor bleed from these deep cries
that resound like the notes of trumpets.

Several camels mutiny, fleeing or stamping in place; some horses
rear.

The wind picks up, making the tatters snap like full sails, in the
rising dust.

The military uniforms, the red or blue burnouses, make colorful
splashes in the midst of this somber, earth-colored swell.

French voices, too weak, try to pierce through the Bedouin cries
and are lost.

And the harsh, wild cries, the plaintive grumbling of the camels
dominate all this noise which rises spreading out over the plain
until it meets the eternal silence of the far horizons.

It is coming to an end, however, this grand spectacle of primitive
life of which we soon will not see the splendor, with the advent of
the colonial regime and the railroad.

The tirailleurs of the escort, wearing *chechias* on their heads and scarlet belts over their white cotton uniforms, mill around and move out with their large, shuffling herds. The sun glints like lightning off the steel of the rifles.

A group of *goumis* head off toward the west, behind the corner of the fort, their tricolor battalion flags flying over the off-white of their burnouses.

Everything is loaded; they are ready.

Slowly the camels go back down into the valley which they cross, heading toward Djenan-ed-Dar.

For an hour, they are deployed into an endless line that winds across the plain through the dust illuminated by the sun.

Then, at the red horizon where an iridescent mirage is floating, the convoy disappears, vanishes.

AT THE HOME OF
BOU-AMAMA'S COUSIN

Amiable smiles on relaxed faces, and slow and solemn gestures beneath white robes. Silence and meditation in the vast courtyards where men slip by noiselessly, like apparitions. The murmur of prayers and postures of ecstasy . . . the permanence of things over the centuries.

At first sight, one sees nothing else in these ancient *zouaoua* of the West, alone impregnable in all the torment that rumbles around and within the ruins of a crumbling world.

Nevertheless, behind this haughty facade of indifference, within this remoteness from things of the present, there is something else: mysterious intrigues in Morocco that often end in blood, secular hatred, absolute devotion side by side with wily betrayals, the terrible violence of passions that lie sleeping in hearts, the ferment of wars and massacres.

But to discover these hidden things, one must gain entrance to the *zaouïya*, live there, build some trust there, because outside all is calm and white.

In the ancient *zaouïya* of Bou-Amama at Hammam-Foukani after a hot day broken by gusts of stormy wind, the evening is heavy, calm, and particularly oppressive in all the silence.

The sun sets without its usual, clear iridescence, without delicacy of tones, in a violent conflagration, changing abruptly from the blood red of the horizon to the sulfureous green of the zenith where several fleshy pink clouds are floating.

The neighboring palm grove sinks quickly under a shadow of deep blue, almost black already, while on the tousled crests of the date palms only a few golden red flames are still racing.

Beyond the low walls of the courtyard, the great plain extends behind Figuig to the rugged Djebel-Grouz. Sandy and slightly rolling, it burns with a dull fire like an immense hearth covered with dying embers.

Toward the right, down below, in the middle of an arid, stony ravine, the *koubba* of Sidi-Abdelkader-Mohammed, patron of Figuig, rises up. Its great white cupola takes on the hue of overheated copper, the reflections of molten metal run down the walls.

Opposite the *koubba*, the far-away villages, beneath the flamboyant crests of the mountains, trace a scarcely visible black line: the palms of El-Ardja.

Closer, there is Dar-el-Beida, the barracks of the *sherifian makhzen*, roasting all alone in the fading light of the plain.

To the left, in the west, the thick wall of Djebel-Grouz darkens and the oblique silhouette of Djebel-Melias is aflame. A great stage upon which fairies of light are dancing.

Night is falling.

The *eddhen* of *moghreb,* the sunset call to prayer, rises in slow notes from the high, white minarets of Elmaiz and Oudarhir. Suddenly, huge, blue shadows reach out from the hollows of the earth toward the summits, which fade slowly, drowning in the diaphanous marine light.

Then, furtively rounding the walls of Oudarhir, bursting forth, unexpected and alarming, a dozen or so gaunt, emaciated men, dressed in nondescript rags. They are armed with Mausers and drive a few skinny sheep in front of them. Near me, one of the keepers of the *zaouiya*, a grave man with impenetrable, gentle eyes, is finishing his prayers.

"Si Mohammed, I say to him, who are those people?"

"Oh, no one, shepherds from Melias."

"But they wear the veiled turban of the Beni Guil."

"No, they are Arabs from here. They dress like the Beni Guil because they lived for a long time at the Tigri *chott*."

Suddenly, Si Mohammed leaves and disappears at the end of the corridor. As the darkness thickens, these shepherds, who look like bandits, enter the covered streets of Hammam-Foukani. After a bit, I hear bleating in the back court of the *zaouiya*.

Si Mohammed, coming back, shuffling in his yellow leather slippers, explains:

"Those poor people, sorely tried by war, are coming here to sell their sheep and to beg for a blessing from the sheikh and his ancestors, — may God have mercy on them! — they have no refuge other than this house."

A long room with bare walls, the floor covered with heavy rugs of thick woolen pile, and, scattered about, long pillows of yellow and green silk brocade with gold flowers.

In a high bronze chandelier, a single candle illuminates the room. On the rug, the faint light flows in purple and green waves, reflecting violet or bronze as it glides over the smooth, warm tints of the wool.

In a corner, a mauve flicker appears on the curved flank of a red copper Moroccan kettle on a high trivet. On the floor, a small plate glows like a pale moon. Adamantine waters stream from a white crystal pitcher, next to the tea cups decorated with multicolored stones.

Si Mohammed ben Menouar, cousin and brother-in-law of Bou-Amama, the actual head of the *zaouiya*, is half reclined on the rug. His strong and supple body is draped in a garnet-red burnous and a *haik* of fine wool frames his thin, tanned face, its pronounced features typical of the villagers. In his black beard several threads of white are beginning to show.

A facade of intelligence, of guile and finesse, by turn affable, almost caressing, and then suddenly harsh, smiles without warmth, often ironic. Multiple and lively gestures, without the solemn majesty and imposing restraint of the other marabouts of the South.

Si Ahmed likes to joke and laugh. When he is with Europeans, he tries to imitate their light bantering style. Si Ahmed expresses favorable feelings towards the French and avows his loyalty to them.

At that hour, at home, he seems preoccupied. He talks to me at length about the palm groves of Melias and the people of Foukani, without my asking him. He talks about it insistently, which is unusual for someone who is good at avoiding topics he does not wish to discuss.

Across from us, Ben Cheikh, the keeper of Sidi Slimane, with whom I came.

Of gaunt and truly ascetic demeanor, he has an extraordinary intensity of life in his fleeting gaze.

He speaks freely in front of the man who replaced the exiled master. He too has his importance because he is the most devoted follower of Bou-Amama at Beni-Ounif.

He tells me that some faithful followers left that morning to go on a pilgrimage to the marabout, out there, at his desert *zaouïya* found at the foot of the Djebel-Teldj, a five- or six-day journey to the northwest of Figuig. With a deep sigh, Ben Cheikh bewails the fate that prevents him from joining his beloved master again. Then for the hundredth time, perhaps, since I met him, he says to me with an engaging smile:

"Si Mahmoud, you ought to go see Bou-Amama. With me and under the protection of Si Ahmed, you have nothing to fear. You will visit his *zaouïya* just as you visit here. As for Bou-Amama, he will receive you with open arms, like his own son. You must do that, Si Mahmoud. Upon returning, you could say to the French: 'I saw Bou-Amama, and he did me no harm. He welcomed me, as he welcomes all Algerian Muslims. He is no enemy of the French, and between him and France there is merely a misunderstanding.'"

I listen and respond evasively:

"In chah Allah — God willing — I will go!"

"And perhaps I will go one day."

Silence falls again. Si Ahmed smiles vaguely. Ben Cheikh seems plunged in the suffering of an unswerving follower. The light wavers, making great deformed shadows prowl on the white walls.

I look at these two men whose polished and personable demeanors hide unfathomable depths, these men whose souls are impenetrable, whose wills tend toward one end: to serve Bou-Amama.

And I prefer them thus, self-possessed, grave and silent, more in harmony with the calm of the hour and the place.

The door is open onto a large covered gallery which surrounds the second floor. Opposite, a heavy square *toub* pillar emerges from the shadows, beneath the red reflection of the candle. A white form is crouched on the ground. Beneath the motionless mass of heavy white robes, one cannot distinguish the face of a black servant. In the courtyard, people speak in low voices. The bare feet of slaves passing by make a slight rustle. A heavy oppressiveness weighs on the sleeping oasis and on this house.

Time passes in the languishing night.

Si Ahmed retires to his quarters, forgetting, as if by chance, his revolver at my side in its green velvet case.

Ben Cheikh rolls himself up in his old burnous, and I stretch out by the still-open door.

Vague images at first, visions glimpsed here, float through my mind. Then it all comes into focus: these shepherds armed with rifles, who came so furtively at nightfall, who can they be? In such a place, where there is nothing to fear . . . where one can sleep in perfect security.

But sleep won't come.

It is hot, and the taint of fever hangs in the air. I get up quietly and go downstairs. On the dark patio, some men are sleeping. I find another door ajar.

There, by the uncertain light of the stars, the shepherds of Melias are sleeping, their rifles under their heads, their cartridge belts clasped to their sunken bellies over ragged djellabas.

Resting, gaunt faces, marked by suffering and hard times, hollow cheeks, sunken eyes closed by fatigue.

In a corner, a soft, whitish mass that ripples occasionally: sheep.

I go back in and lie down, above, in the gallery. Soon after, two servants who were sleeping downstairs, awaken. They speak in low voices:

"Are the Beni Guil leaving tomorrow morning?"

"Sidi said they would leave at dawn."

Then they continue talking in Berber dialect and I understand only vaguely. They speak of the pasha of Oudarhir and of Sidi Bou-Amama.

Those whom I had thought were shepherds are actually Beni Guil dissidents, the remnants of some *djich* broken off by death and hunger, and who arrive perhaps from far away, with these sheep acquired God only knows how.

They come with news from the West, and for some supplies.

But finally I am overcome by sleep, so calm and gentle, at this cooler hour of the night.

In the purple light of dawn, with the joy of a new day, the court-yard of the *zaouiya* is empty: the Beni Guil have vanished with the last shadows.

FIGUIG

The valley of Figuig opened out like a great, white flower under the sun.

I was sitting on the parapet of a high, crumbling tower made of gold-colored earth, so old and fragile that it seemed ready to fall into dust. The tower was mirrored in the dark water of a pool at the edge of the gardens of Oudaghir. It was situated on high, dominating the whole valley.

I was alone in the splendor of the dawning day, and I was dreaming as I gazed at Figuig, queen of oases which had never looked so beautiful to me before, perhaps because I was leaving the next day.

In the distance, toward the South, beyond the mountains of Taghla and Melias, the red desert was climbing high into the sky, marking the horizon with a dark, clear line as on the high seas.

The impressive cleft of the Zenaga pass opened like the bed of a river in which floated waves of black date palms, between the intense indigo tone of Djebel Taarla and the obliquely lit rose color of Djebel Zenaga.

To the right, the pass of the Jewess, arid and stony, between barren hillsides, and the pass of the Moudjabedine, where the mirages play in the blinding noon of summer.

The flat, sterile entrance to the valley glittered in the sun. Closer, beneath my feet, the palm groves of Zenaga rolled in huge waves, undulated, broke against the *djorf*, the high, gray cliff that separates the two terraces of Figuig.

The spreading crests of the date palms took on hues of pale blue velvet upon which glints of silver played. To the right, the old *ksar* of Zenaga made a splash of tawny gold that glowed intensely among all these delicate, pale tones. On the mountain and in the valley, the morning sun was sending out azure waves of light, a dynamic, immaculate light. At the foot of the tower, his back against the rough wall, an old blind man stood, holding his hand out toward the road where the faithful passed by.

He was tall, attractive, and his emaciated face with its empty eyes was as impassive as dark bronze. His bony body was draped magnificently in earth-colored tatters.

Farther, on the sunlit road, two Berber women had stopped, and the light played in the heavy folds of the purple wool of their garments that swept the ground.

Above a wall, the small, gentle head of a dromedary swayed, complaining hoarsely and grimacing strangely with long yellow teeth.

A fragment of dried *toub* broke off from the top of the tower and fell into the still water of the pool, making silver ripples that expanded, coming to an end at the humid banks.

I went down toward Zenaga by the cliff path where horses slide and tremble along the edge of the abyss. As I descended, a wall of murmuring date palms rose, hiding the blue clarity of the distance.

Down below, in the blue shade of the palm grove, a *seguia* was flowing over the moss. The village gardens were putting on display their luxurious pale sea-greens and darker russet greens. The sun, filtering through the angular palms that barely rustled in the breeze, scattered golden dust on the red sand and the white rocks. Nearby, inviting paths, shadowy and cool, opened out between the light-colored *toub* walls of the gardens.

Under the arching palms, fig trees leaned toward the sun, their leaves gilded by autumn and mixed with the rusty leaves of grapevines, and next to them, like flowers in full bloom, the red of pomegranates and peach trees.

A penumbra full of charm blurred the lines and colors in this maze of paths without habitations, so tranquil wild turtledoves could be heard cooing softly in the surrounding trees.

Sometimes, at a sharp turn, there was a large blue pool, a still mirror reflecting leaning date palms, their trunks overrun by climbing weeds.

And everywhere the continuous murmur of the running water of the *seguia*, gushing from a wall, disappearing suddenly underground with the cool sound of a waterfall, then reappearing two steps farther on, beneath the delicate lace of green ferns.

The sun climbed slowly, triumphantly, over the peacefulness and joy of the delightful oasis.

After the palm grove, I entered the perpetual shade of the covered streets of Zenaga, where white shapes passed silently, almost furtively, clinging to the walls.

Massive doors, opened a crack, let in chinks of blue light.

In the midst of all this distrust, in all this silence, one only heard now and then, through the thick, sightless walls, the dull humming of an old African hand mill and the monotone chant, in Berber, of some invisible village woman.

Upon leaving, I dreamed sadly that, without doubt, in several years, the lust for money, the stupidity and the alcoholism that had polluted Biskra would come to destroy the still untainted charm of this old Saharan refuge.

Preserved jealously through the centuries, in its isolation, the oasis of Figuig seemed to me a pearl of perfect beauty.

Along the dusty path, through the burning emptiness of the valley, some inhabitants of Figuig were herding donkeys loaded with sacks of barley and wheat, driven by black *khartani* slaves.

The Berbers, white and serene beneath their robes of wool,

approached slowly, the reins draped on the necks of their submissive mounts.

The vague gaze of their black eyes wandered over the mountains of their land in the distance, where the rose enchantment of the morning was dying out.

Passing in front of me and my companion clad in a blue burnous, they greeted us distractedly with the word of peace that is the watchword of Islam, the sign of solidarity and fraternity between Muslims, from the borders of China to the shores of the Atlantic, from the banks of the Bosphorus to the sandbars of Senegal.

Watching these men pass through the valley, I understood more intimately than ever the soul of Islam and felt it resonate within me. I tasted the harsh splendor of the landscape, the resignation, the vague dreams, the profound indifference to things of this life and of death.

I understood also why the blind beggar was so dignified and serene, his hand stretched out toward the passersby whom he could not see in his eternal sightless night, and why, instead of becoming agitated and laboring with the sweat of their brows, the Arabs slumber, throughout the monotone course of the still days, stretched out in the shade of ancient walls that crumble to dust and which no one will repair, on the bare ground that welcomes them.

THE *DJICH*

The Ouled Daoud, a faction of the Amouria dissidents, numbered not more than a dozen. They held the mountain for months, starved, on the lookout for scanty herds of sheep to raid.

Their rags had taken on the red tint of the earth. Unkempt beards bristled on their bony faces burned by the sun and the wind. Over their frayed *abeyas* and their fawn-colored burnouses, old cartridge belts in red *filali* were cinched around their sunken bellies. They were miserable and fierce, suspicious like all creatures of the desert, pursued by hunger and surrounded.

After the Taghit affair, the southern route had become too dangerous for them and they had returned to the north, prowling around the *douars* and camps, appearing everywhere where there was gunpowder.

They had suffered greatly from hunger, holed up in the narrow gorges and underbrush of the Beni-Smi.

One day, in luck again, they had stolen several sheep and camels from around Ich. Then they had moved back down toward Figuig. By nightfall, they were walking along the tawny-colored, high *toub* walls outside the *ksar* of Oudarh'ir by the deserted valley. Their black eyes looked avidly at the fertile gardens, at the great mud houses, closed and silent, and joy lit the depths of their vulture eyes.

High and round, pierced by small loopholes, the guard towers of mud which flank the walls stand out, dull gold against the red of the evening and the black fronds of the date palms. At the foot of the ramparts were about twenty low gray tents, the Amouria camp, a place of untamed wretchedness and prostitution. Small, smoky fires cast images of flame on the tents and walls, illuminating at times, in the growing shadow, the black silhouettes of women draped in somber tatters.

The starving *djich*, like birds of prey, swooped down near the tents, exchanging joyous salaams with the women of their race and with several skinny nomads stretched out by the fires.

Dry palm fronds thrown on the embers suddenly caught fire with a high, bright flame reaching straight up into the still air. Giant, the deformed shadows of men and things danced on the muted, dusty earth. Voices and joyous cries rose in celebration of the return, the temporary security of the moment.

The thin women with tattooed faces were coming and going, wishing the prowlers welcome, recognizing them, asking them for news of their companions. And as most of them had died, sowing their unburied bones on the mountain, the women invoked God's mercy on the dead.

The Amouria avidly devoured spicy couscous and stringy meat, grains of sand cracking between their teeth. Then, gravely, they prepared the tea themselves, a task reserved only for men.

They settled their tired bodies on an old rug in attitudes of well-being. However, they kept their rifles close to them out of habit and also because the *makhzen* of the pasha of Oudarh'ir, friend of the Christians, was near.

The flames of the fires made blood-red shadows wander over their sere, falcon-like profiles; of the tall, black *khartani* who slipped among them, only the whites of his eyes and the dull white of his teeth were visible.

They exchanged news of the *bled*, recounting stories of pillage, exalting the glory of some, cursing the defection of others. In all this talk, the name most often repeated, piously, evoking the memory of the master, was that of the venerated sheikh: Bou-Amama. Each time his name was mentioned, they all touched their foreheads and lips with their right hands, a sign of submission and respect. And this name Bou-Amama came up constantly. Some children of the Ouled Daoud and even tiny little bronze Amouria were named Bou-Amama.

A lot of tea was consumed that night in the women's camp. Then a chant arose, cadenced and monotone. The voice, at regular intervals, ascended hesitantly with the clear resonance of an oboe, then it slowly died out in a desolate plaint.

The prowlers were singing: "Yesterday, all day, I cried, I moaned: today the sun came up and I smiled. Our country is the country of gunpowder and our tombs are marked in the sand." And the muted tones of small reed *djouaks* accompanied with their sad, immaterial whisperings, the song of the prowlers' death.

The silent hours of the night crept on; the fires died down. Then, slowly, stretching their supple bodies like cats, the Amouria got up and followed the women into the warm shadows of the tents for ardent embraces after the long abstinence of war. For a brief moment there was the jangle of silver jewelry. A gentle murmur, discreet and voluptuous, hovers over the tents, over the uncertain fate of these nomads. The plaintive bleating of a few awakened sheep, the hoarse barking of dogs, uneasy around all these strangers.

Then, all these noises stopped and a great silence reigned over the prostitutes' camp, over Figuig asleep in the warm shadow of its palm groves amid the stillness of large, bluish ponds.

Day broke, all rose and lilac, upon the harmonious contours of this valley. Red gleams illuminated the jagged mountains summits, and metallic reflections glided over the blue velvet of the gardens.

The tawny villages flamed gold in the joy of the morning.

Men with striking and solemn faces, clad in dark blue djellabas and armed with rifles, emerged from the walls of Oudarh'ir. In the front of them there was a tall, thin Moroccan wearing a white djellaba and a red *chechia* creased down the middle over strange loops of graying hair. His pale face was ugly, and his gaze evasive.

The Amouria jumped for their rifles. The police officer of the pasha's *makhzen* came forward: "Peace be on you! Who are you and why are you here? — We are of the Amouria and we come from the north to ask asylum and hospitality from the people of Figuig.

The pasha had pledged not to give sanctuary to dissidents or to bandits: "Get out of here!"

With downcast faces and fierce looks, the Amouria listened; there were only ten of them; if gunfire started, it would be death.

So, without a word, they gathered their dusty rags and they went off down the valley, toward the west, toward other pillages.

The women and the pasha's *makhzen* followed them with their eyes as they disappeared into clear, rose-colored dawn that broke quietly and joyfully.

OUDJDA

Tlemcen, 27 March 1904

Over the course of passing years, the jaded eye gets used to the most vibrant colors, the strangest decors. It ends by discovering the deceptive monotony of the world and the homogeneity of peoples — and that is one of the most profound disenchantments in life.

However, some remote corners of the country remain pristine: those places alone can bring to weary souls a thrill they had thought lost forever.

Oudjda is one of those forgotten corners, a rock standing against the current of a devastating century.

This impression grows stronger as you arrive after passing through scenes of great but well-known beauty, none of which prepares you for the vision of Oudjda.

First there is the brief glimpse of Tlemcen, fog-bound, drenched in rain, buried in green and laughing gardens, with its high, gray walls, its narrow streets and small shops, its yellowed and antiquated look, with the minaret of Sidi-Bou-Medine sketched in black against a disconsolate horizon.

Upon leaving, then, under the feeble rays of the sun, furtively shining like a smile through a veil of tears, the impressive silhouette of Mansourah, ruined and blasted, still endures, proud while on the brink of annihilation, in the midst of the burgeoning African spring.

Beyond the underbrush and the gentle hills, beyond the muddy and insurgent Tafna, Lella Marhnia, a small military town with wide, straight streets lined with enormous *fondouks* (inns), overflowing with the vast waves of a Morocco in ferment, breaking and foaming in rough eddies.

Behind Marhnia, the immense plain of Angad with its large chain of mountains.

There, nothing more than sadness and monotony, gray skeletons of barren jujube trees and long red wounds — gouged out *oueds* furrowing the wet grass.

On the winding trail, gaping corpses expose the horror of their torn-out entrails under the caressing rays of a pale sun, veiled with thin, white haze.

A thick belt of olive orchards, fertile gardens, and small, green velvet fields of barley with, at times, in the corner of a mud wall, the carmine flowering of a peach tree: a tranquil landscape reminiscent of the Tunisian Sahel.

But suddenly there is an opening among the olive trees. A high, dull white rampart rises up, fierce and inaccessible, pierced by a sturdy, arched doorway. It is Oudjda.

Sitting or lying back on the ground, the *askar*, soldiers of the sultan, wearing red jackets and *chechias*, guard the entrance. Indifferent and empty-eyed, these men watch us go by and distractedly answer our *salaam*.

At sunset, when the *moueddhens* send forth the drawn-out notes of their prayer calls, the doors of Oudjda will shut, grating on their ancient, iron hinges. The keys will be brought to the casbah, to the amel's house, where they will be kept until dawn. From sunset to sunrise, Oudjda will thus be isolated from the rest of the world, and no human being can enter or leave.

As soon as we pass through the archway, a penetrating smell nearly chokes us, a composite odor made up of the musty smell of rot, musk, corpses, and soaked olives.

It was into this mud and stench that we entered, amid stagnant ponds embellished with greenish efflorescences in which waste, dead animals, filthy debris, and rags floated.

Instead of the silence and contemplative mood of other Islamic cities, here there is a dense noisy rumbling, a mob that churns and swirls, bottled up in the streets. It is as if a fever-bearing wind had passed through Oudjda. The people we'd expected to be calm and dignified seemed hurried.

They crowded and jostled. On what urgent errands, with what destination, given that it was evening and the gates were going to be inevitably closed?

First, a few miserable, little streets, then the first public square lined with houses, once white, now crumbling, pitted with large leprous black patches, and deep crevices like wounds. The boutiques, opening on to the black mud of the streets, are narrow cavities crammed with merchandise and foodstuffs: glistening black olives, packed brown dates in tan skins, jars of greenish olive oil, sugar cakes wrapped in blue paper.

All along the dried-out footpaths, the crowd hugged the walls, polished and soiled from the continual friction of hands.

What a mixture of races, types, and dress! City-dwellers from Fez and Oudjda are draped in fine djellabas, their faces blank and impassive, their eyes wily and proud. Nomads, in earth-colored tatters, wearing turbans and hoods, with prayer beads around their necks, their profiles harsh but regular, are more familiar and likable, however. Wretched-looking women in rags, wrapped in old *haiks* of dusty wool, dragging their shoes in the mud.

Running among the pedestrians, fleeing like bands of mice under the feet of horses, are clusters of begging children, brazen but polished, with their sweet faces, their wide, caressing eyes. And then, there are the soldiers and the bandits, scarcely distinct from one another, with gaunt and dangerous faces, the Gueballa from the Center above all, with their bony faces, sharp teeth, and burning eyes, are still hardy after long months of atrocious misery. Several wear the red jacket of the *makhzen*, beneath indescribable rags.

All these people talk at the same time, argue, sing, laugh, joke. Because, in this miserable, rotting town, at the end of day, gaiety, bursts of laughter, and singing reign.

Strangely enough, this gaiety augments our sinister first impression and our fear of these exasperated beings, pushed to the hilt, reverting to savage animality.

Among the children, women, and soldiers, jeers and dirty jokes are traded. These men, dying of famine, still dream of the promised pleasures that glittered in their avid eyes throughout the long journey from Taza that has brought them to this hell where so many of their people have died of hunger and illness in the rising tide of filth.

Two cavalry men of the Beni-Ouassine near the frontier and I cross all the way through town looking for a safe, quiet refuge: the *zaouiya* of Sidi Abdelkader of Baghdad.

Suddenly, as the sun sets, purple in an ocean of greenish gold, in those out-of-the-way quarters where crowding families no longer swarm, Oudjda lifts its veils of sorrow and grief. Oudjda smiles, white and rose, embraced by the saracen walls with their elegant ramparts and by the murmuring olive trees. Everything is quiet as the *moueddhens*, the only human voices, call the faithful to evening prayer.

On the crumbling, curved arches, where grass has grown, ringdoves preen their iridescent feathers, cooing gently.

The immense peacefulness, the stillness and dignified serenity of Islamic towns, I suddenly find here, quite unexpectedly after a nightmarish arrival.

The night is pitch-dark, beneath a sky overcast with clouds.

I cross Oudjda on horseback, with a black slave from the *zaouiya*, a giant with a hoarse voice, to visit the small French mission in charge of training Moroccan artillerymen.

And it is then that this city of hallucinations reveals to me another aspect, more lugubrious and fascinating.

The coming and going continues in the shadows where lanterns with red, green, and blue glass waver, throwing long phosphorescent trails of light on fetid pools from which bubbles arise, bursting.

The passersby wave their lanterns, suspended from the ends of sticks, in order not to be engulfed.

A square, an irregular marketplace, crisscrossed by stinking ditches and piles of filth. In a corner, in a pile, two or three corpses of dogs that the living begin to sniff, taking flight afterward, appalled, tails between their legs, with gruesome howls.

Beneath the lurid glowering of the lanterns, vegetables, oranges, olives, lemons, dates, old clothes, and kif are sold; only bread is impossible to find at this late hour, the bread the famished soldiers long for. Deformed, miserable, and menacing figures multiply, emerging from obscure corners to which they quickly return, leaving the ghost of a sinister profile half glimpsed, then gone, which you feel to be somewhere, quite near, perhaps behind you.

My horse slips, shudders. He is afraid of these lamps and all this din. He rears and we have to get out in order not to crush the pedestrians and the street urchins, shouting out beneath our feet.

There, at night, you feel the hunger, the raging hunger that tortures the soldiers, the vagabonds, and those others who have sought refuge here since the war.

A clamor arises, a monotone lamentation, from all the squares and streets: "In God's name, some bread!" "In the name of Sidi Abdelkader Djilani, some bread!" And beyond the marketplace, in the shadows, one voice dominates all the others, the importunate voice of a blind man, hammering away to infinity at the same prayer in a staccato monotone: "Who will give me the bread of charity in the name of Sidi Yahia!"

And the name of Sidi Yahia, patron of Oudjda, coming back in refrain, sounds such a harsh note that it finally makes the beggar's entreaty ferocious.

Finally we find the kasbah, a house shut off like the others in

Oudjda. There, abandoned by their students since the bread shortage, two French officers and a sergeant, as well as two non-coms from the local Algerian tirailleurs, stay alone, exiled, reduced to inaction, in this sad, grim corner of Oudjda. They stay at their military posts and resign themselves, given the uncertainty and uselessness of their presence, poor sorry souls who tomorrow perhaps will be the victims of some Moroccan quarrel or pillage.

In an ancient room, I stretch myself out on a rug and fall asleep. As if in a dream, half-asleep, I hear an indistinct voice that rises from the anguished silence of an Oudjda finally at rest. The voice rises, rises, climbing with the clear sonority of an oboe, to end on a sweet, dying note, a sigh: it is the Aissaouah who are praying and chanting their *dhikr* in the modest calm of the night, hiding the decay of things and the decadence of beings.

Again, as at sunset, there is an impression of immense peacefulness, of immobility, an intense impression of ancient Islam, indifferent before death, unconscious of ruin, following its great dream of a serene eternity, through the centuries of blood and war.

Day breaks clear and radiant on the small garden of rosebushes in the courtyard of the mission, in the shade of a giant aspen, all silvery, and the ancient ramparts of the kasbah, consumed by moss.

I return to the marketplace, still on horseback, for fear of walking in the liquid muck of soot and pus.

Oudjda comes alive: at dawn, the four thousand famished and menacing men of the army of Taza, almost all recruited from among the fierce Gueballa, leave. The *mahalla* leaves, heading out, in search of promised bread, and does not come back. Woe to whomever should encounter this horde of tribesmen on deserted byways!

However, today again, men run about, auctioning off their useless rifles and blood-colored jackets. They sell these things with a sort of furious desperation, for any price, with insults and jeers for the lying and impotent *makhzen*. Their hate explodes openly.

The more we push ahead, the narrower the streets, the denser the crowds. Here and there, in the overheated mud, a corpse bloats. A horse's shoe, an avid dog's claw, tear off strips of dead flesh, letting flow blackened blood and pus.

And the people of the town, distinguished and dignified, overrun for months by the *berrania*, the strangers, do not even try to clean up their town: they walk by the filth and turn away in disgust.

You see also, in these streets, interrupted at every step by archways and receding series of walls, an extraordinary vagrancy — blind men, lepers, cripples, imbeciles.

It is like a den of thieves, a sink of corruption, a Court of Miracles; disgust, fear, and pity all coalesce within me and oppress me.

Muscular men, almost all wearing the red, cast-off jackets of the *makhzen*, run across the city, bumping into people. Attached around their necks by a long, thin chain are a mess-tin and a small bell, all of yellow copper, that bounce and jangle. On their back they carry full goatskins: they are the *guerbadjia*, the water merchants, who, with their outlandish noise add another alien note.

Suddenly, in the midst of all these peddlers, a tall, handsome, tanned soldier in a scarlet jacket holds a bristling, barking dog by the scruff of the neck, at arm's length. At the top of his lungs he cries derisively:

"Five cents, *azizi*, for this dog! A good watchdog — he never bites the hand that feeds him, this dog!"

And everyone understands the insulting allusion to the lying *makhzen*. There is a thunder of laughter as the dog, finally delivered, flees howling furiously.

At the *zaouiya*, spacious courtyards, long rooms, clean and white, silence and peaceful contemplation.

Surrounding the very young son of the absent sheikh, a pale and sickly child in a djellabah of dark cloth, are grave, deliberate individuals with welcoming smiles and gentle ways. They talk — as if they were reciting a lesson — of the Sultan, of his ideas about beneficial reforms and the crimes of Rogui.

But, at base, they are too intelligent to get involved in all these quarrels. They want to isolate themselves from them, in their closed and unchanging world, to live as their pious ancestors lived and to conduct in silence and shadow the affairs of the faithful, without being bothered one way or another about the master of the Mogh'rib, always so forgotten and distant.

Superb black women slaves serve us tea and some *diffa* made of milk and peppered meat. The perfect forms of their strong, supple bodies beneath their dark linen *mlahfas* are revealed by each movement. And they half smile, rolling the whites of their big eyes full of a caressing animality.

How distant this *zaouiya* is from the horrors outside, hidden as it is behind its walls, and successive enclosures, and courtyards, and corridors! How immaculate and serene it is in the midst of the putrefaction and howls of Oudjda!

With this impression of profound calm, covering deeper mysteries, I take my leave.

For the last time, we cross again all the chaos of Oudjda, beneath the noonday sun, and leave by the eastern gate where we had entered.

It is the end. The sumptuous green and silver curtain of olive trees falls back on all these fleeting visions, on this dream of a few hours, made up of both intoxication and nightmare.

And, despite everything, with all its contrasts, Oudjda the sordid, the famished, the prostituted, Oudjda the city of putrefaction and death, made on me one of the most profound and compelling impressions of Africa. I left it without fleeing, almost with regret, harboring the nostalgic memory of those rare moments when, almost furtively, she revealed herself to me, calm and smiling with the melancholy beauty of a fallen princess plunged fully into the terror and ruin of Morocco, this country that sleeps and decays, slowly, under the indifferent gaze of men who do not try to fight against destruction, who do not put faith in the power of humankind.

Sud Oranais: Part II

AIN-SEFRA

Ain-Sefra, May 1904

I left Ain-Sefra last year just at the first breath of winter. The city was numbed by cold, and howling winds swept across it, bending the frail, naked trees. I see it again today in a new light, having regained its customary aspect, beneath the mournful rays of summer: very Saharan, very sleepy, with its tawny *ksar* at the foot of a golden dune, with its sacred *koubbas* and its bluish gardens.

It is the "capital" city of the desert portion of the region of Oranie, isolated in a valley of sand between the monotone immensity of the high plateaus and the furnace of the south.

The place seemed morose to me, without charm, because the magic of the sun did not envelop it in the luminous atmosphere that is the splendor of desert towns. But now that I live here in a small, rented house, I have begun to love it. Thus, I will not leave it again for a boring trip back to a too familiar Tell, and that is enough to make me look at it with new eyes. When I do leave, it will be to push on further, to go beyond into the great South where the *hamada*, the stony desert, sleeps beneath an eternal sun.

Among the poplars whose white trunks follow in long rows along the first curves of the dunes, I have the illusion of losing myself in a forest. This sweet, chaste sensation is colored, in sensual moments, by the distant scent of a bouquet of acacias in flower. How I love this exuberant greenness and these living trunks, wrapped in elephant-skin bark, these fig trees swollen with bitter milk around which golden swarms of flies are buzzing!

In this amazing garden, in the middle of the desert, I have spent long hours stretched out on my back, drunk with inactivity, under the warm caress of the breezes, looking at the branches, barely moving back and forth against the bedazzling depths of the sky, like the rigging of a ship gently tossing.

Beyond the last poplars, now more spindly and stunted, the sandy track rises to end suddenly at the foot of an immaculate dune that seems made of finely powdered gold.

There, capricious winds from the heavens play freely, building up hills, digging out valleys, opening up precipices, creating daily, ephemeral passages.

On high, precariously perched on a slope only a bit more stable, ridged with black stone, a reddish garrison watches over the valley, an empty-eyed sentinel who has seen the passage of armies and bands of marauders, and who now surveys the silence and peacefulness of the vague horizons.

The brilliant golden red dune clashes violently with the stark blue of Djebel Mektar in the background. The day draws to a gentle close over Ain-Sefra, drowned in light haze and aromatic smoke. I feel a delicious melancholy, the strange exhilaration of the eve of departure. All the cares, the oppressive discomfort of the last few months spent in fastidious, enervating Algiers, everything that is my bane, my "blues," has stayed there.

In Algiers, I must have looked down on people and things. I don't like contempt. I would like to understand all, forgive all. Why must

I defend myself against the forces of stupidity, when I have engaged in no quarrel with them, when I am not even in the same game! I don't know anymore. — Those things do not interest me: the sun shines on me and the road calls to me. For now, that is philosophy enough.

Closer to me I have had the chance to see growing in a soul that I thought more free, a great and pure passion, and I said to my friend: "Watch out, when you are happy you no longer understand the suffering of others."

He has gone to find his happiness, at least he thought so, and I to follow my destiny.

Now I am far away, and I feel my soul becoming healthy again, innocently taking in all the pleasures, all the sensual delicacies of visions and dreams.

I find once more, in the only Arab street of the town, the reassuring sense of being "at home" that dates from the month of ramadan last year.

So many familiar faces, on the benches and mats in front of the *cahouadji*. So many friendly greetings to exchange.

And also private joy in knowing that I am setting off tomorrow, at dawn, and leaving all these things that, nonetheless, please me tonight and that I find comforting.

But who, besides a nomad, a vagabond, could understand this double pleasure?

With a heart still full of all that has happened to me and all that I have left, I tell myself that love breeds disquiet and one must love leaving as well, for the beauty of beings and things is only ephemeral.

Against the iron bars of the window in a Moorish café, in front of the pots of basil, a group is gathering little by little.

Someone is playing a reed flute, and I go in: this sad, monotonous music gently rocks my dreams and above all frees me from talking.

A HALT IN THE DESERT

Last year, to get to Bechar, we went east, behind the mountains, passing by the small post of Bou-Yala, since abandoned, to extend the edge of the protected zone at the frontier more to the west. Now it is Bou-Ayech that is the first stop after Beni-Ounif, thirty-five kilometers away.

It is ten o'clock and the valley is afire. Ruddy haze trembles on the wavering horizon. The heat is now burning. A thin trickle of blood runs from the dried-out nostrils of our mares. Lethargy invades me, and I let myself drift in my Arab saddle, comfortable as an easy chair.

Ben-Zireg is only twenty-eight kilometers away, and we have plenty of time to get there to sleep. But what good is it to hurry?

We have to reach the entrance to the village of Bou-Ayech before we can see it; it looks so much like the earth around it.

About a dozen wooden sheds, a fortress of yellow earth and about a hundred formless *gourbis* made of brush, where the Moroccans who work on the construction of the railroad live. Within a hundred meters, all blends in with the alfa grass and the dust, so this corner of the valley seems as deserted as the others.

The state railway line ends, for the time being, a few kilometers beyond Bou-Ayech, and all the construction work gives an air of commercial vitality to this out-of-the-way post.

Already the terrain takes on a more Saharan aspect, less lugubrious than at Beni-Ounif; the pale sand, beneath a golden-green mantle of alfa grass, does not provoke the same sensations — painful to the point of anguish sometimes — as the black *hamada* of Ounif.

In one of the shacks of the "village," on a wooden table, some Spaniards are drinking anisette.

Roughly hewn figures, shaven, tanned, and well-tempered, large black felt hats, short jackets, espadrilles — a distinct race, simple and unpolished, that accustoms itself to all solitudes, to all privations, to the most inclement sun.

From a cashier's window in the wall of a shed, the clerk of the French depot at Beni-Ounif distributes supplies to the workers. I notice that they have all shed their beautiful, earth-colored tatters for horrible, second-hand European workers' clothing that clashes with their white turbans.

Almost all the Moroccans are from the North: energetic, bearded faces, many of them with regular features, quite handsome, with their fierce, elongated eyes.

Some are blond Berbers with blue eyes of the sort one finds in Kabylia, who are certainly the inheritors of a distant line of Germanic blood.

Among these workers, only those from Figuig and the guys from Tafilala keep their tattered Arab dress. They have only come temporarily to earn a few pennies and then return to their villages.

Bou-Ayech was a stopover for us.

As we were cooking potatoes in a hole in the sand, a bit away from the sheds of the post and the Moorish café, in the circular shade of beautiful mastic trees tall as oaks, men in pea jackets and gray berets passed near us, guarded by legionnaires. I recognized them as the "outcasts" of the army, the lowest category, the court-martialed men, who were used for public works at faraway posts.

Several of them were naked to the waist. Of a different savagery in this savage land, they displayed incredible Parisian tattoos, embellished with pessimistic mottoes both rebellious and obscene.

Bored, the outcasts and the legionnaires came to talk with us. I am amused at first, and I scarcely can keep from laughing when I hear them say to each other:

"He's good looking, that little spahi, he has smooth skin!"

Several *mokhaznis* join us. They are from Beni-Ounif and I recognize in them friendly faces from last year.

Together we prepare coffee in a mess tin and chat in the way that all people from the South do, with brief remarks, simple, inoffensive pleasantries.

The *sokhars* of Doui-Menia, camped on the heights in the full sun, come to sit next to us. The *mokhaznis* tease them, ridiculing their strange dialect. The nomads give their best comebacks, seemingly without anger. But beneath the surface the ancient hate that divides the people of the high plateaus of Algeria from the Moroccans can be clearly felt.

The *sokhars* finally leave, and the *mokhaznis* turn to preparing *mella*, bread eaten during Saharan crossings.

On a haversack, one of them kneads the semolina with water from a goatskin. Djilali digs a hole in the sand with his hands while the others bring armloads of wood.

They make a roaring fire at the bottom of the hole, and on the embers they spread large, gray cakes that they cover with leaves or just fine sand. Then another fire is built above all that, and in a half hour, the *mella* is done. It is a bit heavy, but it is hot, better than the disgusting tinned foods.

Mella, Djilali claims, is to men what alfa grass is to horses: it won't make you fat, but it gives you strength.

MIRAGE

Today, the journey will be long. For hours we will travel slowly, at the steady, regular pace of our mares.

From the time we left the spectacular black cliffs of Ben-Zireg, the valley continued to open out; here and there an *oued* with a bit of greenery and beautiful mastic trees; then, suddenly, nothing but dust and stones to infinity.

At Hassi-en-Nous, at the halfway point, we eat lunch and then have coffee with the *mokhazni* at the Bel-Haouari post, nomads of the "Rzain" from near Saida, camped out in makeshift *gourbis*.

One could easily mistake them for a *djich*, these courageous men who, being in the desert, again put on their earth-colored Bedouin burnouses.

Beyond Bel-Haouari, facing an immense, open, incandescent horizon, we walk along a double line of hills that are both singular and amusing. As it is wise to learn from a journey, I ask my companion the name of the geological formation.

Take a good look, he said, and you will understand why the people here call them Bezaz el Kelba (dog's teats).

As we pass by, he points out to me a black line amid this valley as wide open as a plain: the palm grove of Ouagda.

Beneath the flaming sun, our field of vision alters and deforms. It is impossible to judge distances: a sort of vertigo dances before our eyes, and always to the left and the right are the fantastic Bezaz el Kelba.

The least variation in the terrain influences the light, hurting my eyes, or at times bringing them relief.

After this stony region, a zone of pure sand opens out. For the first time in the Sud Oranais, I find again the profound sensation I have experienced before at the entrance of other parts of the Sahara.

I see the desert in all its splendor, with all its mournful, magical enchantments, the land that swoons in an eternal solar caress, without any volcanic tremors, without the immense weight of mountains.

Suddenly, the horizon oscillates, the distances become distorted and the red sand disappears. Far away a great sheet of blue water spreads out, reflecting date palms on its surface.

The water scintillates beneath the sun, infinitely pure. Djilali begins to laugh, great child that he is.

"Si Mahmoud, you see how the mirage makes fun of our thirst! If we just had this accursed sham water to quench our thirst, we'd have been sticking our tongues out in distress or nursing at the dog's teats."

At the edge of this watery chimera, a troop of cavalry in red advances. Above their tight ranks, a scarlet flag flew in the wind. The squadron passes by and disappears. It was a herd of donkeys returning to Ouagda, and also the high tripod of a Saharan well upon which the mirage had hung shreds of purple.

Our arrival at Bechar brings back to me memories of far away Oued-Rir' and the *chotts* of South Constantine, another land of fever and mirage.

We follow from afar the palm grove of Ouagda, between graves scattered all along the road. Opposite us, at the bottom of a ruddy dune, there is a white spot: the fortress of "Collomb."

Bechar, Taagda, Collomb, all these diverse names get confused. In fact, Bechar is the name of the country, just as it is the name of the mountain that blocks the horizon.

Taagda is the *ksar* and the upper palm grove above Ouagda.

An alien name, "Collomb" designates the city under construction.

BECHAR

From Bechar, at the foot of the dunes, the valley slopes gently toward the green belt of the *oued*.

On the bank, beyond the large cemeteries where bit by bit the winds and the shuffling of camels have erased the tombs, is the *ksar* of Taagda, flanked by square towers, surrounded by high, gray, unbroken walls that are entered through low arched doorways; Taagda has the ferocious appearance of a citadel.

Inside, across the silent, smooth earth, we follow small streets in ruin, long covered passages, so dark that we have to feel our way. Where are the handsome lines and full curves of Figuig? Here, everything is a jumble. The high houses of *toub*, some having two stories, lean against one another, straddling the streets.

At Bechar, as in all the villages, everything dozes and disintegrates. The town's waning activity is dying out slowly, the sources of energy drying up, and an agonizing silence weighs on these abortive attempts to maintain this sedentary and laborious life, in the midst of a desert meant for nomads.

Black *kharatins* for the most part, but Arabic speaking, the inhabitants of Bechar are silent and suspicious. They have already taken on a bit of Moroccan arrogance, that aversion for the peoples from the East, the *m'zanat;* however, they are villagers, peaceful gardeners, and not men of gunpowder.

Last year, during the occupation of Bechar, Taagda and Ouagda were raided by the *makhzen* and the tirailleurs. This year, slightly more secure, the villagers regain courage and return to the gardens.

The center of Collomb is still a jumble of partially finished buildings, of materials and debris. The ugly *toub* huts are still standing, whitened like the pale earth; they are found in all the posts of the Sud Oranais, shelters built in haste to house canteens, bric-a-brac and Moorish cafés.

The Spanish and Jewish peoples are dominant, here like everywhere else in this new territory.

The Jews of Kenadsa, clad in green and black rags, come to pitch their worn-out tents, and quickly they light their small forges where they transform the officers' and spahis' *douros* into jewelry.

I rediscovered, in the gardens of Bechar, sensations I had experienced earlier in the *oued* at the unforgettable pearl of the South — Bou-Saada.

There, crouched over rocks, some women clad in blue or black *mlahfas* wash tattered clothes that they beat with palm fronds . . . yes, those are charming memories of Oued Bou-Saada, during the bright days of summer, but with a more distant, more somber feel — the Moroccan feel — brought back by the sight of the sleeping palm groves of Bechar.

In the gardens, beneath the leafy pomegranate trees and in the sickly shade of the fig trees, here and there inviting corners under the pale sea-green vaults of the date palms have something of the mystery of real forests. Irrigation *seguias* whisper in the short grass and, from all sides, the sad, little voices of the toads of the South rise, a single note, infinitely repeated, as far as the arid dunes on the road to Kenadsa, where the last irrigation ditches are already half-filled with silt.

LEGIONNAIRES AND *MOKHAZNIS*

On the heights, the fortress of Bechar, with its low, masonry walls and its wide, well-guarded doors and, on the inside, building materials, piles of stones, all the chaos of a town under construction.

To the left, the great courtyard where the wiry little hobbled horses of the French *makhzen*, slowly chew dried-out alfa grass. In the *gourbis*, the *mokhaznis* stretch out, their heads resting on the bows of their saddles, their guns at arm's reach, clutching their cartridge belts upon their earth-colored *gandouras*. They laugh, joke, and sing, waiting nonchalantly for orders to move out — who knows — perhaps never to return.

So what! What is written has to happen, whatever one does. So, they do not think about it, except to compose plaintive songs about the uncertainty of their lives in these faraway outposts, where at every moment death stalks them.

Arabs recognize manly honor, and they wish to die bravely, facing the enemy, but they know absolutely nothing about posthumous glory, particularly these simple men, rough nomads, who willingly dedicate to the service of France their valiance, their wonderful audacity, their untiring endurance.

Beside the *mokhaznis*, other reckless souls, other lost children, but much more complex — the legionnaires — were erecting the buildings of the Bureau Arabe. Everywhere in the outposts of the Sud Oranais, they are the ones who raised the first wall, with their energy and their patience, sowed the first seeds in the small gardens that appeared as if by magic in the most arid of places. They raised the walls during troubled periods when they had to defend themselves against raiders, after nights passed on the alert, in fear of possible sneak attacks.

There is not a wall, not a *toub* hut at Bechar or elsewhere in this country, that is not the Legion's work, an anonymous work, perhaps more difficult and meritorious than the brave acts of courage carried out every day, in this lost territory where nothing leaves a trace.

KENADSA

Kaddour or Barka, the head of the *khouan* Ziania of Bechar, gives me as a guide a black slave, the *khartani* Embarek. We leave the *douar* of the *makhzen* at the rose and green hour of dawn. The air is clear, without any sign of sirocco. Only a light fog veils the palm groves at the bottom of the *oued*.

Like all the valleys in the Sud Oranais, this one we are passing through, me on horse and Embarek on foot, extends between two rows of hills. On the left, above these low valleys, rises the imposing silhouette of Djebel Bechar.

The golden sand, the soft undulations, always, from Bezaz el Kelba, the same landscape, the same monotonous harmony of great lines without angles, gaps, almost without unevenness.

As we move west, the hills get lower.

We follow, on the right, the strange dune crowned with cantilevered stones, commanding Bechar. This goes on for a long while, and the sun, now burning hot, rises behind us and casts our long shadows on the ground that grows paler.

Finally we arrive at the summit of a stony slope, strewn with flint and slate, like the mournful valley of Ben Zireg.

On the horizon, misted with rosy haze, Kenadsa appears: black dots of scattered trees, the bluish line of a great palm grove, and, rising above the sands, a broken minaret that, in the still oblique rays of the sun, seems made of ruddy bronze.

Farther on, we follow a path bordered, for more than a kilometer, with a row of tall date palms, all alone in this empty valley.

Beneath their shifting shadows, an underground *seguia*, glimpsed here and there, flows fresh and clear.

Kenadsa rises before us, its great *ksar* made of warm, dull *toub*, preceded, on the left, by beautiful green gardens. The *ksar* descends in a graceful disorder of superimposed terraces, following the slope of a large hill. To the right, the golden dune, with its slabs of stone, rises up almost abruptly.

A *koubba*, very white, shelters the tomb of Lalla Aicha — a Muslim saint from the family of the illustrious Sidi M'hammed-ben-bou-Ziane, founder of the Ziania brotherhood.

Around the *koubba* innumerable tombs are scattered in the sand which encroaches upon them little by little.

We pass by vague cemeteries, we walk along this human dust accumulated over the centuries, abandoned and forgotten, and we take the road that follows round the town ramparts, made of dark mud walls, without crenellations or loopholes.

In a small square men are lying down, *kharatines* for the most part.

We enter the town through a large open, square gate with two heavy doors. Next we cross the Mellah, the Jewish quarter, where they live in tiny boutiques opening onto the street.

Here, in contrast to the mores of Figuig, Jewesses, although dressed the same way, are not cloistered. They chatter, cook, and wash in front of their doors.

Another turn, and we enter into a narrower, cleaner street that ends in the distance in half-shadow beneath houses that straddle it.

ARRIVING AT THE *ZAOUIYA*

We dismount and go through another door: we are in the *zaouiya*.

The marabouts of the Ziania support France. They are gentle and humane people who welcome the dominion of justice. Each day they bring new proof of their deference and their respect for a sworn oath.

Kenadsa is beyond the colonial frontier and recognizes the suzerainty of the Sultan of Fez. Here we are, then, in Moroccan territory, twenty-five kilometers from French territory at Bechar.

In reality, where is the border? Where does Oranie end and Morocco begin? No one seems to worry about it.

But what useful purpose does a carefully delineated border serve? The present situation, mixed and vague, fits the Arab character. It hurts no one and satisfies all.

Three or four black slaves greet us. My guide repeats to them what Kaddour or Barka told him: I am Si Mahmoud ould Ali, a young Tunisian student going from *zaouiya* to *zaouiya* to gain knowledge.

They ask me to sit down on a sack of folded wool, on the ground, while going to inform the marabout in charge, Sidi Brahim ould

Mohamed, to whom I give a letter of introduction from one of his *khouan* (brotherhood) in Ain-Sefra.

All along the wall, slaves are waiting, silently. Two among them are *kharatines*. Young, beardless, they wear gray Moroccan djellabas and scarves of white muslin around their shaved heads. The third, darker, taller, dressed in white, is Sudanese, and his face bears the deep scars of a branding iron. All three are armed with *koumias*, long knives with short blades, in sheaths of etched copper, held on by a brightly colored silk cord used like a bandolier.

Finally, after a good quarter of an hour wait, a tall, black slave who is shockingly ugly with small, lively, but furtive eyes, comes to kiss the cords of my turban respectfully.

He leads me into a vast, empty, silent courtyard whose floor slopes gently away.

I was absorbing with every breath now the somewhat disquieting atmosphere of peace. This succession of doors that closed on me added to the distance I had just traveled.

Yet one more low, narrow door, and we enter a large, square room that resembles the interior of a mosque. The light of the fading day is diffused through a quadrangular opening in the ceiling made of beautifully meshed beams.

Rugs are spread out; I am at home. Here, I will live. God only knows how long.

While the blacks go to bring me coffee and fresh water, my eyes become accustomed to the shadows, and I examine my lodgings — a bit of reconnaissance for security's sake.

A narrow, steep stairway of black stone leads to the terrace. To the left, a deep recess, furnished with an iron hearth for making tea placed so that its smoke escapes through a hole in the ceiling. In the middle of the room, a small, square basin, and, to one side, a clay pitcher full of water: necessary items for ablutions. The tranquil water in the basin can serve as a mirror. Four columns embedded in the wall support the ceiling. At the back of the room, a wooden door with painted panels displays simple flowers in faded colors.

This guest room must be quite ancient, as the *toub* walls and the beams of the ceiling have taken on a blackish-green hue. The columns, about a man's height, have been polished by the rubbing of hands, and clothes.

THE MARABOUT'S INDIGNATION

Yesterday, during the siesta, Sidi Brahim comes in suddenly, a letter in his hand, upset.

Si Mahmoud, I have just received a letter from Oudjda, in which I am told that Hadj Mohammed ould Abdelkhaut, head of the Qadriya, has been assassinated by the men of Bou-Amama — may God punish them.

And the marabout dropped to the rug, holding out the letter to me.

This letter, written on a crumpled scrap of gray paper, was brought by a messenger sent from the *zaouïya* of Oudjda to the *zaouïya* of the Ziania.

The messenger tells of the death of Hadj Mohammed, who had gone to Bou-Amama to bring offers of peace to him and urge him not to bring desolation and war to Angad.

Bou-Amama welcomed the emissary and made promises to him. But on the return, on the plain, one of the men of the old robbers joined Hadj Mohammed and led him far from his companions on the pretext that he had something secret to tell him. In the *oued*, bandits in ambush massacred the unfortunate marabout.

I finish deciphering the barely legible scrawl, and in my mind's eye I see again sad Oudjda prey to famished, exasperated soldiers, the beggarly, menacing mob slipping in the mud where carcasses rotted and, at the end of all that horror, behind the ruins where the rosy peaches were in bloom, the white, imposing *zaouiya* of the Qadriya, so serene, directed by Hadj Mohammed so traitorously assassinated and with whom, scarcely three months earlier, I had found such secure and fraternal refuge.

"Si Mahmoud, the Maghrib is lost if they begin killing inoffensive creatures of God over there, men of prayer and charity, who carry neither gun nor sword," Sidi Brahim says to me. "God must have struck blind the sons of the Mogh'rib for them to abandon his path in this manner, for them to betray their Sultan who is the descendant of the Prophet — blessings and salvation upon him — by Mouley Idris; and to follow whom? miserable impostors like Bou-Amama and Rogui Bou-Hamara!"

In a soft, deliberate voice, Sidi Brahim continues to lament the fate of Morocco.

"In truth, what could explain, if not folly, the popularity of Bou-Amama, son of a second-hand dealer in Figuig, a man without family name or education, fomenter of discords and massacres, dispenser of false miracles, of deceptive promises. By God, the house of Bou-Amama is built upon a shaky foundation of lies and iniquity. But isn't this typical of the nomads of the desert, the more improbable what is preached to them, the more likely they are to believe it. As for the one who announces the truth to them, misfortune awaits him: they ridicule him and, if they can, they exterminate him.

And what do you say, you who read God's teachings, have visited many cities and countries, what do you say about Rogui? How do you explain the incredible rise of this man whom no one knows and who, overnight, has appointed himself Sultan, emir of the faithful? He claims to be Moulay M'hammed, brother of the deposed Mouley Abdelaziz. How is it that there is not one trustworthy man among those who knew Mouley M'hammad, who would say to the believers, "in truth, this is he" or would unmask the imposter?

Others claim that Bou-Hamara comes from the Sanhadja of Djebel Zerhaoun. How can it be that no one, from the Sanhadja or the Beni-Zerhaoun, knows this man? Really, one would think that this Bou-Hamara is not a son of Adam but a *djinn*, a fire spirit, a sign of the times, an arrow from God, come down from the heavens or come out of the earth to punish a depraved, criminal Mogh'rib! You others, sons of the East, you are happy. You enjoy in peace blessings given by God. As for us, cursed sons of the Mogh'rib, we live in a country of hungry wolves, where the rivers overflow with blood and iniquity triumphs. At every moment, day and night, we fear for our lives and for our well-being.

"You see, Si Mahmoud, we had important revenues in Tafilala, El-Outtat, Fez, and above all in the region of Angad. Now that the armies of the impostors have invaded the country, we receive only a quarter of the former revenues. And here, the poor, the orphans, the women without protection, the students, and travelers abound and ask us for asylum and bread, that we must give them according to the sacred rulings of our master — God be pleased with him. — Ah, Si Mahmoud, let us pray that God annihilate Bou-Amama, son of a junk dealer, master of deceit, and Bou-Hamara, the shadowy character who, on the back of a donkey, longs to scale the steps of a millenial throne and conquer the heritage that Mouley Idris left in legacy to his posterity by the grace of the Inheritor of Worlds.

And thus, every day Sidi Brahim comes to tell me the news from the West, the sad news, and the gossip from elsewhere. However, in this isolated retreat, they reach us quite diminished, those echoes of the torment that groans across a decaying Morocco.

Here, nothing happens, and news from the exterior world, coming into this warm and pure shadow, no longer bears the glacial shudder of that tragic reality.

In the monotony of my life at Kenadsa, I am losing little by little all feelings of agitation or uncontrolled passion. It seems to me that everywhere, men and things ought to be as still, as sleepy as they are here.

FRIDAY PRAYER

Today, Friday, went to the mosque, to public prayer.

A little after noon, in the oppression and the silence of siesta time, from far away, as if in a dream, a lingering voice reaches to me: it is the *zoual*, the first prayer call.

I get up and try to dissipate my heavy sleepiness a bit with a cool bath. I walk ahead of Farradji, a silent Sudanese, through the blinding light of the courtyard. We follow narrow, little streets, walking along the crumbling fences of gardens to avoid the dark passages that traverse the *ksar*. We emerge into the valley of sand.

Everything in the landscape is burning and glistening, with metallic reflections on the arid rocks of the Barga and on the salty sand of the *sebkha*, where rusty heat waves dance, outlining vague mirages.

It is the deadly hour of sunstroke and fever, the hour when one feels crushed, oppressed, chest on fire, light-headed.

We arrive at last. We enter the *ksar* where there is a bit of shade. As the faithful pass by, blind beggars chant their supplications. The door to the mosque is locked with a high crossbar to keep out children and animals. We take off our old yellow shoes and, carrying them in hand, we cross the courtyard, barefoot, almost at a run, to escape the intolerable burning of the red-hot sand.

From the time we enter, we feel the wonderful atmosphere of coolness, of blue chiaroscuro, of infinite peacefulness.

All is white and bare in this ancient Saharan asylum, the walls, the heavy, square, paired columns that support a ceiling made of planed trunks of old date palms. Diffuse daylight sifts in from high, cut-out peepholes, leaving the lower part of the mosque in shadow. On the old mats, the people of Kenadsa and the nomads pray. To the right, in a large recess, bathed in warm light, the students and the teachers of the *medersa* (school), chant the Koran. Behind them, schoolchildren repeat the lesson of their elders.

Here and there, crouched near a pillar, a lone *taleb* (student) recites aloud the litanies of the Prophet.

And all these voice — the solemn voices, some quite pure and beautiful dominating the others, and the clear voices of children — mingle in a great confused murmur, repetitive and melancholy with drawn-out endings.

It lasts a long time, this lullaby in the sonorous nave.

Then suddenly, on high, in the minaret, the *moueddhen* intones the second call. His voice seems to descend from unknown spheres, simply because he is very high and no one can see him.

At the end of the last verse, the students' voices linger, dying into a final sigh. With a loud clatter of boards, the children take off running.

All is quiet now, all heads bowed, attentive.

From the shadow where the mihrab is in a large recess facing Mecca, the broken and quavering voice of the imam rises. He reads the *khotba*, a long psalm mixed with exhortations, a sort of sermon, and we listen, seated, in silence.

The imam is not a priest — Islam has no regular clergy — he is simply the best informed of the congregation. Any literate man can be imam: he need only recite the prayer.

In Islam, there are no miracles, no sacraments, nothing that requires a priest as intermediary.

During the *khotba*, there are still moments of vague dreaming, of sweet, fulfilling calm.

A man in a white shirt tied with a simple cord, head bare, carries a pail of fresh water and a clay cup: he gives water to the old and the sick. It is an act of charity he imposes upon himself each Friday.

A last call from the *moueddhen*, and the old imam finishes his reading and begins to pray.

A young man with a strong, sonorous voice is next to him and repeats his invocations in plain-chant.

All stand, raise their hands to the level of their faces, and then let their hands drop to their sides, saying with the imam and chanter: Allahou Akbar! (God is Great!)"

They kneel down and prostrate themselves . . .

The prayer ended, I stay with the students and the marabouts, who chant again the rhymed litanies of the Prophet.

"Prayer and peace be with you, O Mohammed, Prophet of God, best of all creatures forever and ever, in this world and the next. Prayer and peace be with you, O Mohammed Moustapha, Arab Prophet, Beacon in the Darkness, Key of the believers, Oh Mohammed the Koreichite, Master of Mecca and Flowering Medina, Master of Muslim men and women, forever and ever."

The marabouts have lovely, solemn voices. They bear themselves with an age-old dignity that so ennobles the sonorous verses of this litany, which the common people are satisfied to recite quickly in a nasal and staccato fashion.

Prayer is over. We get up and take our slippers from the mats where we'd laid them down, one set face down upon the other.

Once more we cross the blinding furnace of the valley.

Courage fails me and I follow Farradji into the maze of black passages, so low we must double over for more than a hundred meters. The darkness is opaque in this passage of rough mud, where the ancient, cave-like humidity reigns.

After the serene hour spent in the blue shadow of the mosque, this return seems like a nightmare in all this darkness.

SAHARAN THEOCRACY

The age-old influence of the Arab marabouts has profoundly altered the institutions and mores of the people of Kenadsa.

Among all the other Berbers, it is the djemaa, the assembly of delegates from ruling village tribal clans that rules. All political or administrative questions are submitted to the deliberations of the *djemaa*. If a new chief is needed, it is the *djemaa* that names him. As long as he holds this office, the chief is obeyed, but he is always responsible to those who elected him.

These Berber assemblies are tumultuous. Passions are given full sway in them; violent, they sometimes end in blood. However, the Berbers have always been jealous of their collective liberty. They fight against autocracy suppressing those who would dare aspire to it.

At Kenadsa, the theocratic Arab spirit has triumphed over the republican, confederative Berber spirit.

The chief of the *zaouiya* is the sole, hereditary head of the *ksar*. He decides all questions and, in the case of war, names the military leaders. He delivers criminal justice while civil affairs are judged by the qadi. But even there, the marabout has the last jurisdiction, and people appeal to him to review the qadi's decisions.

Sidi M'hammed ben-Bou-Ziane, the founder of the brotherhood, wanted to make his disciples into a peaceful, hospitable association. The *zaouïya* enjoys the right of giving asylum: any criminal who has taken refuge there finds himself sheltered from human justice. If it is a thief, the marabout makes him return the goods he has taken. If it is an assassin, he must pay the price for shedding blood. Under these conditions, the guilty undergo no punishment once they have entered the walls of the *zaouïya*, or even its land.

The death penalty is not used by the marabouts. If it happens that a criminal is put to death, it is by the relatives of the victim or sometimes by his own relatives, never by the sentence of the marabouts.

The descendants of Sidi ben-Bou-Ziane, however, showed themselves to be quite severe in the case of thieves and scandalmongers among the village people or the slaves, whom they punish by flogging.

Customarily, during punishment, one of the people attending gets up to ask pardon for the guilty person. Sometimes women send a slave or a Negress to ask this favor: the marabout always grants it.

Thanks to the *zaouïya*, misery is unknown in Kenadsa. There are no beggars in the streets; all the unfortunate seek refuge in its friendly shadow, and they live there as long as they please. The majority make themselves useful as servants, workers, or shepherds, but no one is forced to work.

The influence of the marabout has been so strong at Kenadsa that the Berbers and the *kharatini* have forgotten their native tongues and now speak only Arabic.

Their mores are gentle and orderly, compared to those of other village inhabitants.

Arguments, and especially brawls, are rare, because the people of the community are in the habit of settling their differences in front of the marabouts, who calm them down and impose mutual concessions upon them.

Since the marabouts began to have friendly relations and even a growing friendship with the French, a secret discontent has invaded the hearts of the common people.

No one dares to raise his voice to criticize the actions of the masters. They bow to them, repeat the opinions of Sidi Brahim, sing their praises, but, at bottom, if not for his great moral authority, the common people would be ready to consider him and his family as *m'zanat*.

What is the future of Kenadsa and what will remain, in a few years, of such a peculiar, closed, little theocratic regime?

Most assuredly, after the harshness of Figuig and the somber chaos of Oudjda, it is truly a singular experience to find, at the entrance to the desert, this tranquil corner, that calls itself Moroccan and that so little resembles other Moroccos.

TWILIGHT

What relief, verging on ecstasy, when the sun sets, when the shadows of the date palms and of the walls lengthen, creeping, obscuring the last gleams!

The grim indifference that grips me, throughout the long, tedious day, dissipates; and once again with avid, charmed eyes I look at the daily splendor of the landscape of Kenadsa, already so familiar, with its simple beauty of strict lines and warm, transparent colors that quickly relieve the monotony of the foreground, while diaphanous mists drown the distant horizons.

How sweet and consoling is this rebirth of the soul each evening.

In the gardens, the last hot hour slips by gently for me, in tranquil contemplation, in lazy talk interspersed with long silences.

At dusk, when the sun has set, we go to pray in the *hamada* just before the great cemeteries and the white, iridescent *koubba* of the blessed Lella Aicha.

All is calm, dreaming, smiling, at this charming hour.

Women pass by, going barefoot to Ain Sidi Embarek. Men who were chatting, half reclining on the ground, get up.

The great murmur of prayer rises from this corner of the desert that dominates the *ksar* and the Barga.

After prayer, they stay seated on their spread-out burnouses, hands telling black prayer beads, red prayer beads . . . lips chanting in low voices the tales of the Prophet.

To be healthy of body, pure of all stains, after the long baths in fresh water, to be simple and to believe, never to have doubt, never to battle within oneself, to attain without fear and without impatience the inevitable hour of eternity: that is certainly peace, Muslim well-being — and who knows? maybe real wisdom, too.

Surely, here, the monotonous hours slide by with the gentleness and tranquillity of a wide river, in which nothing is reflected but the vaporous clouds that pass and never return.

Little by little my regrets and desires fade away. I let my soul float away into emptiness and my will soften.

A dangerous but delicious numbness, leading surely, but insensibly, to the edge of nothingness.

These days, these weeks, when nothing has happened, when I have done nothing, not exerted any effort, not suffered, scarcely thought, must they be written off, must I deplore their emptiness? But after the inevitable return to activity, must they, on the other hand, be longed for, perhaps as the best days of one's life?

I do not know anymore.

As soon as the sensation of ancient, unchanging Islam streams through my blood, this Islam that seems to be the very breath of the earth; as tranquil days slip by, the need to work and to struggle has less and less appeal. To me, who not long ago still was dreaming of traveling always farther, who longed for action, to me the desire comes, without wishing to acknowledge it to myself too openly, that the drunkenness of the moment and the somnolence of today might last, if not for ever, at least for a long while yet.

However, I know that the fever for wandering will overtake me again, that I will take off; yes, I am still far from the wisdom of the fakirs and Muslim anchorites.

But the inner voice that drives and disturbs me, that will tomorrow push me again along the paths of life; that voice is not the wisest one in my soul, it is the spirit of agitation for which the earth is too narrow and which has not known how to find its own universe.

To find an end in the peacefulness and silence of some *zaouiya* in the South, to spend the last moments reciting ecstatic praises, without desires or regrets, looking out over splendid horizons.

That would be the sought-after end when, after long years, weariness and disenchantment set in.

DEPARTURE

For the last time, I wake up on the terrace to the hoarse voice of the *moueddhen* trailing off in the night.

It is cool. Everything is asleep.

The Berber El-Hassani and the black Mouley Sahel get up. Like me, they must leave this morning, but are going in the opposite direction.

I am going back to Bechar, Beni-Ounif, and from there to Ain-Sefra to cure myself for the rest of the summer so that I can take advantage of the first convoys of autumn.

My companions are also getting ready to travel to Bou-Dnib. They would like to take me with them and I would like to have the strength to follow them.

"Think about it, Si Mahmoud," the Berber says to me, "there's still time. We will travel for a month, crossing many countries where there will be numerous chances for you to see things and educate yourself. We will go as far as Guir, Tafilala, or maybe even Tisint. You will be received everywhere as our brother."

The temptation is great. But to leave in this condition, still feeble, without permission, without telling anyone. This voyage of study and inquiry, wouldn't it be misinterpreted? Sick at heart, I resign myself to retracing the road to Bechar today.

How different this return voyage will be from my arrival when I was traveling toward unknown territory!

"No, El-Hassani, I cannot. That will be for later, in a while. When I am able, I will let you know."

"May God help you to achieve what you want!

Two other blacks, who will be going on foot, are there, sitting still against the wall, their guns across their knees. They scarcely understand Arabic, because they were born and grew up on the road to Fez, with the Ait-Ischorouschen tribe, the strictest and most isolated of Berbers.

One of them keeps a fierce silence and looks at me askance. In his eyes evidently, I am nothing but a reprobate, a cursed *m'zani*.

At a quick word from El-Hassani, the blacks saddle the horses. With a pointed finger, my companions from the *zaouiya* show me the direction to Guir that they are going to take. However, they do not leave me suddenly. They insist on accompanying me for a while, doubling back later on their route.

"We will go with you," says El-Hassani, "up to the entrance of the cemeteries."

We leave. My throat is so tight with emotion I can scarcely answer the words addressed to me. I must, however, maintain manly emotions to the end.

Among the small, sharp flagstones stuck into the ground like slates, in hard clay, that mark the length of the tombs jutting out and against which the horses rarely stumble, being accustomed to the terrain, we dismount, according to the ancient custom, at the moment of leave-taking, and we embrace three times.

"Go then in the peace and security of God!"

"May you encounter only the good!"

Remounting, we go in opposite directions: El-Hassani toward the unexplored West, where I would have liked so much to follow him, and me toward the disenchantment of familiar territories.

From a knoll my eyes follow the people going to Bou-Dnib for a long time as they disappear into the distance. They vanish finally into the labyrinth of dunes under the rose-colored rays of the rising sun. With them the last gleam of hope fades for me: not for a long time, and maybe never, will I penetrate further into Morocco.

While my mare ambles along at a slow pace, my desolate gaze loses itself in the valley that I found so beautiful in the splendid birth of the summer sun, when I just arrived. And because I am traveling backwards, because, perhaps, a long exile far from the beloved desert is beginning for me, I find the countryside quite unappealing, almost ugly, scarred with a multitude of nooks and crannies where the sun doesn't reach. A great enchantment has vanished.

Then, angrily, pressing the flanks of my white mare, I throw myself into a mad gallop, and the wind of the desert dries the tears from my eyes.

Reports from the Sud Oranais

BENI-OUNIF

Beni-Ounif, 30 November 1903.

At Figuig I was able to see several natives who were familiar with events in the West, probably through contact with the emissaries of the nomads.

According to them, discord is rampant among the hostile tribes: Berbers, Ouled Djerir, Beni Guil, and the dissidents of Doui Menia.

Since the attack on Taghit, when they had by common accord elected Mouley as their head, the nomads formed a sort of association or federation. Naturally it was both chaotic and anarchic.

Now, probably under the pressure of the extreme misery to which they have been reduced and the defeats they have suffered, the nomads are disbanding and serious quarrels are breaking out among the different groups.

There can be no doubt that all these hostile factions are looking unfavorably at our installation at Bechar and at the creation of the military post at Taagda.

Lately, the rumor has gone around among the natives that the nomads had threatened Commander Pierron, the head of the detachment at Bechar. The nomads supposedly threatened to attack if the detachment did not pull back. These rumors seem unlikely given that this sort of threat would certainly have provoked active repression.

On the other hand, they say that the Beni Guil will be gathering around Bou-Amama with the hope of satisfying their hate for the Hamyan and taking revenge for the latest *harka* by the Hamyan, which has cost them a number of tents.

The occupation of outposts in the Southwest Oranais is today already a fait accompli.

This element of our African policy has given rise to numerous controversies, to polemics in the press, and to recriminations. Many have debated its adequacy and wisdom.

Whatever our opinion on this question, it is nonetheless evident that the expansion of our territory in the Oranais has created an extremely grave situation. In fact, we find ourselves not only in permanent contact with the Moroccan state, which is in complete disarray, caught in a perpetual civil war; but in addition we are face to face with numerous, turbulent nomadic tribes who have never recognized any form of sovereignty, neither that of Morocco nor our own and who have remained until today resistent to all organizing efforts.

What makes this situation singularly complicated is that the greater part of these tribes have traditional migration patterns that cross territories, some said to be Moroccan, and others that are under our control. Consequently, we have to take care of these tribes so that they do not remain a perpetual cause of bloody turmoil.

It is, thus, the means of obtaining as soon as possible, and with the least cost in human life and money, the pacification of the Southwest Oranais that we are trying to determine after returning from a long visit to Figuig, the center of contact with our neighbors, for the moment.

In order to approach this question and to show clearly the phases of its solution, we will say a few words about the region and its inhabitants.

Starting at Ain-Sefra, the country takes on a clearly desert character: largely unproductive lands, except for certain areas where one finds Saharan pastures adequate for raising sheep and camels. Alfa grass, *drinn,* and several types of sprawling, stunted, shrub-like trees are almost always good as feed for camels. As for sheep, their existence is completely dependent upon winter rains that help more tender, nutritive, grassy vegetation to grow.

Water holes become farther and farther apart as one moves south. Many of them, especially the most important, are inhabited. Sedentary Berber tribes have built small *ksour* there and cultivated several crops: date palms, vegetables, fruit, and sometimes, a bit of cereal, mostly barley.

Figuig, and its neighbors now controlled by France, Beni-Ounif, Taghit, Igli, Beni-Abbes, and so on, are important water holes. The water table in these locations is close to the surface, which has facilitated to a great degree the installation and development of towns, permitting the *fellahs* a more extensive, if not more varied, cultivation.

The desert territories, except for the *hamada*, are stony, sterile regions that furnish the village people with precious construction materials: *toub*, mud mixed with manure. *Toub* is, depending on the sort of earth used, sometimes very solid and allows the building of multistory houses very cheaply; they are weather resistant and often not without elegance. Date palms furnish material for beams strong enough to support roofs and terraces.

Let us focus more closely on Figuig, which describes quite accurately the general situation in the Southwest.

Figuig is an agglomeration of seven villages: Zenaga, Oudar'ir, Ksar el-Abib, El Maiz, Ouled Slimane, Hammam Foukani, Hammam Tahkoui.

These occupy two levels of a splendid valley: Zenaga is lower down, to the southwest, and the *hammamine* are on the western slope below the upper terrace, where the other *ksour* are located.

An impressive chain of mountains protects the valley on all sides: the Grouz to the northwest, the Beni-Smir chain to the northeast, the *djebel* Ta'la toward the southeast, and the *djebel* Melias to the west.

Several large, deep passes lead into the valley of Figuig: the Ta'la pass to the east, the Zenaga pass to the south, the pass of the Jewess to the southeast, the pass of the Moujahdine to the west. The *ksour* are close to one another except for Zenaga, isolated at the foot of the cliff, which is the southern edge of the upper terrace.

A magnificent palm grove surrounds the *ksour* of the southwest, south, and east.

The water table is near the surface. A remarkably ingenious water system irrigates the palm groves. In addition to rectangular ponds lined with *toub*, there is an elaborate network of underground canals, accessible channels, where the trenches are regulated and the springs carefully tapped. The water is excellent.

The palm groves are cultivated with extreme care. In their shade, fruit trees grow: figs and pomegranates, and local vegetables: peppers, melons, onions, turnips, etc. The people of Figuig grow a bit of barley in irrigated fields that are cultivated with pickaxes in perfectly straight rows of great beauty. The gardens of Zenaga and those of the section called Baghdad, below the *ksar* of Ouled Slimane, are the most beautiful.

In this desert area, the valley of Figuig is unusually fertile, and only a long-felt insecurity has stopped the *fellahs* from extending their cultivations far beyond their present boundaries.

Because Morocco never has had more than nominal authority in this Saharan region, Figuig has remained autonomous, conserving a roughly republican and confederated political structure involving, in each *ksar*, a council of the delegates, or *djemaa*, as the body that deliberates on its own all the village affairs. Justice is in the hands of the qadi and the *djemaa* represents executive power. Today, anarchy reigns because of the turmoil throughout the region.

For some reason, it occurred to our diplomatic core to further confuse the imbroglio at Figuig by establishing at Oudar'ir an *amel*, or Moroccan governor, who in actuality has no authority whatsoever and, consequently, could not and will never be able to be of any use in the effort of pacification and organization that France must accomplish there. This innovation, while irritating the inhabitants of Figuig, who have no love for the Moroccans, has had no result other than to display to European eyes and to the Makhzen itself a similacrum of Moroccan domination at Figuig.

Action must then be taken, just as it has been to this point, outside the jurisdiction of the *amel*.

It is also absolutely useless to dream of pacifying the region by means of the supposed influence of the Pretender: just like the Sultan, the Rival is powerless to organize this vast Moroccan hinterland.

As for Bou-Amama, his political influence is hardly even felt. He has grown old and tired, and an alliance with him could not guarantee us peace.

At present, we are obliged to take care of everything by ourselves, relying only on our own forces.

We have before us two populations which are absolutely distinct and whose interests are more often than not opposed: the sedentary village people, tied to the land they cultivate and own, thus having a direct interest in the pacification of their country; and the nomads. It is a mistake to think that famine alone is the cause of nomadic raids: by tradition, from the earliest times, the nomads have always been quarrelsome and predatory. This is accounted for by their very way of life itself.

It is the nomads who are the cause of all the strife, all the spilling of blood that have afflicted the region that concerns us.

Only the rapid organization of conquered territories leading to a new era of prosperity can legitimate, in the eyes of reason and fairness, our push forward into these desert regions.

Peace and security are, after all, the primary conditions of any progress.

Should we continue the costly and bellicose practice of expeditions against this or that tribe, whom we rarely conquer and who will reappear tomorrow?

Should we remain on the defensive, having to deal with repeated hostilities?

Or should we, as some have dared to propose, especially in Algeria, engage in the complete extermination of the dissident nomads?

All these plans of action are equally bad.

There is another plan, more economical and humane, that greatly limits the use of armed intervention, regrettably rendered necessary by the continual incursions of armed, marauding hordes.

General Lyautey, who commands the subdivision at Aïn-Sefra, breaking with the old military routine, has had the happy inspiration of putting this new system to the test recently at Figuig, and it is beginning to yield excellent results.

We are speaking here of the *isolation* and *surveillance* of the *Saharan markets*.

In fact, in order to survive, the nomads — shepherds, caravanners, escorts, or bandits — need the Saharan markets where they buy provisions, sell their flocks, and where they serve as intermediaries between the *ksour* and the Moroccan Tell, especially Ouezzan.

Without these markets, the nomads would be reduced to famine and could not exist; besides, their transhumance patterns, although vast, are actually limited because each tribe is attached by its traditions to a certain *ksar* or market.

It is easy to understand, therefore, why, once these markets are under surveillance and off limits to any dissident tribe or tribal clan, that clan must very quickly submit, being unable to subsist otherwise.

Thus, instead of innumerable military operations that are complicated and incur colossal expense, in men and money, there would only be a few police actions to take, rapidly and at small cost.

Figuig has been placed under the surveillance of the French commissariat headquartered at Beni-Ounif. To the North it has been isolated by the creation of the outpost of El Ardja. By these measures, the market at Figuig has been cut off from all contact with the dissidents and, after several months, the tribes have begun submitting and soliciting access to the market. The Beni Guil especially have recently begun talks with the French authorities at Beni-Ounif.

But Figuig, pacified and now an instrument of pacification, is not enough.

Herein lies the greatest difficulty brought about by our presence. One measure is absolutely necessary; without it we will never obtain a lasting peace: the pacification of Tafilalet, the hub toward which all the nomadic tribes gravitate.

The railroad is being extended toward Bechar, and an outpost was recently established at Taagda. The railroad will bait the nomads using the route to Tafilalet. This route will, then, be razed and Tafilalet isolated, an action that will lead quickly to the submission of the nomads: Ouled Djerir, Doui Menia, even the Berbers of the area.

It is up to our diplomatic corps to explain to the Sultan that it is not a question of conquest here, that we do not envision taking away his nominal authority over the frontier lands, but that clearly it is a question of cleaning out an old haunt that has traditionally served as an asylum for all those bandits who continually make incursions against us.

Tafilalet pacified, thus prosperous, commerce reestablished and developed significantly by the nearby railroad, all these improvements will benefit the Sultan as much as ourselves.

In order to convince our readers that the pacification of Tafilalet is indispensable, that without it we would be in a perpetual state of war to no useful end, let us remind them that the misery that has held sway at Tifilalet for the past year and has starved the nomads who are cut off from their resources at Figuig is the sole reason for their apparent quiet today.

But given a good year at Tafilalet, the nomads, having provisions once more, will begin their *razzia* (raids) which only dire necessity causes them to renounce.

It is, therefore, urgent to assure the protection of Tafilalet from any contact with the dissidents and marauders.

Weakened by famine, worn out by almost a year of continual fighting, the nomads will offer only feeble resistance this year. As for the village people, those of Tafilalet like those of Figuig now will understand quickly that it is absolutely in their interest to reestablish commerce and maintain a lasting peace. Practical and hardworking, they will become an invaluable tool of pacification and of economic penetration.

The rapid construction of the railroad is, it goes without saying, the necessary guarantee of the future structure of the Southwest.

The people of Figuig have begun to buy supplies from us. They go to the market at Beni-Ounif, and they bring about six wagonloads of goods per week.

The Taagda station at Bechar will become a very important commercial depot if the pacification of Tafilalet is accomplished. It will be necessary to pursue the construction of the Saharan railroad to the furthest points Southwest, all the way to Ain-Beni-Abbes, via Taghit and Igli, which would noticeably diminish the burdensome cost of supplying by convoy and would secure the Southwest route.

In summary, to justify our presence in the Southwest Oranais, France absolutely must ensure that a beneficent peace reign there and must use all its economic means to better the lot of this country and to lead it to normal economic development.

Without that, this conquest, whose advisability has been so challenged, will remain an escapade without any redeeming aspect, one that any intelligent mind would not hesitate to condemn severely.

Beni-Ounif, February 1904

La Dépêche coloniale publishes a letter from one of its correspondents who recently returned from a tour of the Sud Oranais. Our colleague's view reflects the utmost optimism. In his view, things couldn't be going better there, and he says that in six months there won't be any more *djiouch*. He even claims that in the same period of time, the moral conquest of the Berbers will have been accomplished.

Our colleague must have raced through the region because otherwise, he would have seen that the situation there is far more complicated and fragile than it seemed to him.

After two months spent at Beni-Ounif, involving frequent, *discreet* trips to Figuig and successive conversations with all the local groups — military, European civilians, natives — here is the actual situation as I understand it.

We find there two groups that are absolutely distinct in terms of their mores, their character, and consequently, with extremely different interests, even conflicting: the village people who are farmers and craftsmen possessing some household goods, therefore, essentially sedentary and peaceful; and the nomads, the Ouled Djerir, Doui Menia, Beni Guil, Amour dissidents, and so on.

The latter, having no attachment to the land — transient shepherds, turbulent, hard to discipline, and who have remained to the present almost completely elusive — are accustomed by tradition to bloody battles between tribes, between tribal clans, even between families. They are also accustomed to *harkas* and *razzias*, carried out for vengeance and also for looting, against neighboring tribes or against the townspeople whom the nomads despise.

In their relations with us, the nomads are simply continuing their traditional way of life, nothing more, nothing less.

The inhabitants of this vague borderland do not consider themselves involved in a holy war against us in any way. This becomes even more obvious when one considers the fact that nondissident groups from the same pillaging tribes speak of us without hesitation and with dignity, as acknowledged by all the officers, with the highest praise.

The people of Southeast Morocco do not, any more than the people of Figuig or Tafilala, consider themselves subjects of the Cherifian *makhzen*. They have always been independent, thus, in warring against us, just as they have warred against each other for centuries, they believe they are serving their own interests, not those of the Sultan at Fez or of Rogui.

We know that even in Algeria there is a certain antipathy between the people of the Tell and those of the Sahara. This antipathy has reached a bitter point in Morocco, similar to how it had been in Algeria before the conquest.

There are then two issues here which are fundamentally distinct, however linked they appear in form — the Moroccan question itself, and that of the Sud Oranais, or more exactly, the Southeast of the Bled Saiba.

It is pointless and remiss at present to waste precious time in vain recriminations or in asking ourselves if we should have gone to Tidikelt, Touat, Beni-Abbes, Figuig.

Haven't some people even gone to the stupefying length of saying the word *evacuation!* Others have pushed naïveté to the point of suggesting we fight the dissidents with all we have. Others maintain that we must exterminate them, "waste" them, as the latest slang puts it.

It serves no purpose to bother with such scenarios. We have, right now, a situation, a reality, that we must deal with. We are faced with vast territories in which there are several clusters of *ksour*. We need to be ready as quickly as possible, at the least cost possible, to be able to gain from the situation, as M. Jonnart already noted in one of his speeches to the parliament.

Groups of towns like Figuig were at the mercy of the nomads, serving them as sources of supplies and as markets for their products, sometimes stemming from commerce in Morocco, especially Ouezzan, sometimes merely involving booty collected in the course of *harkas*.

The existence and free operation of these large markets in the *ksour* are then the sine qua non of the current existence of the nomads. Without these markets, they could not maintain their anarchic lives and their age-old pillaging.

If we want to be pragmatic, we should not be dreaming of Bou-Amama, old, tired, surrounded, as a matter of fact, by the more French-leaning influence of his son Si Taieb, nor engaging in an ill-considered flirtation with Rogui: neither one nor the other will give us, or the Sultan, what we most need: peace.

We have a task to accomplish — complex and delicate but not impossible.

In this context, we couldn't have done better than to entrust this mission to General Lyautey, young, unmatched in energy, who has been able in so few months to grasp clearly the condition of the region and figure out a plan of action. It has proven equally wise to have given the General the freedom and independence he clearly needed to accomplish this task which requires perfect unity of leadership, constant oversight, personal vision, and above all, a fit spirit always on the alert.

Very soon we can hope to see accomplished, thanks to the actions of the General and his collaborators who are as intelligent as they are dedicated, not — as our colleague from *La Dépêche coloniale* called it — "the moral conquest of the Berbers," but rather the pacification and *economic* conquest of the region.

Quite impressive and truly handsome is the *miad* (delegation) of the Beni Guil, who have come today to bring to conclude five days of talks with General Lyautey. There are five chioukh and the great caid Abderrhamane who announced this evening that they have accepted the conditions imposed on them and who gave the kiss of peace to their enemies of yesterday, the caids of the Hamyan from around Mecheria.

These men, clad in long djellabas of fine cloth and white turbans, have beautiful dark faces, impassive and energetic because of their pronounced traits and the fiery gaze of their elongated, untamed eyes.

The severity of their somber dress from the Moghrib adds a particular dignity to their faces, so dissimilar from those of the chiefs of the Hamyan, wearing long scarlet burnouses embroidered with French decorations.

They have come from their refuges in the West in order to announce finally a new era of peace in this country that is so much in need of it after months of bloody quarrels, of *djiouch*, of *harkas*, skirmishes, a whole strange and outmoded epic that Bedouin minstrels, camel drivers, and illiterate *mokhaznis* are beginning to sing in naive ballads.

Following these harmonious and solemn words, following these accolades that nevertheless preserved an aftertaste of blood, we have to wait for action.

The Beni Guil have accepted the conditions offered them, of which the main ones are first the reintegration of their traditional territory of migration, shared with the Hamyan, which they had abandoned when the quarrels broke out between the two tribes, the serious attempt to bring their fellow, still dissident, tribesmen to peace with us, and finally, the actual and sincere abandonment of Bou-Amama around whom they were pushed by their mass exodus.

If they carry out these, and come under the control of our posts, surrounded by Hamyan who have long been faithful and led by admirable men — the high commander of the group at Mecheria and the agha El Hadj Habib, and thus under constant, steady surveillance, they could hardly revert to instigating trouble and internecine struggles in the region.

Moreover, the Beni Guil themselves will soon feel the benefits of peace and their example could be beneficial for the other dissident tribes.

This sort of declaration of peace by the Beni Guil, it seems to me, is the direct result of the ingenious and firm policies that General Lyautey has maintained toward the nomads: reduce them to extreme weakness by cutting off their supplies, that is by depriving them of the Saharan markets where they restock and they sell the merchandise brought by caravans, stolen or bought, and their livestock, which enables them to remain in a state of rebellion. Accept straight-forwardly, though prudently, their offers of peace when their truthfulness is guaranteed and they include acceptable conditions. As long as the nomads keep their promises, treat them with regard, so as to prove to them the extent to which their interests are served by remaining on good terms with us. The moment they demonstrate bad faith in their actions, show them, with great energy, that we will not allow them to betray their sworn oath. Never compromise our dignity either by acts of brutality, any other provocation, or by weakness. Respect rigorously our promises to them, in order to demand in return the same respect and loyalty.

Unfortunately, behind the Beni Guil there is an old agitator who is still venerated: Bou-Amama, whose influence remains hostile.

Even granting, which is somewhat less than certain, that the Beni Guil represented by the *miad* are sincere today, spurred on by need, isn't it fully possible that tomorrow they could switch sides, with their versatility and their usual inconsistency, and this, either because abundant rains have brought back prosperity to their herds, or because of the influence of Bou-Amama?

That the influence of Bou-Amama is hostile to any accord between the Beni Guil and ourselves is understandable given that the Beni Guil constitute the majority of Bou-Amama's people.

All you need to do in order to convince yourself of these arguments is to go to Figuig, as we have just done, and to talk with the Zoua, followers of Bou-Amama and his brother-in-law residing at Hammam Foukani, Si Ahmed ben Menouar. The Zoua engage in the bitterest mockery of the *miad;* they consider the chioukh and the caid Abderrhamane as impostors who falsely claim to represent the majority of the Beni Guil. In this context, one of the most important members of the Zoua told us: "I bet whatever you wish that the Beni Guil of Abderrhamane wanted to swindle the French, promising whatever they demanded, in order to get resupplied and ready, only to return to a state of dissidence at the first opportune moment."

Even though the opinion of this *amaoui* was dictated by hate and anger, it may well be true.

What seems to indicate that the Beni Guil are still pretty far from the promised peacefulness is that another *miad*, led by the son of Bou-Amama, Si Taieb, left twenty days ago for the encampment of the Pretender (the Rogui Bou-Hamara) . According to the latest news from Figuig, an agreement would have been reached through the mediation of Si Taieb, between the Pretender and Bou-Amama. Bou-Amama would help the Pretender, by means of his influence and his men, to get rid of Mouley Abdelaziz, the Sultan of Morocco, and in return, the Pretender would give him some sort of control over the south of Morocco.

The first act of Si Taieb in this situation would be to move on to Oudjda to fight the Sultan's *makhzen* there.

What truth is there in this news? At least it contains nothing that is implausible.

If indeed this alliance between the Pretender and Bou-Amama takes place, then, at the first success, won't the Beni Guil abandon us to follow their kinsmen who remained faithful to Bou-Amama?

One can see the extent to which the situation is both complex and delicate.

While counseling in our dealings, with tribes like the Beni Guil, not only the utmost prudence, but even a constant suspicion, nevertheless, we would not hesitate to say that it would be most undiplomatic to reject the *miad* who come to us and that it would be better to try to bring this event to our advantage so that we can say to the nomads: "Every time you have come to us with acceptable propositions, we have received you and we have always honored our commitments."

Coming back to the Beni Guil, it is interesting to note the contrast between the pessimism of the people of Figuig, whoever they might be (except, of course, the governor's people), on the subject of the Beni Guil and the optimism of the Hamyan and the Amour from Ain-Sefra. This contrast is natural, however: beneath the pessimism of those from Figuig rests a loyalty to Bou-Amama. Underlying the optimism of the Hamyan there is flattered vanity because of what they consider a putdown for their enemies. As for the Amour, they are under the influence of the agha, Sidi Mouley of Tiout, who played an important role in the negotiations with the Beni Guil.

As for us, after many conversations with the most diverse elements, we think that the present period should be seen only as a wait and see period during which we should keep up our guard, carrying on an active surveillance of the activities of the Beni Guil while obliging the Hamyan, who are almost as turbulent as the Beni Guil, to respect our agreements by not engaging in any acts of violence.

Above all, we must profit from the few months of peace that, in any case, will be the result of the truce with the Beni Guil, by improving and reinforcing our guard posts in order to demonstrate to the Beni Guil that we will be in a position to punish them should they attempt to betray us.

It would be essential also, beyond action, to work morally on the Beni Guil, to counterbalance the influence of Bou-Amama by showing them how much interest they have in remaining loyal to us.

In my next letter I will speak to you about the other tribes and the situation in general.

Mission Civilisatrice

EBERHARDT'S JOURNEY FROM ANARCHY TO COMPLICITY

Laura Rice

Isabelle Eberhardt dreamed throughout her teenage years of escaping from the gloom of the Villa Neuve, where she grew up outside Geneva, to the exotic South, to Dar el Islam. As the nineteenth century drew to a close, Eberhardt realized her desires by traveling to North Africa with her mother, whom she would always later refer to as the "White Spirit." They arrived in Annaba, Algeria, in May of 1897, and Eberhardt began to live the existence she had longed for; she shed her European clothing for a white burnous, moved to the Arab quarter of the city and immersed herself in the language and culture. The sudden death of her mother in November of 1897 cut short this idyll. Eberhardt was in despair. Her father, the old nihilist Alexander Trophimovsky, arrived in Algeria only in time to attend the funeral. Inconsolable, Eberhardt sobbed that she longed to join the "White Spirit" in the grave, and Trophimovsky is said to have calmly handed her a revolver. By 1904 when death did find Isabelle Eberhardt at age 27, in a flash flood in the Sahara, she had led a tempestuous life that encompassed both the subversive political anarchism of her father and the religious mysticism of her mother, but only at a high price — a price finally dictated by the French colonial authorities.

Eberhardt spent the first four months following her mother's death in a state of shock; her moods shifted from exaltation to despair, from melancholy to apathy, and she took to drinking as well. It was anarchy, rather than religion, that finally jolted her out of this aimless circle of emotions. During the time she had spent in Annaba, Isabelle had made friends with Muslim students there who were beginning to complain about the indignities the colonizers heaped upon all Muslims. In early March she noted in her journal that although she felt it unwise for the Muslims to openly attack the French, she had no doubt about whose side she would take in such an event: "Perhaps I shall be fighting for the Muslim revolutionaries like I used to for the Russian anarchists . . . although with more conviction and more real *hatred* against oppression. I feel now that I'm much more deeply a Muslim than I was an anarchist."[1]

When the students revolted against the French colonial authorities on the night of March 14, 1898, Eberhardt was among them. She later wrote: "My chest was pounding and my head spinning, deliciously . . . I saw [the *khalifa* of the Aissaouas *zaouiya*] in front of me brandishing a truncheon. . . . At every moment it slashed into the surrounding police, cracking into skulls and arms raised in self-defense. [The *khalifa*] seemed transfigured: He seemed to me to have ineffable mystical beauty." Seeing a friend of hers, all bloodied, trying to fend off four policemen with a short Moorish dagger, Isabelle picked up a sword and went to help: "For the first time, I felt the savage intoxication of battle, bloody and primitive, of males, body to body, wild with anger, blinded by fury, drunk on blood and instinctive cruelty. I knew the consuming voluptuousness of streaming blood, of the atrocious brutality of *action* triumphing over *thought*" (Kobak, *Isabelle*, 64). Setting aside the purple prose of the passage, it is not difficult to see several themes that would sketch out the boundaries of Eberhardt's brief life — adherence to Islam, siding with the underdog, hatred of the vulgar colonial mentality, love of anarchy and battle, and a impulse to record it all in writing. Eberhardt left Annaba the next day, without being called in by the police, but not without it being noted in her police file that she had been implicated in an Arab insurrection against the colonial authorities.

A central contradiction of Isabelle Eberhardt's life in North Africa is her simultaneous allegiance to radical individualism and to the defense of the oppressed. While vocal in her disgust at the arrogance, ignorance, and acquisitiveness of the French colonists, she did not embrace any formal social causes, but rather was attracted to those figures who seemed to have turned their backs on the routine of civil society — vagabonds, legionnaires, nomads, outcasts. One key to her attitudes is found in the depiction of Dmitri Orschanow, the main character of a novel reworked up to the moment of her death. In the novel *Trimardeur* (*The Vagabond*), Dmitri yearns to change the world and so becomes a medical student and joins the humanitarian movements of the times: "From the start he took part in all the revolutionary meetings and projects, but he soon found that the socialist ideal didn't suit his nature. His ideas were changing and developing, and finally he gave his full allegiance to the anarchists, with their demand of complete freedom for the individual."[2] But the anarchists, too, end up accusing Dmitri of being withdrawn, of not fully involving himself in the group's activities, of having a private life that could endanger the group. For Dmitri, true freedom was to be found in the accumulated and separate liberties of individuals. While drawn to human suffering — the misery of poverty, alcoholism, and prostitution — Dmitri discovers that he not only wants to alleviate it but to partake of it, to immerse himself in the antisocial, in degradation. Eberhardt seems to have shared this double impulse to help the underdog — and to be the underdog. She wrote in her journal dated Cagliari, 1 January 1900:

> For the gallery I put on the borrowed mask of the cynic, the dissolute, the I-don't-give-a-damner . . . So far no one has managed to pierce the mask to see my true soul, this sensitive and pure soul that hovers so high above the baseness and degradation through which I choose, out of disdain for the conventional and also out of a strange need to suffer, to drag my physical being [in the mud].[3]

Both Dmitri and Isabelle attempted to escape the petty judgments of the "gallery" and all its bourgeois conventions by going to Africa. As Dmitri sets sail on the Mediterranean heading for Oran, Algeria, we are told: "This was certainly the classic sea, the glistening sea, revelling in the glory of the sun, the deep purple sea-swell which had lapped against the sunny shores when human thought was first born. It was also the high road which led to all the dream-countries" (Eberhardt, *Vagabond*, 83–84). In her journal entry on New Year's Day 1900, Eberhardt dedicates herself, too, to the vagabond life: "As a nomad who has no country besides Islam and neither family nor close friends, I shall wend my way through life until it is time for that everlasting sleep inside the grave." Of her dedication to social justice she writes: "My heart is in fact a pure one filled with love and tenderness, and with boundless compassion for all who suffer injustice, all who are weak and oppressed . . . a heart both proud and unswerving in its commitment to Islam, a cause for which I long to give my life some day." So, like her hero Dmitri, Eberhardt turned to the colonies of France in North Africa — Tunisia and Algeria — to find the "right path" toward knowledge and social justice. Unfortunately, the geography through which she planned to make her spiritual pilgrimage was one administered and patrolled by other forces, those of the colonizing power.

During Eberhardt's lifetime, Europe as a whole extended its colonial claims more than it had done in the previous three-quarters of a century. France alone added 10,000,000 square kilometers of overseas territories (about 20 times its own size) to its holdings.

This expansion was generally unplanned, having been carried out by military officers acting on their own. Many in the metropole did not favor colonization — not because they respected the autonomy or intelligence of peoples overseas — but because they favored spending government revenues on domestic programs or because there simply was more money to be made in other markets. The colonial lobby, dating from 1889–90, demonstrated at least three reasons why France should colonize: 1) the need for France to protect her economic well-being (this was argued mainly by smaller, seaport entrepreneurs); 2) France's need to compete with England as a world power with vast overseas colonies; 3) France's *mission civilisatrice*, that is, France's obligation to carry "civilization" to the more "primitive" peoples of the world.

The National Colonial Congress held in Paris in 1889–90 developed a resolution favoring the "assimilation" of peoples in overseas colonies into the body politic of France through the civilizing mission: "The efforts of colonization should propagate among the natives the language, the methods of work, and, progressively, the spirit and civilization of France."[4] These high ideals (however ethnocentric they may be) were not representative at all of the colonial reality. Even an imperialist like French prime minister Jules Ferry found the gap between policy and practice to be a yawning chasm. Visiting Algeria as head of a Senate commission in 1892, Ferry noted: "Very few colonists are committed to the educational and civilizing mission which is the duty of the superior race; fewer still believe that it is possible to improve the conquered race. On the contrary, they proclaim ever more loudly that the conquered race is incorrigible and ineducable, despite the fact that in thirty years, they have made no attempt to rescue it from its moral and intellectual poverty."[5] Isabelle Eberhardt points to the disjunction between the arrogance and self-serving behavior of the French colonists, on the one hand, and the helplessness, gullibility, and, often, the dignity of the oppressed Arab colonized, on the other.

As the Tunisian writer Albert Memmi demonstrates in his well-known study, *The Colonizer and the Colonized*, the basic reason the colonizers come to the colony is because it is "a place where one earns more and spends less."[6] This is true because the colonizer enjoys special privileges that are dependent upon the oppression of the native inhabitants: guaranteed jobs; high wages; rapid career advancement; the right to buy expropriated land cheaply; the security of belonging to the group whose language, mores, dress, flag, and laws are privileged at every moment. Eberhardt's stories often turn on this inequality of circumstances. Eberhardt's more admirable European characters are those who, like herself, long to assimilate the "wrong" direction. Characters like Tereneti Antonoff (and later his son Andrei) in "The Anarchist" flee to Algeria "looking for a new land, a chosen country where, under a merciful sky, men would be less crusted over by routine." When Tereneti Antonoff dies, his last words to his son are: "Always be true to yourself . . . Do not bend before the hypocrisy of conventions, continue to live among the poor and to love them," and that is precisely what Andrei does — but he is a rarity.

Most of the French colonists depicted in Eberhardt's stories are unintelligent, fearful, prejudiced, and brutal. The petty landowners in "Native Exploits" look out for number one. The dialogue between Perez, a violent and stupid man, and Durand, a less physical but equally violent man, centers on how they are going to take the law into their own hands and punish the "dirty Arabs" who live near their town, Alfred de Musset. "We won't have another Margueritte here," they exclaim. The Margueritte Affair had taken place on the 26th of April 1901 when the colonial settlement of Margueritte was attacked by one hundred members of the Righa tribe; they killed one shepherd and five Europeans who refused to convert to Islam. All the rest converted and the killing stopped at that point.[7] Then, the inhabitants of Margueritte banded together, taking the law into their own hands, to hunt down the guilty parties. Oddly enough, they rounded up *one hundred twenty-five* natives, who were tried and convicted. The Margueritte Affair brought to the surface, on the natives' side, an awareness of the injustice they were doomed to suffer, and on the colonizers' side, the fear and paranoia that accompany usurpation. The disagreement between the French settlers and the Arabs was at least as much about land grabs as it was about religion, as two other accounts, one contemporary and one recent, would indicate. Victor Barrucand, the left-wing newspaper editor who employed Eberhardt and remained her staunch friend, was editor of *Les Nouvelles* at the time of the Margueritte Affair; his editorials address the repressive tribunals that were created after the incident, the kangaroo courts where the colonists could see their hatred of Arabs institutionalized and their paranoic feelings of insecurity assuaged.[8] Rana Kabbani, editor of a 1987 English translation of Eberhardt's journals, describes the incident as "a nationalist revolt against the French in which a group of North Africans attempted to destabilize colonial rule by attacking a French garrison."[9] There is no question in this account of unarmed "Europeans" attacked by religious fanatics. Eberhardt's own attitude toward the Margueritte Affair, as we will see, was that the attack was an unwise but not an unmerited form of action.

Eberhardt's story "Native Exploits" focuses on the mentality of the French settlers, a group she had always despised for their vulgarity, lack of imagination, and repressive social codes. The natives of "Native Exploits" are completely absent from the story, except as the future recipients of the rough "justice" of the settlers, underscoring the displacement in the story from "exploits" to "exploitation." The only reference to French military presence is an oblique one. Durand says, "Over there in France they could care less about it. There's nothing left for us — only for the *bicots*. They acquitted the assassins at Margueritte, they want to strip us of our disciplinary courts and allow the natives to crush us." At the time Eberhardt wrote this story, the French colonial lobby had been working for a decade to implement a two-pronged shift in colonial policy: 1) the centralization of the offices dealing with colonial policies inside France; and 2) the decentralization of administrative power in the colonies. This shift had, in the eyes of the colonial lobby, two advantages: centralization at home would enable the lobby to locate, pressure, and hold accountable those French officials who oversaw colonial affairs; decentralization in the colony would actually reduce the power of the Bureaux Arabes run by the military and increase civilian administrative control, thus increase the power of the settlers. The military goal of "law and order" represented a different (and in times of peace, more avoidable) form of control than did civilian aims based on economic motives. The military wanted to police the land and the natives; the civilians wanted to own the land and exploit native labor power. "By the year 1900, the coastal regions of Algeria had passed under civilian control with native representation [like the *caid* in "The Marabout"], while the region south of and including the line formed by the towns of Tiarit, Saida, Bou Saada, Biskra, were administered by the military, each region being under an 'Arab Bureau.'"[10]

The resulting combination of the two was yet worse, as Eberhardt demonstrates in stories like "Forced Labor in the South" and "The Seduced." In an earlier collection of stories also published by City Lights, Eberhardt's story "Criminal" summarizes the dynamics between even well-intentioned colonists and the dispossessed natives. In the story, Mohammed Achouri loses his part of the communal land because he cannot prove on paper that it is his; his complaints about the inapplicability of the criteria to his situation go unheeded as the minor officials in charge of this decentralized expropriation point out that they are "only doing a job" and they "don't make the rules." Achouri strikes out against the colonial system by setting on fire the barn of Monsieur Gaillard, a well-meaning colonizer who has bought the land that was once Achouri's from the government and who has hired Achouri on as a day laborer. Eberhardt writes: "They could not know that they were indivisible, both victims of the same grotesque and evil game. The law makers sat far away in their palaces high above Algiers. Crime, particularly among the poor and downtrodden, is often a last gesture of liberty."[11]

Eberhardt's sympathy and identification with the natives is unmistakable, but her assessment of the civilizing mission is less unambiguous. Writing to her husband, Slimane Ehnni, an Arab and former spahi from Constantine, on July 15, 1901, Eberhardt exhorts him to prepare for the civil service exam so that he can get the post of *khodja* (clerk) once he is no longer in the military:

> Imagine that in working toward the goal that I set out for you here that you are working for all your Arab brothers, for all our Muslim brothers. You will provide for these French gentlemen — disdainful and arabophobe — the example of an Arab who, having begun as a Spahi of the second order, has raised himself to a rank envied and respected, by his intelligence and work. If there were many such Arabs in Algeria, the French would have been obliged to change their minds on the subject of "dirty Arabs." That is how you must serve Islam and the Arab nation, and not by fomenting useless and bloody revolts which serve only as ammunition for the enemies of all that is Arab, and not by discouraging those honest French who would like to be brothers.[12]

Once Slimane Ehnni attained the post of *khodja* in Tenes, Algeria, he and Eberhardt were plunged once again into the morass of paranoic colonial attitudes and practices. Eberhardt's unquestioned assumption of the value of Western literary and humanistic traditions, and her assumptions about "well-meaning" colonists need more scrutiny. Memmi, in *The Colonizer and the Colonized* had sketched out a portrait of the "well-meaning" colonizer, whom he called "the colonizer who refuses," pointing to the inherent contradictions of this position: "It is not easy to escape mentally from a concrete situation [the inequality inherent in colonialism], to refuse its ideology [Western superiority], while continuing to live with its actual relationships [Western privilege]" (Memmi, 20). As the trials of those accused in the Margueritte Affair approached, Eberhardt knew that she should side with them:

> Algiers, Wednesday 13 October 1902, 5pm.
>
> I may have to go to France this winter to see about writing a piece in defense of the Margueritte rebels. Oh! if I could only say everything I know, speak my mind and come out with the whole truth! What a good deed that would be! In due course it would have positive results and establish my reputation too! Brieux [French socialist-realist playwright] was certainly right about that: I must start my career by coming out openly in defense of my Algerian Muslim brethren." (Eberhardt, *Passionate Nomad*, 100)

Eberhardt never did write about the Margueritte Affair. And although she did want to make her mark on the literary scene, she seems to have been driven far less by a desire for literary fame than the quest for spiritual fullness, on the one hand, and the search for adventure, on the other. Brieux encouraged Eberhardt to write about a cause when what she really wanted to write about was her interior and exterior world. Her writing, finally, is far more autobiographical than social, even at its most "ethnographic" in the travel sketches or "objective" in the journalistic descriptions of conquering the Sahara with General Lyautey.

Rana Kabbani suggests that Eberhardt never wrote about the Margueritte Affair because of her fear of displeasing the colonial authorities. Eberhardt had good reason to fear these powers: her name appeared on the Algerian police record after her involvement in the uprising of March 14, 1898, at Annaba; in July of 1899, she was harassed by the officials of the Bureau Arabe — especially Captain Susbielle whom she had scorned — when she visited El Oued at the edge of the Sahara; she was kept under close surveillance when she revisited El Oued in 1900 (but luckily for her Captain Cauvet, head of the Bureau Arabe in El Oued, saw nothing politically threatening in her unconventional life); an anonymous letter (probably from Susbielle) eventually caused Governor-General Jonnart to recommend that Eberhardt be expelled from El Oued and Touggourt and that Slimane Ehnni be dismissed from El Oued; before the Bureau Arabe succeeded in driving Eberhardt out of El Oued, she became the victim of an attempted assassination and spent several weeks recovering in a military hospital; she left Algeria to avoid deportation, was called back for the assassin's trial, which gave the press and the colonial system an excuse to try Eberhardt informally, and then she was formally expelled from Algeria; returning to Algeria finally as the wife of Slimane Ehnni, now *khodja* of Tenes, she became the target of a scandal there, instigated by the colonial settlers who feared and resented her association with the natives of the region. In short, at age 26, Eberhardt had had a number of run-ins with the authorities and had ample reason to fear them.

The stories and travel sketches collected in this book go a long way toward charting Eberhardt's attitudes toward the colonial project during the period from 1898 to 1903. Her early interest in indigenous peoples is balanced by a romantic fascination with outcasts, especially those European men in the French Colonial Army who, because they are more intelligent and less prejudiced than their peers, do not fit in, even in the military. Typically, these characters are seduced by the sun and sand of North Africa, attracted by the landscape more than by the people. The character Andrei, like the character Jacques in "Yasmina" and in "The Major," begins a liaison with an Arab woman. The women in all three stories are also outcasts of some sort.

It is in the midst of uncanny landscapes that these characters are most at home. At the desolate Legion outpost in the Sahara, Andrei undergoes a "blazing revelation": "There Andrei understood the reverence ancient peoples had for the great celestial bodies, the all-powerful fire, both generative and destructive." Following his tour in the Legion, Andrei moves permanently to the oasis of Tamerna Djedida on the oued Rir': "He loved this mysterious, visionary country where all the hidden chemistry of matter was spread on the surface of the ground; where the iodized saltwater made whimsical, white arabesques on the fragile grasses of the murmuring *seguia*, or tinted rusty red the bottoms of the small walls made of *toub* that made the gardens into true labyrinths of shadow." Andrei's love of the landscape extends to an empathy with the black inhabitants of the oasis, and finally to Saadia. The daughter of a midwife, Saadia has been repudiated by her husband, now dead. Significantly, the two women are "of mixed race, almost Arab." Eberhardt recognized and deplored the racism of the European colonists toward the Arabs of North Africa, but she herself tends to make Arabs more important or worthy than blacks. Her bias is not by any means comparable to the overt racial hatred of the settlers, rather it appears in the quite secondary roles she assigns to blacks in her work. While she may be reflecting a bias that operated in Arab society, it must be noted that she herself is clearly less sympathetic to her black characters than to her Arabic ones.

Andrei's story ends with his romantic embrace of both Saadia and the land; other similar characters do not attain this completion. The character Jacques — a figure Eberhardt worked and reworked — thinks himself more attuned to native life than the other Roumis, but in the end, Jacques has alienated himself from the European legionnaires, betrayed the native peoples and jilted the woman who has been foolish enough to fall in love with him (in "Yasmina" the woman ends up dead; in "The Major" she ends up in jail). In "The Major" Jacques's alienation from the Europeans takes the form of a rejection of their banal adherence to routine in both thought and behavior: "More and more what disgusted him was their vulgarity, their dedication to be, think, and act like everyone else, to look like each other, to impose on one another the same orthodox and narrow point of view. This appropriation of each other's liberty, this meddling in one another's thoughts and actions appalled him . . . Not content to be nonentities themselves, these people wanted to annihilate his own personality, regiment his ideas, check the independence of his actions." In his rebellion against the repression of the Bureau Arabe, Jacques frequents the natives whom he imagines accept him. He starts a liaison with a girl who has been left unprotected in the world and has been surviving by occasional prostitution. Jacques, certain of the love and fidelity of Embarka, defies his critics at the Bureau Arabe. His contact with the natives gives him the idea that he has escaped the narrow-mindedness of his countrymen: "What made Jacques like [the natives] was that they were *different*, they didn't possess the thick-headed vulgarity he had detested so much in Europe. And the gray, sandy horizon surrounding the dreary town didn't distress Jacques any more: his soul communed with the infinite." In short, hating the Europeans, Jacques believes that he loves and understands the natives. The depth of his misunderstanding and lack of empathy is revealed when Embarka is thrown into jail on fabricated charges, and Jacques asks for a transfer: "He looked at the familiar landscape with the same dreary indifference one feels when looking at a strange port, where one has never been, would never go, from the deck of a ship, during a short layover." The military is the "ship" that allows Jacques to leave Embarka — but not without his laying the blame for disillusionment on her first. When she lashes out at him for leaving her moldering in jail, he feels his alienation from the place has been corroborated, and he can leave the town and the people feeling sad but somehow vindicated.

On his way out of town, resigned to his fate, he has a sudden insight: "Undoubtedly, he was made that way, and all his enterprises would be aborted . . . all his dreams would end up like this, and he would go into exile, more or less driven out of all the corners where he would try to live and love. Indeed, he would never be like the *others*. He would never submit to the tyrannical yoke of mediocrity." Jacques's relations with the natives and Embarka are shown to be based less on affection for the unknown than on disaffection with a world he knows all too well. Jacques is much like Dmitri in *The Vagabond* — an elite among souls, condemned to a life of wandering across foreign and forbidding landscapes. Jacques's self-serving romanticism, however ethnocentric it may seem to us today, was perhaps more appealing to Eberhardt. In her journals, she often presents herself in a similar role. For example, as she prepared to leave for Kenadsa on April 8, 1904, she wrote: "I am leaving once more to go again into the sad Mogh'reb, land of mystery and death. . . . This evening, rereading these old journals, full of dead things, felt an intense obsession and a deep melancholy, coming across the names almost already forgotten of Souf, Bordj-Ferdjeun, Ourmes with its enchanted gardens, El Oued, Behima. In two years, in five years, names familiar today like Ain-Sefra, Figuig, Beni-Ounif and Djebel Amour will have the same nostalgic music in my ears. So many other corners of Africa still charm me. Thus, my solitary and dolorous being will erase itself from the land where it will have passed among people and things as a mere spectator, a stranger."[13] In many ways, the travel sketches Eberhardt wrote in the last two years of her life reflect this vagabond perspective.

The sketches translated here from the collection *Sud Oranais* depict life in the Sahara on the border with Morocco in 1903–1904. Eberhardt describes the native soldiers — *goumis*, spahis, *mokhaznis* — with whom she identified, and with whom she traveled. She also depicts life in the oasis villages of the regions and the life of the nomadic tribes. "Reflections of War" presents the *mokhaznis* as simple, straightforward people caught up in the colonization process as the French move into the Sahara under General Lyautey's command. Interviewing some of the wounded after the battle of El Moungar in which the Legion fought desert tribes, Eberhardt writes: "How congenial these poor devils [the *mokhaznis*] are who have suffered and almost died for causes that are not their own, that leave them indifferent." She goes on to explain that for the *mokhaznis*, just as for their brothers, the nomads, battle is a traditional fact. "For them, it is neither a question of war with Morocco, nor above all of a holy war. The region has always been *bled-el-baroud* (The Land of Gunpowder), and the tribes of this vague frontier land have always raided each other . . . [The *mokhazni* Mouley Idriss] thinks of the current military operations quite simply as counter-raids and reprisals against the *djich*." Mouley Idriss has historical fact on his side in this case. What the

French may have looked upon as a rural social and economic back-
water was, for the natives, a vital region crossed by important caravan routes. The oasis complexes of Tafilalet and Figuig were active
markets and entrepots.

This area was also tied by tradition to political life of central
Morocco where the government (*mahkzen*) was located:

> Since the ninth century the control of Sijilmasa [a city in the
> Tafilalet grove] and its commercial revenue was crucial to any
> group wishing to seize and retain the rulership of Morocco. Thus,
> the tribes and communities of [Tafilalet] and a wide surrounding
> area were frequently enmeshed in dynastic politics, sometimes sup-
> porting the incumbent sultan, sometimes making common cause
> with pretenders and rebels. In the 1630s [Tafilalet] was thrust into
> an even more prominent position when one of its native sons,
> Mawlay 'Ali Sharif, launched a new dynastic movement for which
> he claimed legitimacy by his status as a *sharif* (plural *shurfa*),
> or descendant of the Prophet Muhammad. The 'Alawi family, as
> Mawley 'Ali Sharif's lineage became known, successfully supplanted
> the crumbling Sa'adian dynasty and established its power in the
> cities of the north of the Atlas. Yet [Tafilalet] remained the ideolog-
> ical headquarters of the new dynasty and the homeland of the
> 'Alawi *shurfa*, the kinsmen of the sultan. It also continued to be
> a breeding ground for court intrigue and conspiracy. Though the
> legitimacy of the 'Alawis was generally accepted in Morocco, no
> rule of primogeniture governed the succession. Consequently,
> members of the *shurfa* lineage, many of whom lived in [Tafilalet],
> frequently vied with one another for the positions of strength nec-
> essary to depose a weak sultan or to assure themselves of the suc-
> cession. A sultan's death invariably unleashed a factional struggle in
> which the populations of the [Tafilalet] area were likely to become
> involved. Thus, from the seventeenth to the twentieth century the
> political disposition of the tribes and communities of the Southeast
> were of constant concern to the sultan as well as to other power
> elements in the country. Conversely, political crises generated in
> central Morocco and the imperial cities quickly reverberated in
> the Southeast.[14]

The people of the Saharan periphery of Morocco, thus, went about
their business outside of the Sultan's control and, while they

accepted the Sultan as their sovereign, they resisted paying taxes, serving in the army, or dealing with central administrators. At the time Eberhardt was in this area, the Moroccan *makhzen* was vying for more control — thus there is mention of impotent *amels* (governors) in oases like Oudarhir and of disaffected soldiers of the *makhzen* discarding their uniforms, as they do in the piece "Oudjda" where water carriers are now wearing the cast-off red *makhzen* jackets. In 1902 the Franco-Moroccan Accords had placed an *amel* at Figuig, but none appointed during Eberhardt's time were natives of Figuig, and none were able to build any independent power base there. At most they had a handful of *mokhaznis* at their command and the right to levy a palm tax, but no means to enforce it. As the *amel* was dependent upon the *ksar* for his support, he ended up having little real power. The *amel* was regarded in most cases as a representative of the central government, there to interfere and threaten taxes, and so was treated with little regard. The *amel* in his turn could irritate the *ksar* in minor ways as a mode of retaliation. The only reason the oases tolerated the *amels* was that they did recognize the Sultan as a spiritual leader, and therefore they also recognized those in his employ — but secular activity was another issue altogether. During Eberhardt's time, the *amel* at Figuig generally took refuge at Oudarhir, which allowed him to live there in the hope that he could somehow be used to threaten the neighboring *ksar* of Zenaga. Zenaga, on the lower terrace, had taken a disproportionate amount of water from the spring, and Oudarhir hoped that by harboring the *amel* they would get the leverage to make Zenaga share the water more equitably.

The *amel* was largely ineffectual. When Eberhardt mentions him in the sketch "The *Djich*," he is a lackey of the *makhzen*, and the *makhzen*, under pressure from the French, have ordered their subalterns not to give amnesty or sanctuary to dissident nomads: Men with striking and solemn faces, clad in dark blue djellabas and armed with rifles, emerged from the walls of Oudarh'ir. In the front of them there was a tall, thin Moroccan wearing a white djellaba and a red *chechia* creased down the middle over strange loops of graying hair. His pale face was ugly, and his gaze evasive.

The Amouria jumped for their rifles. The police officer of the *makhzen* of the pasha came forward:

"Peace be on you! Who are you and why are you here?"

"We are of the Amouria and we come from the north to ask for *aman* [asylum] and hospitality from the people of Figuig."

The pasha had pledged not to give sanctuary to dissidents or to bandits:

"Get out of here!"

In this sketch, Eberhardt keeps her distance from both the dissidents and the representative of the *makhzen*. The French harbored deep suspicion of both, and Eberhardt begins to reflect this perspective in her work.

Before 1902, only a handful of Europeans and no military had gotten into Figuig. This oasis was alternately intransigent or cooperative, depending upon the pressures and imagined advantages of the moment. When Eberhardt visited Figuig, she did so as a sort of spy for Lyautey. This oasis complex especially interested the French because it harbored the aging Bou-Amama, a marabout who had led an uprising against the French in 1881–1882. Because the French had been expropriating land and water holes, the displaced tribes were more than happy to join Bou-Amama. According to a book written in 1905 by Commander E. Graulle, former head of the Bureau Arabe, entitled *The Insurrection of Bou-Amama*, Bou-Amama was, at the beginning of his career, "a good man at bottom, who generally advocated peace, harmony, and love of one's neighbor; he had, therefore, nothing in common with the fanatic and bloody marabout that legend has chosen to depict."[15] Bou-Amama's uprising drew a wide number of supporters, but it was over as quickly as it began. Nevertheless, his challenge to the French was threatening enough that the French still were wary of him in 1902. Following his rebellion, the French began building forts in the South, beginning at Ain-Sefra. Bou-Amama settled at Figuig at the *ksar* of Hammam-Tahtani (his birthplace) from 1896 to 1902. He made overtures both to the Moroccan *makhzen* and to the French while keeping his independence. Hints of this intrigue are obvious in the sketch "At the Home of Bou-Amama's Cousin," which takes place in a *zaouia* at Hammam-Foukani where the Beni Guil dissidents have taken a night's sanctuary.

Eberhardt is astute about the political and social changes taking place in the Sud Oranais. Her romanticism seems limited at this point to regret for a way of life that was disappearing before her eyes. In *"Douar* of the *Makhzen,"* she describes the newly arrived *mokhaznis* as those who "remain most traditional, preserving their local customs. They remain attached to the Muslim faith . . . Five times a day one sees them withdraw into the desert to pray, grave, indifferent to all that surrounds them; and they have a certain beauty in their noble gestures." Unfortunately they soon take on the loose mores of a soldier's life: "Without any moral gain, they rid themselves of some of their ancestral traditions."

The large caravans Eberhardt describes in this piece were also on the edge of extinction; the *sokhars* (camel drivers) were "men who remain unchanged from the time of the patriarchs and prophets at the dawn of the world." A colorful chaos is the order of the day as complaining camels "stand for hours between the railway station and the fortress, in the midst of swollen packs, planks, canteens, and crates bearing faraway addresses: Taghit, Igli, Beni-Abbes, In-Salah, Adrar . . ." As Eberhardt watches the caravan finally move out, she notes, "This great spectacle of pure desert life will come to an end, and with the advent of the colonial regime and the railroads, one will no longer see its unforgettable splendor." She had already traced the economic effect of the railroad in pieces like "Ghost Town" where hasty villages appear and then fall into ruin as European merchants and the Foreign Legion follow the progress of the railroad, always in search of a quick profit to be made. In "Figuig," Eberhardt notes sadly that "without a doubt, in several years, the lust for money, the stupidity, and the alcoholism that had polluted Biskra [a military headquarters] would come to destroy the still untainted charm of the old Saharan refuge."

It was, in part, her search for a refuge that led Eberhardt to collaborate with the French army. In General Lyautey, she found a kindred spirit, a rebel. Lyautey met Eberhardt at Ain-Sefra in September of 1903, when she was interviewing the wounded of the battle of El Moungar. Lyautey had just been assigned to the region and had been given free rein by Governor-General Jonnart (the same one who had urged Eberhardt's expulsion from El Oued in 1900) to carry out his new ideas about how to control this ambiguous frontier. Lyautey had his strategy clearly in mind — the policy of "pacific penetration" — which involved cutting the nomad dissidents off from their lifeline, the markets of the oases, thus isolating them. The railroad would be brought in simultaneously, creating new economic opportunities for the people of the oasis complexes. However, Lyautey knew little about the geography and language of the region, and less about the marabouts and religious brotherhoods, the effective political powers in the area. The marabout at Kenadsa, where Eberhardt longed to go, was especially powerful. So not only did Eberhardt and Lyautey hit it off personally, but also they were most useful to each other. Eberhardt's knowledge of the desert and her membership in the Qadriya brotherhood made her an ideal scout for Lyautey. Lyautey's power and protection gave Eberhardt the first real security she had ever had in Algeria, and because she needed permission from the military to travel to the religious retreat at Kenadsa for her own spiritual quest, she was especially grateful for Lyautey's support.

As the last pieces in *Sud Oranais* indicate, Eberhardt finally did reach the *zaouia* at Kenadsa. And the last piece in the volume, "Reports from the Sud Oranais," indicates the high price Eberhardt paid for this access: in essence, she lost her voice. Writing as a special correspondent for *La Dépêche coloniale*, Eberhardt uses for the first time the pronoun "we," meaning "we French." Here the avid, pseudo-objectivity of the journalist attached to a military campaign drowns out the voice of the rebel who earlier had empathized with vagabonds, rebels, and dissidents. Eberhardt explains clearly Lyautey's plan of "pacific penetration," which he also referred to as the "tache d'huile," the spot of oil. French influence would spread slowly but indelibly into the oases, by creating a dependence on outside markets and starving out those nomads who rebelled against foreign control. Eberhardt had come around to finding in Lyautey's a "humane" form of colonialism. She writes at the end of her report:

> Above all, we must not profit from the few months of peace that, in any case, will be the result of the understanding with the Beni Guil, by improving and reinforcing our guard posts in order to demonstrate to the Beni Guil that we will be in a position to punish them should they attempt to betray us. It would be essential also, beyond action, to work morally on the Beni Guil, to counterbalance the influence of Bou-Amama.[15]

Eberhardt's early death in the flash flood at Ain-Sefra in 1904 prevented her from the pain of seeing that Lyautey's colonial policy amounted to a colonialism like any other, where peace is based on intimidation and prosperity is only for the few.

1. Cited in Annette Kobak, *Isabelle: The Life of Isabelle Eberhardt* (New York: Knopf, 1989), 63.
2. Isabelle Eberhardt, *Vagabond*, Annette Kobak, trans. (London: Hogarth, 1988), 9.
3. Isabelle Eberhardt, *Lettres et journaliers*, présentation et commentaires par Eglal Errera (Aries, France: Actes Sud, 1987), 85. Our translation.
4. Martin Deming Lewis, "One Hundred Million Frenchmen: The 'Assimilation' Theory in French Colonial Policy," *Comparative Studies in Society and History*, 4, 2 (January 1962), 143.
5. Cited in Alec G. Hargreaves, *The Colonial Experience in French Fiction* (London: Macmillan, 1981), 12.
6. Albert Memmi, *The Colonizer and the Colonized* (Boston: Beacon, 1965), 4.
7. This account is given by Françoise Renaudot in *L'Histoire des français en Algérie* (Paris: Robert Lafont, 1979).
8. Christine Drouet and Olivier Verniot, "Victor Barrucand: Un indésirable à Alger" in *Le Maghreb dans l'imaginaire français: la colonie, le desert, l'exil* (Paris: Edisud, 1984), 31-36.
9. Isabelle Eberhardt, *Passionate Nomad: The Diary of Isabelle Eberhardt*, forward and notes by Rana Kabbani (London: Virago, 1987), 113.

10. Cecily Mackworth, *The Destiny of Isabelle Eberhardt* (New York: Ecco Press, 1975), 57.

11. Isabelle Eberhardt, *The Oblivion Seekers and Other Writings*, Paul Bowles, trans. (San Francisco: City Lights, 1972), 50.

12. Archives d'Outre-Mer / Fonds Isabelle Eberhardt (23 x 21; 23 x 22). Our translation.

13. Isabelle Eberhardt, *Lettres et Journaliers*, présentation et commentaires par Eglal Errera (Arles: Actes Sud, 1987), 246. Our translation.

14. Ross E. Dunn, *Resistance in the Desert* (Madison: University of Wisconsin Press, 1977), 17–18.

15. Le Commandant E. Graulle, Ancien Chef du Bureau Arabe, Insurrection de Bou-Amama (Paris: Henri Charles-Lavauzelle, 1905), 8. Our translation.

Eberhardt and Gender

EBERHARDT AS SI MAHMOUD:
TRANSLATION OR TRANSGRESSION?

Laura Rice

In the winter of 1896–1897 Monsieur and Madame Casson, potential buyers of the Villa Neuve in Geneva, visited the house several times because they shared an interest in botany with Alexander Trophimovsky, Eberhardt's father. Many years later, Mme. Casson would remember how Eberhardt looked that winter, prior to her departure for Algeria:

> A young fellow of about sixteen was sawing wood in the court-yard. His delicate, elegant hands and his refined manners should have told us his sex, but we had no idea. It was only on the third visit that Monsieur [Trophimovski] revealed the disguise to us.[1]

According to most of Eberhardt's biographers, however, her "disguise" consisted of the clothes she had grown up wearing. Thus, they were not a disguise to her; this was not a case of "dressing up" in someone else's clothes, nor was it a misrepresentation of herself. But, given the strict, asymmetrical gender divisions which were signified by the clothes one wore, the work one did, and the places one traveled, it is little wonder that Eberhardt's self-presentation — in her dress, her behavior, and her writing — led to considerable discussion of her motives and character. An example of the stringency with which the late nineteenth century drew gender demarcations can be found in Otto Weininger's book, *Sex and Character*, written during this period. Weininger, a young Austrian philosopher, seemed to feel that the security and meaningfulness of Western society itself was bound up in the character differences between men and women. Women did not simply differ from men in their dress and behavior, they embodied the metaphysical polar opposite of the male principle that underpinned European civilization:

> Women have no existence and no essence; they are not, they are nothing. Mankind occurs as male or female, as something or nothing. . . . The meaning of woman is to be meaningless. She represents negation, the opposite pole from the Godhead, the other possibility of humanity.[2]

If as Weininger posits, women have "no essence," then they are condemned to perpetual masquerade, to perpetual deception. In Weininger's world view, Eberhardt would double this deception by being "on the other side of the looking glass" so far as gender training is concerned: that is, she is not merely covering up her lack of an essence with her clothes, she is, by wearing masculine clothes, attempting to appropriate the male's privilege of having an essence.

This issue of the relation of one's dress to one's self — whether an essence is posited or merely an identity in the continual process of construction — has been explored by contemporary feminist critics. Sandra Gilbert, in "Costumes of the Mind: Transvestism as Metaphor in Modern Literature," opens her essay by quoting Virginia Woolf's *Orlando:* "There is much to support the view that it is clothes that wear us and not we them. . . . we may make them take the mould of arm or breast, but [clothes] mould our hearts, our brains, our tongues to their liking."[3] Gilbert goes on to point out that the male modernists of the early twentieth century tended to oppose the self (one's essence) to the mask of the self one presented to the outside world. Eliot's Prufrock, for example, needs time "to prepare a face to meet the faces that you meet." The deception of costume is played off against the truth of the naked self. For women, so often posed nude in art and so constantly chastised or counseled about the cut of their clothes, nakedness was just another costume. Given this awareness of the continual posturing inherent in human self-presentation, women of the period, when they cross-dressed as men, were not trying to become male, rather they were donning the signifiers that would give them license to engage in male-gendered behavior. Thus, when the writer George Sand dressed as a male, she did so in order to be able to go out on the streets at night in Paris where the writers of the mid-nineteenth century frequented cafés and carried on their literary discussions. For Sand, cross-dressing was a matter of practicality and convenience — male dress translates into the sign of male privilege; for the philosopher Weininger, Sand's dress signified a sort of hermaphroditic abnormality: "some anatomical characters of the male" lurked beneath those trousers.[4]

While Weininger's male contemporaries who were engaged in criticizing Eberhardt's cross-dressing were less literal in their interpretations, many tended to see her dress as a sign of transgression rather than mere translation of privilege. Eberhardt herself gave practicality (that is, access to the world she wished to write about) and economy as her reasons for dressing as a male. Eberhardt is caught on the cusp of two centuries, caught between Weininger's clear-cut division of genders and Woolf's complication of the signifying system of clothing in general, and most especially when it defines gender. Gilbert's point in "Costumes of the Mind" is finally that "for the male modernist . . . gender is most often an ultimate reality, while for the female modernist an ultimate reality exists only if one journeys beyond gender."[5]

A constant theme from the opening pages of Eberhardt's journals is the search for a "true" identity that would be beyond the dichotomies of the sensual and the intellectual, and would be fulfilled ultimately by its merging into the oneness of Islam. Writing on January 1, 1900, Eberhardt says, "The knowledge I have acquired of the human heart is now so keen that I know the two months ahead will only bring me more sorrow, for I simply pay no attention to anything other than the dreams that make up my *true* personality. I seem to wear a mask that bespeaks someone cynical, dissipated . . . No one so far has ever managed to see through it and catch a glimpse of the sensitive soul that lives behind it."[6] Eberhardt's quest was to take her on a journey beyond gender. Her journals were to be the record of this journey: "All I want to do is work in peace and develop what intelligence I have. Such apparent egocentricity to be found on every page of this diary should not be taken for megalomania . . . oh no . . . to begin with, loners are given to constant introspection; and I do need to compile a record that will give me, later on, a true image of my soul as it is today. That is the only way I shall be able to judge my present life and to see whether my character has progressed or not" [30 July 1900, 8 p.m.]. Her soul's progress was to be filled out, paradoxically, through a continual shedding of the unnecessary baggage of European civilization. The end goal was to reach the pure, barren state where self and other merge in Islam.

Eberhardt's journey into the desert is both physical and metaphysical: "As a nomad who has no country besides Islam and neither family nor close friends, I shall wend my way through life until it is time for that everlasting sleep inside the grave" [1 January 1900]. The quest for ultimate meaning had several stages for Eberhardt. First she had to leave the shelter of Villa Neuve: "Ever since I walked out of it, I have lived as if in a swift and dazzling reverie, moving through varied scenery under different names and guises. Her aim in "[donning] the cloak of the rootless wanderer" was to find herself: "the further behind I leave the past, the closer

I am to forging my own character. I am developing the most unflinching and invincible will, to say nothing of integrity, two traits I value more than any others and, alas, ones that are so hard to find in women" [18 January 1900, 5:30 p.m.].

Eberhardt seems misogynistic at times, but looking at her work in its entirety, it becomes clear that she criticizes both men and women who lack the intelligence or will to break out of the mundane, gendered lives of European society. In choosing to follow the spiritual nomad's life, Eberhardt sees the necessity of escaping the domestic hearth of the female gender role, the division of labor that would assign women to the role of, as Woolf puts it, the "angel in the house." Eberhardt notes: "I have given up the hope of ever having a corner on earth to call my own, a home, a family, peace, or prosperity" [18 January 1900, 5:30 p.m.].

Eberhardt criticized the woman's role in both European and Arabic societies circumscribed by the gender entrapment of the hearth, but the fact that she longed to get beyond gender is clear when she writes, as she did in Marseilles, 21 November 1901: "How it rankles the common man to see anyone — and a woman at that — depart from the norm and be herself!" The process of becoming oneself was not a matter of collecting disguises and accumulating experiences, rather it was a process of divestment, of stripping away all unnecessary or accidental elements to reach the core of being: "I am full of the sorrow that goes with changes in surroundings, those successive stages of annihilation that slowly lead to the great and final void" [29 January 1900]. It is true that Eberhardt associates her path into the desert with her adoption of male garb and male behavior — "life in the Desert will be a bit less exhausting [this year] as I will not have to stay up all night, but it will complete my education as a man of action, the Spartan education I need" [16 June 1900] — but often it seems that her attitudes are based at least as much on position as on gender. That is, she identifies with outcasts, wanderers, loners who embody otherness, and these marginal people are both male and female. Nevertheless, Eberhardt's long established custom of dressing and writing as male did shape her experience ("[clothes] mould our hearts, our brains, our tongues to their liking"), especially in the more sexually segregated world of North Africa. She spent much of her life in arenas delegated to men.

Eberhardt's attitudes toward gender early in her life seem relatively unambiguous although unorthodox. Because she had grown up wearing male clothing, doing chores society had defined as men's work, and studying subjects usually associated with male education, she saw her activities as a normal part of her identity and never identified with the hausfrau mentality. Yet her romances with various men, her love of sentimental literature like that of Pierre Loti, and her "boundless compassion for all who suffer injustice" [1 January 1900], may be seen as "feminine." Eberhardt's unusual upbringing, then, gave her the self-confidence and the physical strength to wander in a fashion usually limited to men. At the same time, the world around her was operating according to traditional notions of gender, and she caused discomfort and suspicion whenever she challenged those notions. In short, as far as gender codes are concerned, she seems to have been deemed "deceptive" according to social standards rather than by her own will to deceive.

In a biography of Eberhardt written in 1975, Cecily Mackworth posits that the true deception — at least in Trophimovsky's eyes — would have been for Eberhardt to wear fashionable female clothing, whalebone corsets, petticoats, and all the other flounces and frills:

> As for her clothes, they were chosen because they were practical. No nihilist, however unmilitant, would admit that a girl might deck herself out with the false seduction that is in itself a lie; and back in Russia the first act of any young woman adhering to the creed would be to put off her pretty clothes, cut off her hair, and don a simple dark frock which could not be suspected as an aid to coquetry. Moreover, men's clothes, according to Trophimovsky, gave "more security when she goes into town."[7]

Her male dress may have increased her security, but it simultaneously aroused the suspicion of the local police. "False seduction" was avoided at the price of perceived deception. In a world like Weininger's that envisions women as having "no essence, no existence," appearance is the only possibility left for them. False seduction and perceived deception are two sides of the same coin in a system where counterfeit currency is the only exchange women have.

The Geneva police were in the habit of keeping dossiers on Eberhardt's eccentric family of Russian emigrés, and Eberhardt's dress came in for its share of comments in the police files. Police reports describe Eberhardt during her visit to Geneva in 1899 as walking "like a man" and "wearing a fez" and "dressed like a man" in "a double-breasted gray suit"; at other times she was spotted in a "dark brown suit."[8] Her escape to North Africa, where she dressed as a Tunisian student named Mahmoud Saadi who was going from *zaouiya* to *zaouyia* to study the Koran, was perhaps less of an escape than she thought, for her dress caused the French authorities to begin surveillance. An anonymous letter sent to General Dechizelle, who commanded the Constantine subdivision of the French army at Batna, lays out Eberhardt's purported motives for wearing male Arab dress:

> Isabelle Eberhardt, born in Switzerland but of Russian nationality, disguised as a man and calling herself Mahmoud Saadi, installed herself in El Oued in order to spy on the activities of the officers of the Arab Bureaux on behalf of the Paris journal *l'Aurore*, with the aim of aiding and abetting the relentless press campaign against the officers of the Arab Bureaux in particular, and the Army in general . . . This woman also has a profound hatred for France and would like nothing better than to excite France's Arab subjects against her. In order to gain the Muslim's trust, she passes herself off as a Muslim, which is not true.[9]

Eberhardt never knew about this letter, but the accusations it contained — about her gender, her nationality, her religion — were reflected in the official French handling of her North African dossier.

The venemous, anonymous letter was sent to the authorities only a few weeks after Eberhardt's arrival in El Oued on August 2, 1900. Eberhardt, who had visited "the city of a thousand domes" a year earlier, had chosen this small city on the northern edge of the Sahara as her refuge, her escape. She envisioned it as a place where she could live simply, write, study the Koran, and devote herself to contemplation. The systematic surveillance of her activity in North Africa began then, just when Eberhardt thought she had finally gotten out from under the weight of European social control. On August 4 she wrote in her journal:

> Here I am, finally arrived at the goal which seemed a little fanciful while it still was a project. Now it's done, and I must act with all the energy I can muster . . . I'm far away from people, far from civilization and its hypocritical shams. I'm alone, on the soil of Islam, in the desert, free and in excellent conditions. Apart from my health, the results of my enterprise now depend only on me.[10]

She could not have been more wrong about her enterprise, for just when she thought she was the farthest from the intrigues that defined European society, intrigue was all around her.

While in El Oued, Eberhardt met the spahi Slimane Ehnni, who would become her husband. She also made contact with the local leaders of the sufi brotherhood of the Qadiriya order, Sidi El Hussein (ben Brahim) and Sidi El Hachemi. By early November she had become a *khouan* (initiate) of the Qadiriya. The romance with Ehnni and her acceptance into the religious brotherhood fulfilled Eberhardt's dreams; they were the stuff of nightmares for the French authorities. Luckily for Eberhardt, Captain Gaston Cauvet, head of the Bureau Arabe in El Oued, was a level-headed man who appreciated Eberhardt's intelligence and overlooked her eccentricities of dress, although he disapproved of her promiscuity. Most other officials were unable to separate the unorthodox style of her dress and behavior from the worth of her character: to be unusual, in their eyes was to be dangerous, deceptive, or perverted. Cauvet's assessment of her notes that "she dresses like a young native man from the Tell, with a *chechia* [a red skullcap] with tassels, a French-style jacket and trousers, and an Arab chaplet," but that "there is nothing that she has been reported as having said or done that has not been perfectly correct." To that he appends the following observation, however: "Physically she is a neurotic and unhinged, and I'm inclined to think that she has come to El Oued principally to satisfy her dissolute tastes and her penchant for natives in a place where there are few Europeans."[11]

In her own acerbic way, Eberhardt would attribute the French establishments' critical attitudes toward her to their ethnocentricity and narrow-mindedness. She noted in her journal when she first visited the territory around El Oued in July of 1899: "Those who are not in the Sahara for their own pleasure do not understand why anyone might want to come here, especially out of season . . . and then I make the mistake of dressing like everyone else in the region."[12] Eberhardt's mistake actually involved much more than cross-dressing, it involved the sort of reverse cultural assimilation that challenged the entire French *mission civilisatrice*. Cauvet's report reflects the more Orientalist assumptions that even the most laconic authorities could hold when it came to explaining her behavior: that she was "slumming," experimenting with the "looser" sexual mores of the Arabs, for example. Cauvet is merely cynical about Isabelle's motives; other French officials, particularly two whose amorous advances Eberhardt had firmly rejected, attacked her more viciously. Captain Susbielle, who had offered to escort Isabelle to Touggourt, near El Oued, in 1899, was put off with vague excuses when she discovered his racism toward the natives. She went with two Arabs instead, a slight which the Captain was never to forget. He is suspected of having perhaps authored the anonymous, poison-pen letter about Eberhardt a year later. A couple of years after her stay in El Oued, Eberhardt was living in the town of Tenes near Oran. Tenes, where Ehnni was a town clerk, was riddled with spiteful infighting among the French colonial functionaries. When Eberhardt rejected the advances of a town deputy, telling him "I'd rather kiss the open mouth of a stiff who had died of Asiatic cholera than sleep with you,"[13] he retaliated by joining a smear campaign against Eberhardt and Ehnni (among others) that involved bribing witnesses and writing pseudonymous letters of accusation. Eberhardt sued and won the battle on paper, but the tension drove Eberhardt and Ehnni out of Tenes finally.

For these men and their kind, Eberhardt's cross-dressing and her preference for Ehnni in particular and for Arab society in general was not merely evidence of eccentricity or bad taste, it was a betrayal of French superiority. If European women were allowed to consort with native men, then the entire civilizing mission would be undermined. Confiscated lands might be regained through marriage, children of mixed parentage would no longer fit conveniently into the administrative structures that allocated privilege and legitimacy according to racial or religious origins. Eberhardt's flouting of gender became a lightning rod that drew the wrath of the colonial settlers and functionaries. Because they could not imagine anyone choosing to follow a path of progressive simplification and elimination (which involved leaving Europe behind and owning very few personal belongings) they made of her life a simulacrum; that is, they imagined a more clichéd life for her that their imaginations could understand. For them, she was a rich eccentric off on a trip to "less civilized" lands where she could indulge her senses through drugs and sexual perversions.

To be sure, Eberhardt was eager to escape the constricted mentality of Europe, and she was fascinated by the part sensuality plays in our lives, but she hardly fit into the "myth" of the rich orientalist that was created for her. Had she been more political and fought for causes — women's rights, Arab rights — she would have been more protected from the mythic simulacrum of the wealthy eccentric, but she still would have been prey to the French colonial system. Eberhardt was, rather, a kind of anarchist, and her spiritual quest was an individual one. In addition, although she flouted many of the rules of gender and was generally opposed to the patriarchal and colonial projects, her record shows her to have been critical of some colonial practices, while she embraced and participated in others. For example, she despised the French attitude of superiority, yet she pushed Ehnni to master the greatness of French literature, and even advised him to read the likes of Loti.

Eberhardt's crisscrossing of boundaries — between languages, cultures, religions, genders — was to cause her trouble in the context of Arab mores as well. Just when she felt her fate was firmly in her control, when she was living in El Oued in August of 1900, other intrigues, beyond the machinations of the Bureau Arabe, were brewing. On January 29, 1901, one Abd Allah ben Mohammed tried to assassinate Eberhardt with a saber as she sat translating a telegram in a house in the small town of Behima. Eberhardt survived the attack, thanks to a metal clothesline that deflected the blow, but was seriously wounded in the arm. After three weeks in a military hospital, she was released but lived in poverty and under the threat of expulsion by the French for having been a victim — a troublemaker. In May, she decided she'd better go to Marseilles before being forcibly expelled from Algeria. She shipped out as Pierre Mouchet, deckhand, so that she could travel fourth-class (women were not allowed to travel steerage class because of its lack of comforts and protection). In her journal Eberhardt notes: "Sitting on my bundle by the windlass, I mulled over the hopeless poverty I have come to, the utter destitution that will now be mine. Thought also of the settings I grew up in, the days long past when I was well off and would indulge my taste for dressing as a sailor, of all things" [22 May 1901, 9 p.m.]. Eberhardt refers here to a picture taken in 1895 in a studio in Geneva; she was very fond of this photograph of herself dressed as a sailor from a ship called *Vengeur*.

The French required Eberhardt to return to Algeria for the trial of Abd Allah ben Mohammed so that she could testify. Her letters to Ehnni indicate that she was once again faced with a situation where her presentation of herself, her identity, in short her character, would be read and translated by a judge and the press. When Ehnni writes to say that he will buy her European clothes for the trial, she replies:

> You absolutely *must not buy European clothes, because you've no idea how much it costs and I formally forbid* you to contract a centime of debts. . . . One can tell you know nothing of what it costs to dress not well, but at least passably as a Frenchwoman: a wig (this costs, for a shaved head like mine, some 15 to 20 francs, because a simple plait won't do) , a hat, underwear, corset, petti-coats, skirts, stockings, shoes, gloves and so on. All I will concede is to stop *dressing as an Arab,* which is anyway the only thing which would prejudice the authorities against me. I shall therefore dress *as a European* [man], now that I'm properly equipped. I swear to you . . . *it's not for pleasure of dressing as a man,* but because it is *impossible* for me to do otherwise. At court-martial, just like with de Susbielle in Touggourt, they always said to me: "We understand that you wish to wear men's clothes, but why don't you dress as a European?" . . . I don't care if I dress as a *workman,* but to wear ill-fitting, cheap and ridiculous women's clothes, no never . . . I'm too proud for that and I hope you won't insist on such shame for me, in a place where I pass for a millionaire, more or less.[14]

Eberhardt finally appeared in court dressed as an Arab woman. In this context, her clothing marked her as a subaltern, both in terms of gender and colonial status.

According to court records, Abd Allah ben Mohammed admitted attacking Eberhardt, but gave the following defense:

> I did not strike a European, I struck a Moslem under divine impulsion. One day I received a mission from God, who ordered me to go to the Djrid, passing by Behima, where I was to meet Mademoiselle Eberhardt, who created disorder in the Moslem religion. An angel also appeared to tell me that Si Mohammed el Lachmi, marabout of the sect of the Qadrya, would be proceeding to Tunisia and was accompanied by Mademoiselle Eberhardt, who wore masculine dress, which is contrary to our customs, and thus made trouble in our religion.[15]

Abd Allah would add that he thought Eberhardt to be the mistress of Sidi Lachmi.

In defense of her actions (given that she was actually on trial too) Eberhardt pointed out that Abd Allah's defense was built on ground that continually shifted, and that although wearing masculine garb might be considered "improper," it was practical for riding. Eberhardt maintained that she and Abd Allah were both tools by which a rival sect, the Tidjania to which Abd Allah belonged, attacked the Qadriya. Although Eberhardt asked for lenience for Abd Allah, given that he had a wife and five children to support, the French court used the trial to affirm the superiority of French ways: Abd Allah was sentenced to prison; Eberhardt was expelled from North Africa, formally this time.

Eberhardt's concern for Abd Allah's wife and children was probably not just a courtroom display. The women Eberhardt writes about in her stories — Yasmina, Fathma, Mariema, Saadia (in "The Anarchist") and Embarka (in "The Major") — are all outcasts or marginal figures with whom she can identify. For the most part, they have come to live outside normal social structures because they do not fit easily into the family pattern. Often, they are widows who have lost the economic support of the men in their families. Their husbands have been sent to jail, their sons have died, their brothers sent to faraway posts with the French military. Left to survive on their own, the women often turn to prostitution, serving the French military system, or take refuge in insanity or death.

In her introduction to an anthology of Eberhardt's works, Simone Rezzoug points out that Eberhardt's female protagonists — often peasants or prostitutes — give rise to stories that are played out in three registers: the sentimental, the erotic, and the philosophico-mystical.[16] Certainly this is true of the first three stories in this collection: "Yasmina"; "The Anarchist"; and "The Major." "Yasmina" and "The Major" are, in many ways, much the same story told from differing perspectives — that of the native girl and that of the French officer who has fallen in love with her. Eberhardt typically presents the officer (named Jacques in both these stories) as being a cut above his mess-mates; he seems less racist, more intellectual, than his fellows. But, after seducing the native girl, the French officer is called to serve elsewhere, forgetting the girl, now doomed to prostitution. Steeped in the romances of Pierre Loti, Eberhardt was telling the same old story, but with a hard edge. Yasmina dies, rejected face to face by Jacques, and Embarka is wasting away in prison as Jacques leaves El Oued, full of self-serving, egocentric melancholy: "all his enterprises would be aborted. . . . all his dreams would end up like this, and he would go into exile, more or less driven out of all the corners where he would try to live and love. Indeed, he would never be like the *others*. He would never submit to the tyrannical yoke of mediocrity." The irony, of course, is that in fact Jacques is not like the others — his racism is refined to the point that he must taste and meddle in the lives of the "Other" — Embarka, in this case — before retreating back into the solid structures that underpin the French notion of their own superiority. Eberhardt's women tend to be double victims of sexual inequality and racism. Only in "The Anarchist" does the love story seem to have a happy ending, but the main characters are depicted as isolated from European and Arab ways, living on the margins of a largely black oasis community that is foreign to them.

When Eberhardt focuses her attention on female protagonists — Fathma, Yasmina, Mariema / childhood, youth, old age — she writes with considerable distance from her characters. Fathma flashes by us. We know that she is a leader among urchins, but see that her poverty, her charisma, and her openness are likely to make her a victim of the French system later on. Yasmina has a pronounced personality — a code of honor — but Eberhardt depicts her as "one of her race," as typically lost in vague dreams and mysticism, as gullible and fatalistic. Likewise Mariema, sunk in her world of madness, is presented to us very sympathetically, but from the outside. Eberhardt seems to feel an empathy with these outsiders, rather than an identity. Despite her ironic criticism of Jacques, there is a narrative level at which she identifies more clearly with his European dreams of the Orient: in short, she understands Jacques more fully, although she does not agree with him.

In stories where women are simply part of the ongoing narrative, they appear in the most clichéd manner as "statuesque" and "biblical." Eberhardt's depictions of women do not have any more depth than those of her contemporaries; rather, the difference is in her attention to those social structures that doom these women to poverty and marginality. Both the native system and the French colonial system play their part in the devaluing of these women. Eberhardt's ambivalence — her incomplete identification with the native female point of view, her incomplete dissociation from the male European point of view — lays her open to attack. In her "Introduction" to the translation of Eberhardt's journals, *Passionate Nomad*, Rana Kabbani sees Eberhardt as a pitiful misfit who "became a mouthpiece for patriarchy, voicing traditional male views on sex, culture, religion and politics." In comparing Eberhardt's stories with those of her less culturally complex contemporaries who treat gender as an essential trait, it is difficult to agree with Kabbani, who goes on to say:

> Her dressing as an Arab man (a two-fold masquerade, since she was posing both [as] a *man* and as an *Arab*) exiled her completely from the society of Arab women, who were socially sequestered from male company. Although no one for a moment supposed she was either male or Arab, courtesy nevertheless required that the pretense of her be respected. She, in turn, was aware that the formal codes of etiquette implicit in this segregation of sexes were to be upheld. This would have suited her perfectly, since she hadn't the slightest desire to associate with women, for whom she felt only dislike and hostility.
>
> Her disguise endeared her to no one. Arab women must have thought her a pitiful and uncouth creature for mixing in male circles which were better left alone; Arab men must have found her ambivalent persona rather trying and her sexual presumptions perverse. French women would have been contemptuous of her for having de-classed and de-sexed and de-raced herself. She was

untouchable as far as they were concerned. French men would have shared the view of their women, while also perceiving her as a dangerous symbol of female rebellion; her taking Arab lovers would have galled them too, for in a colonial society, miscegination — if it occurred between a white woman and a non-white man (rather than vice-versa) — was considered a deadly sin. (ix–x)

Like those works about Eberhardt which see her only as a symbol of liberation, Kabbani's depiction erases all the complexities of gender and nationality that Eberhardt embodies. She is certainly not the psychically twisted, dissolute adventurer Kabbini wishes to present; and it is difficult to maintain that Eberhardt "felt only dislike and hostility" for women. But Kabanni's depiction does amply reflect one aspect of Eberhardt — her ability to outrage her judges. Surely Eberhardt aroused these sorts of venemous attacks, in her own time as well as in ours, because she did violate the norms. Yet, to present her actions as the mere sum of disguise, of playing with appearances, is to ignore the extent to which she did assimilate into Arab culture. Treating Eberhardt's dressing as a *man* and an *Arab* as merely a two-fold masquerade empties her experience, devalues it completely; but to do this is also to posit some sort of essence for the man and for the Arab that goes beyond the constructions of gender and the practices of culture. Eberhardt's strength is precisely her ability to depict the limiting nature of social boundaries. Her attempts to forge a self — beyond gender and cultural origin — were complicated and failed in many ways but her attempt has merit. The amount of critical work done on Eberhardt, the fascination with her cross-dressing, the eager defenses and angry attacks she still arouses, all attest to her ability to challenge comfortable political positions — patriarchal or feminist, colonial or post-colonial.

1. Annette Kobak, *Isabelle* (New York: Knopf, 1989), 49.
2. Cited in Eva Figes, *Patriarchal Attitudes* (New York: Stein & Day, 1970), 132.
3. Sandra Gilbert, "Costumes of the Mind: Transvestism as Metaphor in Modern Literature," *Critical Inquiry*, 7, 2 (Winter 1980), 391.

4. Cited in Fige, 132.
5. Gilbert, 394.
6. Eberhardt, *The Passionate Nomad: The Diary of Isabelle Eberhardt*, Nina de Voogd, trans., forward and notes Rana Kabbani (Boston: Beacon, 1987) , 1. This version of Eberhardt's diaries has been severely edited and suffers from that fact. However, since this is the available English translation, I will use it, when possible, and cite the page numbers parenthetically.
7. Cecily Mackworth, *Isabelle Eberhardt* (New York: Echo Press, 1975), 19-20.
8. Edmonde Charles-Roux, *Un désir d'orient: Jeunesse d'Isabelle Eberhardt 1877-1899* (Paris: Grasset, 1988), 16.
9. Kobak, *Isabelle*, 142-43.
10. Cited in Kobak, *Isabelle*, 131.
11. Cited in Kobak, *Isabelle*, 129-30.
12. Isabelle Eberhardt, *Lettres et journaliers*, ed. Eglal Errera (Arles: Actes Sud, 1987), 56-57.
13. Recorded in Robert Randau's *Isabelle Eberhardt: Notes et souvenirs* (Paris: Editions Charlot, 1945), 76.
14. Kobak, *Isabelle*, 166.
15. Mackworth, 128.
16. Simone Rezzoug, *Isabelle Eberhardt* (Alger: Publications Universitaires, n.d.), 37.

Eberhardt and Mysticism

THE INTOXICATED MYSTIC: EBERHARDT'S SUFI EXPERIENCE

Karim Hamdy

The question of whether Isabelle Eberhardt was truly a Sufi, and if so, how much of an Islamic mystic she was, will remain for the time being without a definitive answer. Facts about her mystical journey in North Africa are scarce, and the available information seems marginal and often contradictory. For example, Eberhardt did not refer directly, anywhere in her extant writings, to Sufism. Indeed, her complicated character was still being shaped when she was killed at age twenty-eight. Much of her life was chaotic, shifting, and fast-paced, like the flash flood that took her life in October 1904 in the Algerian Sahara. In spite of these vexing difficulties, light can be shed on Eberhardt's mystical experience as a Muslim convert who was formally accepted and inducted in the Qadiriya Sufi brotherhood.

We cannot naively rely on the dominant representation of Islam in the West, and still claim to contribute to the understanding of Eberhardt's writings. The typical Western scholarship about Islam, in the unfortunately still thriving Orientalist tradition, goes back a long way to the single-mindedly crusading travelers and self-proclaimed scholars of the eleventh and twelfth centuries (see Yusuf Ali's comments on the history of translation of the Koran into European languages, introductory chapter). These pioneering Orientalists laid the massive intellectual foundation for dealing with the "infidel Saracens"; their biases later became commonplaces in Europe. More writings, voluminous but riddled with distortions about Islam and the Arabs, were produced during the so-called European Renaissance through the colonial period. Even now, the misrepresentation of Islam is carried on with the added potency of today's large-scale dissemination through Western academic work and in popular culture.

Isabelle Eberhardt herself. beyond the truism that she was a product of her time, was deeply influenced by the general fascination in Europe with the so-called "exotic East" fueled by writers, poets, "explorers," and artists such as Burton, Lane, Beckford, or Byron in Britain, and Chateaubriand, Flaubert, Loti, Delacroix, or Gautier in France. Geographical societies sprang up all over Europe in the nineteenth century to finance expeditions throughout the world. Solemn conventions were organized at the conclusion of these adventures. "Explorers," hailed as superhuman heroes, gave titillating reports to home audiences, often pandering to Europeans' prurient tastes. And Eberhardt was an eager member of those audiences, through reading if not participation. She was also an eccentric rebel who reveled in living on the fringe of whatever social system she happened to be wandering through. She was a dreamer who thought up schemes of escape from the decadent *mal de siècle* in Europe at the turn of the century, and who acted on these schemes. She wanted

> to be free and unencumbered, a nomad in the great desert of life
> where I shall never be anything but an outsider. Such is the only
> form of bliss, however bitter, the Maktoub will ever grant me, but
> then, happiness of the sort coveted by all of frantic humanity, will
> never be mine. (Eberhardt, *The Passionate Nomad*, 2)

Free and unencumbered she was indeed. But her rejection and rebellion were not directed at one suffocatingly limiting social system in favor of another. She was destined to live an uprooted life from the time she was born, in Geneva, as the illegitimate daughter of Mme. de Moerder, a German Lutheran aristocrat, who had been married to a tzarist general in Russia, and a family tutor, Vladimir Trophimovsky, a Russian convert to Islam who may formerly have been a Russian Orthodox priest. Under her father's tutelage she learned a number of languages, including Arabic, and most importantly, she was introduced to the Islamic precepts. Bookish, lonesome, and dressed from an early age as a male, she felt and soon became conscious of her marginality and discomfort in *fin de siècle* Geneva. She later thought of herself, after officially converting, "as a nomad who has no country besides Islam."

This culturally nomadic woman in the skin of a European moved with her mother, in 1897, to Algeria in North Africa, a land of Islam with an "intoxicating expanse" of the Sahara desert, which France had begun colonizing in the 1830s. It is tempting at this point — the temptation was irresistible for some critics (see Kabbani, for example) — to add Eberhardt's name to the legion of European (and later American) lady travelers and camp followers in the Islamic East. Although of no particular nationality that she could call her own, she must have been, in the eyes of the indigenous Algerians. the privileged and powerful European who used the language of the despised but feared colonizer. While not as wealthy as some other travelers, she managed to eke out a living by becoming an enterprising writer-correspondent. She was able to travel extensively throughout Algeria and Tunisia, and back and forth between Europe and North Africa. Notwithstanding French suspicions toward her, the apparent privilege of being European in a French-imposed social order that professed and believed that there should be "no humanity for Arabs," must have been a factor in making possible and fairly safe Eberhardt's movement among the indigenous population. The settlers had raw and ruthless power backing them and, thus, were untouchable.

However, for these indigenous people, who had more than a passing encounter with this wandering woman, it became less and less obvious that he as just another *colon*, or settler. She professed to be a Muslim, went through an officially sanctioned conversion, and was even initiated, in 1899, into the powerful and secretive Qadiriya Sufi brotherhood. Such an action convinced the native Muslims around her of the sincerity of her protestations that, unlike the arrogantly superior settlers, she was "filled with love and tenderness, and with a boundless compassion for all who suffer injustice, all who are weak and oppressed," and that she had a heart "both proud and unswerving in its commitment to Islam, a cause for which I long to give my life some day" (*The Passionate Nomad*, 1). This closeness and acceptance between a rootless, non-French woman and the so-called *indigènes primitifs*, whom the *mission civilisatrice* had yet to lift to human levels, as Ernest Renan, the ideologue of French racial superiority put it, drew the ire of petty colonial officers. They had her followed and spied upon by their agents. They even suspected that she was an *agent provocateur* for the British. What intrigued them most, however, was her seemingly symbiotic interaction with the members of the Qadiriya brotherhood, who, unlike the competing, and by that time obediently pro-French Tijaniya brotherhood, had bitterly resisted the French military domination and the encroachment of the alien French culture in the land of Islam. One of the leading members of the Qadiriya was the heroic Abdel-Kader, the nemesis of French colonial designs if ever there was one, during the first two decades following the French landing at Sidi-Fraj, east of Algiers, in 1830.

At the time, Europe and the West in general possessed the power of scientific and technological achievements. Europeans had an unshakable belief that, with diligently meticulous science, "man" could dominate nature to his advantage, that there was no limit to progress, and that those indigenous peoples encountered during conquests and discoveries were either part of nature, and hence had to be tamed and dominated, or were, as the science of eugenics had proven, lesser humans, who needed to be proactively civilized by outside agents. In the words of Kipling, colonial mouthpiece that he was, the agents on whom this thankless burden fell were white European men. So diligent, French ethnographers doubling as military interpreters and forward scouts observed and documented all kinds of indigenous traditions, beliefs, ways of living, kinship systems, and so on. The purpose was not human understanding. No illusion about that. It was technical facilitation of conquest and control.

These military and colonial ethnographers soon discovered that there was a preestablished social order in Algeria, and that it was based on the Islamic religion. For Europeans, in whose society the pre-eminence of secularism and the relegation of religion to the private sphere, away from the public affairs of government, had long been a well-established fact, the indigenous social order must have seemed antiquated and easily dismissible as primitive, irrational, backward, and inherently weak. One more reason for the *mission civilisatrice*.

A classic of the genre that was published in Algiers in 1897, the same year Isabelle Eberhardt landed in North Africa for the first time, was the encyclopedic *Les Confréries Religieuses Musulmanes*. Its authors were Octave Depont and Xavier Coppolani, two military bureaucrats assigned by the Service des Affaires Indigènes et du Personnel Militaire du Gouvernement Général de l'Algérie to produce a meticulous and utilitarian account of Muslim brotherhoods in Algeria. Already in the introduction, they let their scientific masks down and explain:

> [These Sufis] are by nature the enemies of all established systems, and the Muslim States, as well as the European powers who have Muslim populations under their control, have to contend with

these anti-social preachers." (Our translation, Depont & Coppolani, *Les Confréries*, xiii, 1987 edition)

In Islamic lands, many local religious leaders were either uncorrupted by the approving power of central but distant authority, or felt unfairly squeezed by that same authority for a disproportionate share of control on their own turf. In either case, religious leaders, reluctant to accept corrupt oversight or to share power with outsiders, seemed inimical and were labeled antisocial. On the other hand, Sufi mystics have been known to be, at times, mysterious, extravagant, and downright eccentric. Eberhardt's personality had the raw material to fit the same stereotype.

She was a self-proclaimed rebel who could not fit, let alone feel happy, in the oppressively tidy social environment in Geneva. She felt marginal and distrusted established power. And certain aspects of her behavior could easily be perceived as antisocial. At the time, rebellious women in Europe who did not accept the norms of feminine conduct imposed by male-dominated society were diagnosed as hysterical or neurasthenic; and more outspokenly radical women were routinely committed to lunatic asylums. It is easy then to see why, for Eberhardt, an escape to North Africa, however precarious and full of dangers, may have saved her from becoming yet another Freudian patient. In Algeria, for the typical officer in the French colonial administration, a woman who not only cross-dressed but seemed to avoid Europeans and quickly built friendships with Arabs "*sans humanité*," was either exhibiting bad judgment or must have an ulterior motive. If nothing else, Eberhardt had these two character traits (rejection of established orders and antisocial comportment) in common with members of Sufi brotherhoods.

One has to grant that, in spite of their bureaucratic pedantry, these military ethnographers were sometimes capable of keen observation. They were able, for example, to identify the seat of power in an otherwise "alien" system, and with it the cracks through which division and domination could be furthered. Again in the same introduction they write:

"Whether he be? a Sufi, a Dervish, or a Marabout, the leader of
an Islamic brotherhood is the representative, the agent of God on
Earth, and the followers' submission to this divine man is such that
they are his property in the absolute sense, for *it is God who commands through the sheikh's voice* ...
We immediately see where a loyalty to a *living God* would lead
... It is their chiefs who actually lead the populations, pacify or
incite at will their khoun (brothers). (My translation, emphasis in
the original, Depont & Coppolani, xiii)

The ethnographers' message to their superiors in the colonial
bureaucracy, although indirect, was clear enough: To subdue the
indigenous population France had to first neutralize the religious
chiefs, by silencing them, corrupting and coopting them, or perhaps making them disappear and be replaced. Coppolani, an arro-
gant, self-promoting colonialist, propounded on this "theory" and
lobbied for it at the highest levels of government. His rising star as
an Islam specialist was short-lived, though, as he was knifed to
death in May 1905 by a Muslim rebel. His violent end swayed the
colonial administration toward more naked bloodletting. This blew
away the final shreds of the masquerade that the Western colonial-
ists would kill only reluctantly.

The established social order in Muslim territories prior to the
French invasion of Algeria had been indeed based on a powerful,
and far-reaching network of franchise-like local *zawiyas* (sufi
lodges) that carried out varied and all-encompassing administrative
roles. The functioned as religious and community centers, tribunals, and, when relations with the Ottoman vassals in Tunis or
Algiers were not sour, served as government offices as well. The
leader was usually a disciple of one of the numerous Sufi *turoq* that
recognize a historic Sufi figure as their spiritual mentor. In Algeria,
as in Tunisia, about two dozen Sufi brotherhoods flourished in the
nineteenth century. The most prominent of these were the
Qadiriya, the Tijaniya, the Rahmaniya, the Taibiya, and the
Shaykhiya.

A brief historic overview of Islam should help explain the promi-

nent status of these *turoq* at the time of French colonialism and
Eberhardt's experimentation with the Qadiriya. Islam is accepted by
the believers as a faith, offering spiritual bearings in times of crisis,
and a way of life as well, defining rules of conduct for material
aspects of daily living. In more political terms, Islam defines itself as
a "religion and a blueprint for government." Over the centuries,
when Islamic rulers succeeded in passing themselves off, however
deceivingly, as true and faithful to Islam, they secured the consent
of their governed subjects, and achieved a fairly high measure of
peace and order. In these instances, their critics were damningly
portrayed as heretics, and swiftly neutralized. The centrality of
Islam in the life of the *umma*, or community of believers, had been
instrumental in the speedy expansion of the Islamic empire into
Africa and Europe in the West, and over large stretches of the Asian
continent within a few decades of the death of the Prophet in 633
CE. Considering the Islamic teaching that "there is no compulsion in
belief," and its clear record of tolerance toward other "peoples of
the book," the peoples whose territories were conquered by
Muslims converted to this new religion in great numbers. At every
stage of the expansion, the newly converted Muslims, with
uncommon zeal born of recovered dignity, swelled the ranks of
Islamic armies, pushing the conquests into new lands and eventually becoming themselves the rulers of the provinces.

Spreading the word of the new faith was the declared goal of the
conquests, and wherever the armies went, so did the learned
preachers. By the third century of Islam (ninth century CE),
preaching became a powerful, well-established institution. The
Islamic state encouraged learning in all fields by funding such centers of higher learning as Beit-el-Hikma (the House of Wisdom) in
early-ninth-century Baghdad, where theologians, scientists, and
rhetoricians had lifelong careers dedicated to intellectual specula-
tion, research, teaching, and translation from Greek, Syriac, and
other languages. In this atmosphere, a number of daring, noncon-
formist individuals pursued a more ambitious but dangerous

endeavor: to wed religion and science by rationally proving the existence and unity of God. A virulent debate between the rationalists and the traditionalists ensued (such as the Mu'tazila vs. Ash'ariya schools, and later, Ghazali's *The Decadence of the Philosophers* and Ibn Roshd's (Averroes) response in his *The Decadence of the Decadence*).

The growth and maturation of Islamic science and scholarship was as swift as the territorial expansion itself. By the late fourth century of Islam (ninth and tenth centuries CE), theological interpretation of the two principal sources — the Koran and the Sunna of Mohammad — had been codified in four dominant juridical schools that became the constitutive groups of the majority Sunna sect of Islam. The Shi'a legal and theological interpretations were to develop at a later stage. In this fertile and esoteric environment of intellect and avid quest for knowledge, Sufism was born and shaped, but independently from the legalistic aspects of theology.

While Malik, Abu-Hanifa, Shafe'i and Ibnu Hanbal each produced a system of laws that translated Islamic teachings into practical how-to guides for society, Hasan al-Basri, Rabi'ah Al-'Adawyiah, Junayd, Abdel-Qadir al-Jilani, and many others pioneered the Sufi path to unity with God. But the latter were more interested in their own inner experience than in setting immutable standards for posterity. The four Sunni theologians functioned almost as a one-man think tank that provided a service to the state. The Sufis, on the other hand, wandered literally and metaphorically off the beaten path; they occasionally risked their lives for doing so. Al-'Hallaj, a major Sufi figure who lived in the ninth and tenth centuries, was one such victim of perceived excessiveness that was not tolerated by the established system. He was executed for purportedly exclaiming "I am the Truth [God]," in a moment of spiritual ecstasy, and also for being a Shi'a spy. These apparent setbacks did not deter later Sufis from pushing forward according to the true Islamic dictum that: "If humans set their sights on the Beyond [the Throne of Creation], they would attain it."

However, Sufism, as it manifested itself in the experiences of numerous masters throughout the centuries, is puzzling to lay Muslims, and can be threatening to Islamic orthodoxy. For non-Muslims it is inevitably strange and unfathomable. The non-Muslim scholars who ventured to study it, mainly Western Orientalists with a few exceptions, had no sympathy for their subject and hence no disposition to grasp the essence and diversity of Sufi experience. Such an attitude was to be expected since the European intellectual battle between reason and religion had already been settled. In France, although the complete divorce between church and state would wait until 1905 to be consummated, the Lois Organiques of 1802 had mortally weakened the hold of Catholicism on society by recognizing the freedom of belief, and the equality of religions, including atheism. In a thin volume, appropriately titled *What is Sufism?* Martin Lings, one of these exceptional scholars who probably would reject the Orientalist label attempted to represent the Sufi path through a powerful metaphor: God is at the center. Believers are conscious that they are at some point on a radius. The radius toward unity with God is the mystical path. The novice believer is quite far from the center and may not even be conscious of the path to God, nor cognizant of the effort required to unite with God. For this novice, the way to Sufi spirituality is discipline. The infinite number of radii is an expression of the diversity of individual mystical experiences, an expression of the paradoxical nature of Sufism as at once particular and universal.

Only novices who have received a number of important gifts from God can start the journey toward consciousness and eventual unity with the Center. These gifts, if utilized with abnegation, discipline, and sincerity, make the journey proceed with success from one mystic state to the next. Ability to meditate, a feeling of nearness to God, love, fear, hope, longing for unity with God, intimacy, tranquillity of the soul, worshipping contemplation, and certainty about the meaning of existence are all wonderful gifts that the novice, now an initiate, uses to journey from station to station. At the first station, conversion, one is a novice. The second station on the concentric path is abstinence from worldly things. Another station is renunciation, then there is the station of poverty. At the fourth level it is patience. Closer to the Center, but not there yet, the initiate who has become an adept somewhere along the path has trust in God. Finally, the adept becomes a master, with "satisfaction" in the unity with God. Such a station is so overwhelming and fraught with danger that only a small number of Sufis claim to have reached it while living.

Was Eberhardt endowed with the "ten gifts of God?" What spiritual station had she reached on the concentric path toward God-the-Center? First, nowhere in her diaries did Eberhardt discuss, or even refer to her mystical experience in Islam (Kobak *Isabelle*, 138). In her shifting moods and constant moves from one locale to another, she behaved like some Sufi and nomadic wanderers:

> Watching these men pass through the valley, I understood more intimately than ever the soul of Islam and felt it resonate within me. I tasted the harsh splendor of the landscape, the resignation, the vague dreams, the profound indifference to things of this life and of death. (Figuig, our translation)

The "harsh splendor of the landscape" that she longed for she found in the "intoxicating expanse" of the desert, where she spent long hours in meditative solitude as she traveled through the Sahara. For Eberhardt, Islam may have been a refrain or a metaphor, not a path, in the search for her lost self. For Sufis, knowing oneself cannot be part of the journey. Quite the contrary, a Sufi seeks to be "drowned" (*Istigh'ra:q*) and to be "extinguished" (*fana:*), hardly a pursuit of self-discovery. Eberhardt, on the other hand, fell in and out of love with fellow humans, but her love of God, or fear of the Creator for that matter, she didn't seem, from all accounts, to have experienced as a true Sufi. Instead of certainty and hope and tranquillity, Eberhardt had clear manifestations of inner turmoil and unsettling doubts about nearly everything in life. Unlike Sufi *muridin* (disciples) she did not devote any significant amount of her time to learn the methods and teachings of her adoptive *tariqa*. While not pettily materialistic, as the petit bourgeois settlers were, she was intermittently highly conscious of her goal to succeed as a *secular* creative writer and reporter. Also Eberhardt's biographers have speculated about her sexual intimacy with the sheikh of the Qadiriya. Were this to be incontrovertibly confirmed, the evidence would indicate that her presence among the Qadiriya was more corrupting to the morals of the group than spiritually fulfilling to her.

We should recall here the destructive and nefarious role played by another "lady of colonial Algeria" — Aurélie Picard — whose marriages, first to a defeated and pliable Ahmed Tijani, leader of the Tijaniya at the time, and, after his death, to his brother Al-Bashir, were blessed by both the colonial bureaucracy and the French Catholic establishment. Tijani became totally beholden to the colonial administration and discredited in the eyes of his fellow Muslims. After his death, his French wife acted for the rest of her life as a dutifully patriotic agent and propagandist for France. She helped rally the Tijaniya to French imperialism in Algeria, and contributed to French expansion into Tunisia, and later into Morocco. Unlike Eberhardt, Aurélie Picard's disdain, haughtiness, and consistent betrayal of the people who adopted her were matched only by her extreme material greed.

Nonetheless, Picard's useful precedent must have been in the mind of Hubert Lyautey when he successfully recruited Isabelle Eberhardt for reconnoitering the Tafilalet, a territory in southwest Algeria, dominated by the Kenadsa marabouts and for strategic intercession with her adoptive Qadiriya brotherhood. Lyautey, lauded by many Western scholars as the mastermind of the "more humane, pacific penetration" of the rest of North Africa, was just another meticulous but ruthless military bureaucrat who was clever enough to push the well-tried colonial technique of "divide and rule" to an efficient extreme. The quality of her mysticism notwithstanding, Eberhardt played straight into Lyautey's hands, and thus became a tool of the tragic "scramble for Africa" that the Europeans

considered manifest destiny. The atmosphere of rumors and con-
spiracies that colored the political debate in France at the turn of
the century following the notorious Dreyfus Affair fed the French
paranoid fear of Islam in Africa; hence the usefulness of any white
European who knew how to gain the trust of the indigenous
Muslims and sap their hostility, turning them into compromised collaborators. One of Eberhardt's contemporary admirers, who wrote
her first biography, spelled out the details of colonial approaches in
dealing with Sufi leaders in his 1906 *Précis de politique musul-
mane*. Arnaud (an anagrammatic pseudonym for Robert Randau)
determined that Sufis were only humans and not above "material
persuasion." He advised potential users of his manual among the
colonial brass that they should get the "maximum advantage" from
Sufis based on judiciously estimated bribes. Isabelle Eberhardt was
not immune to pressures from Lyautey since she was still struggling
to make a name for herself, which her daring journalistic excur-
sions eventually allowed her. Lyautey, being the highest colonial
officer in the region she was covering, had her on a short leash
by controlling her permissions to travel in "military" zones. In
any case, Lyautey and Randau, as well as Eberhardt, were of one
mind as regards the way to proceed to expand the French
"dominion of justice."

Considering then Eberhardt's free-spirited youth, aimless wanderings, financial and professional insecurity, we can see how her
Sufi journey looks more like an opportunistic "meandering line that
sometimes moves towards the center and sometimes away from it,
crossing and recrossing various radii but following none with any
constancy" (Lings, *What is Sufism?* 21).

Historically Sufis were nomadic wanderers in their lifestyle but
doggedly consistent in the pursuit of their goal. They would, so to
speak "cross several radii" in their journey, but would, nonetheless,
slowly inch their way, one station at a time, toward "trust in God"
and "satisfaction." In comparison, Isabelle Eberhardt may have crisscrossed the Sahara, endured a great deal of suffering, gone every-

where in the land of Islam, but ultimately she was nowhere near spiritual satisfaction in the Sufi sense. Was she then like the mythical Mimouna who, although ignorant of the basic tools of worship, was considered by believers including Sufis more capable of nearness to God? Indeed the North African old adage says: "God knows Mimouna, and Mimouna knows God." In other words, if Sufi experience is at once extremely particular and universal, why wouldn't Isabelle's experience, in spite of her many idiosyncracies, be legitimate? A number of aspects of her experience point to the fact that she was not disciplined enough to follow the Sufi path. Unlike Mimouna, Isabelle was highly intelligent, driven, and cognizant of the machinery of power and domination. She was literate not only in the colonizer's language and culture, but she had also learned to read and write Arabic; she could read the Koran and recite portions of it. And that's much more than the average Sufi initiate usually starts with.

In spite of Eberhardt's acute intelligence and her ability to persevere in her actions when she chose to — as in her writing — we still cannot totally dismiss her mystical experience as mere flirting with an alien philosophy for the purpose of professional observation. Rather than having made a conscious decision to not devote her life to seeking communion with God, she seemed to be distracted by her youthful restlessness as much as by her vague ambition. She died young, much too young to have had time to sort out her beliefs and to reflect on her way of life in light of those beliefs. In Islam, it is said 'Innamal-a'ma:lu binniya:t,' or, "the intent counts more than the actual deeds." Given what is available from Isabelle's writings and in her biographers' work, her deeds are not completely known. She was often meditative but also recklessly intoxicated with kif (hashish) and alcohol. She was supportive of her fellow Muslims, but also dismissive and critical of those who stood against French rule. More complicated than her deeds, her intent toward God, as a Muslim convert and a Qadiri member, was prematurely buried with her at Ain-Sefra, in the Algerian Sahara.

There is no clear and objective testimony from other Muslims concerning the sincerity of her devotion.

Ironically, the closest Eberhardt came to Sufi communion that could have developed into a discipleship later was not with her adoptive brotherhood, but with the Rahmanyia at the *zawyia* of El-Hamil, which had been led by a woman since 1897. This leader, Lalla Zaynab, was nobody's fool. Strong of character, learned in theological matters thanks to her late father's benevolence, and uncommonly astute at exploiting the weaknesses of domestic and colonial authorial systems, she succeeded in imposing herself as the deserving heir of her father's leadership position after his death. Although Eberhardt reported that Lalla Zaynab was her father's designated successor, it seems that the French authorities forced him, shortly before he died, to name his nephew instead. Lalla Zaynab stood up against patriarchal instincts of the Rahmanyia brethren and pleaded her case at all levels of the colonial "justice" system and won. At the time of her struggle for control of the *zawyia*, the circumstances were in her favor as the higher echelons of colonial Algeria were sold on Coppolani's theory of corrupt and co-opt. The year 1897 was also Isabelle's first year in Algeria, and Lalla Zaynab's fame and reputation of *baraka* (God's blessing) must have reached her through newspaper reports and through the Sufi grapevine. When Eberhardt undertook her first visit to El-Hamil in 1902, Lalla Zaynab greeted her with an open heart, and the two women developed a mutually sincere liking of each other. Lalla Zaynab, "saintly," childless, and almost twice Isabelle's age at the time, may have extended a motherly affection toward her young European guest. In "A Visit with Lalla Zaynab," Eberhardt reports that

> . . . suddenly, [Lalla Zaynab] becomes sad, and I see tears in her eyes. — "My daughter . . . I have devoted my life to doing good in the sake of God . . . But men do not recognize my efforts to help them. Many hate me and are jealous of me. This, despite my total renunciation: I was never married, I have no family, no joy . . ."
> (My translation, Eberhardt, *Notes de Route*, 293)

That Lalla Zaynab, the wise, ascetic, and cautious Sufi leader, allowed herself to confide in Isabelle about her innermost feelings, testifies to the trust established between them, and the quick, but genuine woman-to-woman communion in a world dominated by men. Given the natural hospitality of Arabs and the recognized function of *zawyias* as a place of refuge for fugitives in general, it would have been unlikely that Isabelle would have ever been made to feel that she overstayed her welcome had she elected to stay and become a devoted disciple of Lalla Zaynab. It wasn't unheard of that a Sufi be a member of more than one order at the same time. Lalla Zaynab, although not lacking in managerial skills and in dealing with the colonial administration, would have found an extended stay of Isabelle extremely useful. Had Isabelle stayed she would have come to terms with the dilemma that she was never to resolve: whether she was totally on the side of her fellow Muslims against colonial France, or only occasionally and conveniently Muslim during her quest to become a famous French writer.

Isabelle was so impressed with Lalla Zaynab's mystical power that she visited her again a year later; and yet again her impression was not overwhelming enough to make her stay on at El-Hamil. The colonial officers in charge at Bou-Saada, close to El-Hamil, had been alarmed by this dangerous communion between a Qadiri trouble-maker and a saintly but unsubordinated Rahmanyia matriarch. Their superiors, equally alarmed, instructed them to keep a close eye on the pair. By 1903, on her second visit to Lalla Zaynab's realm, Isabelle had her sights on yet another adventure. She was in the process of getting an assignment from *Al-Akhbar* newspaper to report, this time from the Tafilalet territory at the southern limits between Algeria and the fragmenting Sultanate of Morocco. Her choice not to stay at El-Hamil but to follow her dream and her career in the Sahara sealed her fate in more than one way. During her incursion into Tafilalet, she met Lyautey, who knew how to work up her ego in favor of his designs. She also was forced by ill-ness to stop at Ain-Sefra. There, her move from the military hospital on the heights overlooking the *wadi* to the Arab sector down close to the riverbed turned out to be the last twist of fate for her, as she died trapped in her room by the freak flood that descended on Ain-Sefra. She died among the people she emphatically preferred over the European settlers, while not being sufficiently committed to their cause to rebel against their enslavement by French imperialism which she opportunistically served. Lalla Zaynab's positive disposition and open hospitality was meant to remain a lost opportunity for Eberhardt's Sufi mystical journey. As the Sufi master Derqawi explained, the undisciplined, superficial seeker is like one who digs a little here and a little there, looking for water, without focus or real conviction, and dies eventually of thirst. Eberhardt's aimless wanderings, even close to the source of heavenly water, did not a Sufi make. She may have drowned as an aspiring Sufi, thirsty for God's love while having willingly walked away from an abundant source at Lalla Zaynab's side in El-Hamil.

References:

Ysaf Ali, *The Holy Quran: English Interpretation with Arabic Text* (Lahore: Muhammed Ashraf Press, 1938, 1969).

Julian Baldick, *Mystical Islam: An Introduction to Sufism* (New York: New York University Press, 1989). Extreme "Orientalist" approach, attributes nearly every defining aspect of Sufism to spiritual traditions other than Islam.

George Chowder, *Classical Anarchism: The Political Thought of Godwin, Proudhon, Bakunin and Kropotkin* (Oxford: Clarendon Press, 1991). Introduction to anarchism, and to the thoughts of Trophimovsky's friend Kropotkin.

Octave Depont and Xavier Coppolani, *Les Confréries Religieuses Musulmanes* (Paris: Edition a Alger, 1897).

Emile Dermenghem, *Le Culte des Saints dans l'Islam Maghrébin* (Paris: Gallimard, 1954). Mimouna's story, pp. 69–70.

Isabelle Eberhardt, *Notes de Route* (Paris: Charpentier et Fasquelle, 1908).

Isabelle Eberhardt, *The Passionate Nomad: The Diary of Isabelle Eberhardt, trans. Nina de Voogd* (London: Virago, 1987).

Isabelle Eberhardt, *Vagabond*, trans. Annette Kobak (London: Hogarth Press, 1988).

Ursula K. Hart, *Two Ladies of Colonial Algeria* (Athens, Ohio: Mongraphs in International Studies, No. 49, 1987). On Aurélie Picard and Isabelle Eberhardt.

Nikkie R. Keddie and Beth Baron, eds. , *Women in Middle Eastern History: Shifting Boundaries in Sex and Gender* (New Haven: Yale University Press, 1992) Chap. 15, pp. 254–274: "The House of Zaynab: Female Authority and Saintly Succession" by Julia Clancy-Smith. About Lalla Zaynab, leader of El-Hamil, her stuggle with the colonial administration, and her meetings with Isabelle Eberhardt.

Annette Kobak, *Isabelle: The Life of Isabelle Eberhardt* (New York: Knopf, 1989).

Martin Lings, *What is Sufism?* (Berkeley: University of California Press, 1975).

Simone Rezzoug, *Isabelle Eberhardt*, (Alger: OPU, 1985).

Leonard Shengold, *Father, Don't You See I'm Burning: Reflections on Sex, Narcissism, Symbolism, and Murder: From Everything to Nothing*, New Haven: Yale University Press, 1991, p. 40, has a partial list of "dark continent" best-sellers, published Europe from 1858 to 1878.

Elaine Showalter, *The Female Malady: Women, Madness, and English Culture, 1830-1980*, (New York: Pantheon, 1985). Hysteria, Neurasthenia, Darwinian psychology, Freud, and radical women.

William Zinsser, editor, *They Went: The Art and Craft of Travel Writing*, (Boston: Houghton-Mifflin, 1991), pp. 13-18. Books on travel in the "Orient."

GLOSSARY

abadan: Never.

abeya: Long cloak worn by women.

agha: Official above the level of *caid*.

allahou Akbar: God is Great.

aman: Asylum or refuge.

amaoui: Spiritual descendent of political dynasty that ruled in the Middle East in the early Islamic period

amel: Moroccan governor; specifically the title of the top *makhzen* official in Oudjda or Fiquig.

araba: Harness.

arouah: Come here!

askar: Soldiers of the Sultan.

azizi (m.) or *aziza* (f.): Darling.

bach-hammar: Head camel driver.

Bedouin: Desert tribesman, nomad.

berdha: Mule saddle; nickname given to their packs by *tirailleurs*.

berrania (f.) or *berrani* (m.): Stranger.

bicot (m.) or *bicotte* (f.): French racist slang, "dirty Arab."

bled-el-baroud: Land of Gunpowder.

bendir: Small drums similar in shape to a tambourine.

bordj: Tower.

Bureau Arabe: French colonial office, run by the military, in charge of indigenous affairs.

burnous: Large hooded cloak made of wool (see *djellaba*).

cahouadji: Waiter or owner of a coffeeshop.

caid: Tribal chief.

chaouch: Guard or porter.

chechia: Skullcap made of red felt.

chih: Medicinal desert herb.

chott: Salt flat.

dar-ed-diaf: Communal house for group of travelers.

diffa: Meal served in honor of travelers.

dhikr: Sacred ritual chants.

diss: Desert plant used for thatch.

djebel: Mountain, hill.

djellaba: Long robe with a hood (see *burnous*).

djemaa: Council.

djinn: Spirit.

djerid: Palm frond.

djich (singular), plural *djiouch:* Armed group (originally, army).

djort: Cliff.

djouak: Flute.

douar: Group of tents, village.
doum: Type of palm.
douros: coins (of five francs each).
drinn: Desert grass.
eddhen: Call to prayer.
erg: Region of dunes.
feggaguir: system of irrigation.
fellah: Peasant.
filali: Red leather from Tafilalet in Morocco.
fondouk: Hotel or inn.
forka: Sub-tribal group.
gandoura: Long tunic of light material.
gasba: Reed flute.
gh'rair or *harair* (plural): Long black and gray wool sacks hung on the pack
   saddles of camels.
goum: Military contingent composed of nomads led by a *caid.*
goumi: Arab or Berber soldier.
gourbi: Hut.
guerbadjia: Water carrier.
hadada: Ambiguous frontier of Morocco.
haik: Light scarf or veil.
hamada: Stony desert.
hammam: Moorish bath.
harka: Armed band, expedition; later gained the connotation of turncoat
   Algerians (pro-French).
hokkam (plural): Administrators.
in chah allah: God willing.
kasbah: Originally Turkish for fort, by extension, old Arab quarter of a city.
khador: Regular inhabitants of Oudjda.
khartani: Black oasis laborer.
khian: Bandits, robbers.
khotba: Iman's speech preceding group prayer.
khouan: Member of a religious brotherhood.
kif: Hashish.
koubba: Sanctuary consecrated to a **marabout.**
koumia: Long knife with a short, curved blade.
kouri: Language spoken in the east Sahara or in Sudan.
ksar (singular), plural *ksour:* Village.
M'zabi (adj. **Mozabite**): From M'zaba, a region in western Algeria.
m'zani (singular), plural *m'zanat:* Literally adulterers, fig. outsiders, riff-raff,
   renegade.
mabrouk: One who brings good fortune.
mahalla: Military detachment, caravan.
makhzen: Central government of Morocco.

marabout: Muslim saint, sacred place, tomb.

mechta: Winter pasture, farm.

medersa: School.

mektoub: Fate.

mel: Fortune, money.

mella: Bread eaten during Saharan crossings.

mercantis: Merchants.

miad: Meeting. (Delegation, in Eberhardt's usage.)

mihrab: Niche in a mosque facing in the direction of Mecca, where the **imam** stands.

mimoun: Someone who is successful and protected (by the will of God).

mlahfa: Dress worn by women in the South.

Moghreb (Mogh'rib; maghreb): Sunset, North Africa.

mokhazni: Horse soldier for the *makhzen*.

moueddhen or *muezzin:* Person who calls the faithful to prayer.

muzhik: (Russian) Peasant.

nana: Mint.

nefra: Battle.

nouba: Sufi Arabic music played with drums and flutes.

oued: River.

pekin: French slang for a civilian.

qadi: Islamic judge.

ramadan: Muslim holy month of fasting.

r'aita: Type of clarinet.

Roumi: Person from Europe or the West (originally refered to Romans).

sabir: Pidgin French.

salaam: Peace.

schritt: String.

sebkha: Salt lake, often dried out in summer.

seguia: Open irrigation canal.

sidi: Sir.

smalah: Invocation of Allah to repel the evil eye, when talking about family members or valuable property; used by Eberhardt as "family retinue."

sokhar: Camel driver.

Souf: Desert valley in southeast Algeria.

spahi: Native soldier.

srab: Mirage.

taleb (singular), plural *tolba:* Student.

tirailleur: Sharpshooter.

toub: Mud building material made of straw and clay.

zaouiya (singular), plural *zouaoua:* Religious retreat or school.

zerbia: Fenced areas around Bedouin shelters where animals are kept.

zoual: First afternoon call to prayer.

CITY LIGHTS PUBLICATIONS

Acosta, Juvenal, ed. LIGHT FROM A NEARBY WINDOW: Contemporary
    Mexican Poetry
Alberti, Rafael. CONCERNING THE ANGELS
Allen, Roberta. AMAZON DREAM
Angulo de, Jaime. INDIANS IN OVERALLS
Angulo de, G. & J. JAIME IN TAOS
Artaud, Antonin. ARTAUD ANTHOLOGY
Bataille, Georges. EROTISM: Death and Sensuality
Bataille, Georges. THE IMPOSSIBLE
Bataille, Georges. STORY OF THE EYE
Bataille, Georges. THE TEARS OF EROS
Baudelaire, Charles. INTIMATE JOURNALS
Baudelaire, Charles. TWENTY PROSE POEMS
Bowles, Paul. A HUNDRED CAMELS IN THE COURTYARD
Bramly, Serge. MACUMBA: The Teachings of Maria-José, Mother of the Gods
Broughton, James. COMING UNBUTTONED
Broughton, James. MAKING LIGHT OF IT
Brown, Rebecca. ANNIE OAKLEY'S GIRL
Brown, Rebecca. THE TERRIBLE GIRLS
Bukowski, Charles. THE MOST BEAUTIFUL WOMAN IN TOWN
Bukowski, Charles. NOTES OF A DIRTY OLD MAN
Bukowski, Charles. TALES OF ORDINARY MADNESS
Burroughs, William S. THE BURROUGHS FILE
Burroughs, William S. THE YAGE LETTERS
Cassady, Neal. THE FIRST THIRD
Choukri, Mohamed. FOR BREAD ALONE
CITY LIGHTS REVIEW #2: AIDS & the Arts
CITY LIGHTS REVIEW #3: Media and Propaganda
CITY LIGHTS REVIEW #4: Literature / Politics / Ecology
Cocteau, Jean. THE WHITE BOOK (LE LIVRE BLANC)
Cornford, Adam. ANIMATIONS
Corso, Gregory. GASOLINE
Cuadros, Gil. CITY OF GOD
Daumal, René. THE POWERS OF THE WORD
David-Neel, Alexandra. SECRET ORAL TEACHINGS IN TIBETAN
    BUDDHIST SECTS
Deleuze, Gilles. SPINOZA: Practical Philosophy
Dick, Leslie. KICKING
Dick, Leslie. WITHOUT FALLING
di Prima, Diane. PIECES OF A SONG: Selected Poems
Doolittle, Hilda (H.D.). NOTES ON THOUGHT & VISION
Ducornet, Rikki. ENTERING FIRE
Duras, Marguerite. DURAS BY DURAS

Eberhardt, Isabelle. DEPARTURES: Selected Writings
Eberhardt, Isabelle. THE OBLIVION SEEKERS
Eidus, Janice. VITO LOVES GERALDINE
Fenollosa, Ernest. CHINESE WRITTEN CHARACTER AS A MEDIUM
    FOR POETRY
Ferlinghetti, L. ed., ENDS & BEGINNINGS (City Lights Review #6)
Ferlinghetti, Lawrence. PICTURES OF THE GONE WORLD
Finley, Karen. SHOCK TREATMENT
Ford, Charles Henri. OUT OF THE LABYRINTH: Selected Poems
Franzen, Cola, transl. POEMS OF ARAB ANDALUSIA
García Lorca, Federico. BARBAROUS NIGHTS: Legends & Plays
García Lorca, Federico. ODE TO WALT WHITMAN & OTHER POEMS
García Lorca, Federico. POEM OF THE DEEP SONG
Gil de Biedma, Jaime. LONGING: SELECTED POEMS
Ginsberg, Allen. HOWL & OTHER POEMS
Ginsberg, Allen. KADDISH & OTHER POEMS
Ginsberg, Allen. REALITY SANDWICHES
Ginsberg, Allen. PLANET NEWS
Ginsberg, Allen. THE FALL OF AMERICA
Ginsberg, Allen. MIND BREATHS
Ginsberg, Allen. PLUTONIAN ODE
Goethe, J. W. von. TALES FOR TRANSFORMATION
Hayton-Keeva, Sally, ed. VALIANT WOMEN IN WAR AND EXILE
Heider, Ulrike. ANARCHISM: Left Right & Green
Herron, Don. THE DASHIELL HAMMETT TOUR: A Guidebook
Herron, Don. THE LITERARY WORLD OF SAN FRANCISCO
Higman, Perry, tr. LOVE POEMS FROM SPAIN AND SPANISH AMERICA
Jaffe, Harold. EROS: ANTI-EROS
Jenkins, Edith. AGAINST A FIELD SINISTER
Katzenberger, Elaine, ed. FIRST WORLD HA HA HA!
Kerouac, Jack. BOOK OF DREAMS
Kerouac, Jack. POMES ALL SIZES
Kerouac, Jack. SCATTERED POEMS
Kerouac, Jack. SCRIPTURE OF THE GOLDEN ETERNITY
Lacarrière, Jacques. THE GNOSTICS
La Duke, Betty. COMPAÑERAS
La Loca. ADVENTURES ON THE ISLE OF ADOLESCENCE
Lamantia, Philip. MEADOWLARK WEST
Laughlin, James. SELECTED POEMS: 1935-1985
Le Brun, Annie. SADE: On the Brink of the Abyss
Lowry, Malcolm. SELECTED POEMS
Mackey, Nathaniel. SCHOOL OF UDHRA
Marcelin, Philippe-Thoby. THE BEAST OF THE HAITIAN HILLS
Masereel, Frans. PASSIONATE JOURNEY
Mayakovsky, Vladimir. LISTEN! EARLY POEMS

Mrabet, Mohammed. THE BOY WHO SET THE FIRE
Mrabet, Mohammed. THE LEMON
Mrabet, Mohammed. LOVE WITH A FEW HAIRS
Mrabet, Mohammed. M'HASHISH
Murguía, A. & B. Paschke, eds. VOLCAN: Poems from Central America
Murillo, Rosario. ANGEL IN THE DELUGE
Paschke, B. & D. Volpendesta, eds. CLAMOR OF INNOCENCE
Pasolini, Pier Paolo. ROMAN POEMS
Pessoa, Fernando. ALWAYS ASTONISHED
Peters, Nancy J., ed. WAR AFTER WAR (City Lights Review #5)
Poe, Edgar Allan. THE UNKNOWN POE
Porta, Antonio. KISSES FROM ANOTHER DREAM
Prévert, Jacques. PAROLES
Purdy, James. THE CANDLES OF YOUR EYES
Purdy, James. IN A SHALLOW GRAVE
Purdy, James. GARMENTS THE LIVING WEAR
Purdy, James. OUT WITH THE STARS
Rachlin, Nahid. MARRIED TO A STRANGER
Rachlin, Nahid. VEILS: SHORT STORIES
Reed, Jeremy. DELIRIUM: An Interpretation of Arthur Rimbaud
Reed, Jeremy. RED-HAIRED ANDROID
Rey Rosa, Rodrigo. THE BEGGAR'S KNIFE
Rey Rosa, Rodrigo. DUST ON HER TONGUE
Rigaud, Milo. SECRETS OF VOODOO
Ruy Sánchez, Alberto. MOGADOR
Saadawi, Nawal El. MEMOIRS OF A WOMAN DOCTOR
Sawyer-Lauçanno, Christopher, tr. THE DESTRUCTION OF THE JAGUAR
Scholder, Amy, ed. CRITICAL CONDITION: Women on the Edge of Violence
Sclauzero, Mariarosa. MARLENE
Serge, Victor. RESISTANCE
Shepard, Sam. MOTEL CHRONICLES
Shepard, Sam. FOOL FOR LOVE & THE SAD LAMENT OF PECOS BILL
Smith, Michael. IT A COME
Snyder, Gary. THE OLD WAYS
Solnit, Rebecca. SECRET EXHIBITION: Six California Artists
Sussler, Betsy, ed. BOMB: INTERVIEWS
Takahashi, Mutsuo. SLEEPING SINNING FALLING
Turyn, Anne, ed. TOP TOP STORIES
Tutuola, Amos. FEATHER WOMAN OF THE JUNGLE
Tutuola, Amos. SIMBI & THE SATYR OF THE DARK JUNGLE
Valaoritis, Nanos. MY AFTERLIFE GUARANTEED
Wilson, Colin. POETRY AND MYSTICISM
Wilson, Peter Lamborn. SACRED DRIFT
Wynne, John. THE OTHER WORLD
Zamora, Daisy. RIVERBED OF MEMORY